PERSPECTIVE. ~~.~~ POLITICS
AND BLACK LEADERSHIP

Edited by
John Davis

University Press of America,® Inc.
Lanham · Boulder · New York · Toronto · Plymouth, UK

Copyright © 2007 by
University Press of America,® Inc.
4501 Forbes Boulevard
Suite 200
Lanham, Maryland 20706
UPA Acquisitions Department (301) 459-3366

Estover Road
Plymouth PL6 7PY
United Kingdom

All rights reserved
Printed in the United States of America
British Library Cataloging in Publication Information Available

Library of Congress Control Number: 2007932868
ISBN-13: 978-0-7618-3716-9 (paperback : alk. paper)
ISBN-10: 0-7618-3716-7 (paperback : alk. paper)

⊖™ The paper used in this publication meets the minimum
requirements of American National Standard for Information
Sciences—Permanence of Paper for Printed Library Materials,
ANSI Z39.48—1984

To Tomorrows Black Leaders

Table of Contents

Introduction
John Davis

During the post-civil rights era a veritable cottage industry emerged in Black Politics with focus on one salient theme: the crisis within black leadership at the elite level. Two scholars, Harold Cruse and Ethelbert Haskins, opined that black leadership envisages an enduring crisis (Cruse, 1957 and Haskins, 1988). Instructively, Cruse expressed the predicament that confronts black leadership this way, as *The Crisis of the Negro Intellectual*. On this point Cruse employs his "triple front thesis" noting empowerment within the black community must simultaneously consider the political, economic, and social parameters in order for any movement to reach its desired outcome. The continued failure of black leadership to incorporate the dynamics of this paradigm into a strategic leadership calculus has led to defeat and incomplete reform movements throughout the civil rights and black power periods, and if we were to apply this methodology from the seventies forward, one would concede it speaks to the ills of post-civil rights leadership as well.

Haskins observed that in the nascent stages of the post-civil rights era, black leaders continued to utilize a declining "psychology of victimization" that left black America without a strategy to confront a myriad of issues in an era absent of Martin, Malcolm, and other leaders of the civil rights movement.

While extraordinary scholarship explicates that old guard civil rights leadership depended on a praxis and time-honored strategy (Walters and Smith, 1999), one could call into question whether the new guard of the post-civil rights period comprehends the importance of theory and practice in developing strategy and scoring significant victories for the movement (White, 1999).

Contemporary scholarship indicates that black leadership remains plagued by a number of additional problems. In the first of many critical assessments, Adolf Reed, Jr. left little doubt of his perception of the state of black leadership: "There is no black presence in national politics besides the Congressional Black Caucus that is capable at this juncture of responding appropriately to the ominous challenge posed by the collapse of Democratic liberalism" (Reed, 1994).

Exploring black leadership from an institutional and organizational perspective, Robert Smith concludes that the black movement has been marginalized by a co-opted cadre of leaders who have been overly enamored by mainstream institutions to the detriment of the traditional path to success: grassroots politics. As a result, black leadership has been unable to develop new organizations and strategies to keep apace with the ever-expanding issues that confront blacks in the post-civil rights era (Smith, 1996).

According to Ricky L. Jones, black leadership failure is due to leadership erosion, cooptation and exploitation. In an important analysis, Jones forcefully argues that:

> When America's historical and contemporary discrepancies along numerous cleavages within liberal structures are examined, it is difficult to deny that a dichotomized oppressor-oppressed society has been established. If it is conceded (and many people certainly do) that this dehumanizing reality does indeed exist, then the primary concern for members of the oppressed group must be the restoration of humanity. In such a struggle, the quality of black leadership's analysis, understanding, and commitment to such a transformation is essential. Unfortunately, on many fronts, current black American leadership falls short (Jones, 2001: 42).

Noting that black leadership is in the midst of a period of "leadership estrangement," Donn Davis makes an important contribution to the dilemmas that confront black leadership with the following polemical statement:

> Black masses no longer have, nor may rely upon, the uncompromised commitment and exclusive leadership of a middle-class black intelligentsia. In far too many instances, in fact, they may expect just the opposite. From the Supreme Court to the Board of Regents of California (and many points in between), blacks may now be certain that other blacks will act against what the majority of them believe to be in their best interest. It is safe to say this would never have occurred twenty-five years ago (Persons, 2001: 15).

In a rudimentary, if not overly simplistic argument, Earl Hutchinson opines about *The Disappearance of Black Leadership* (Hutchinson, 2001). His central hypothesis enlists a return to an incessant debate among black intellectuals: leading civil rights era organizations—NAACP, Urban League, and SCLC, to name few—are less inclined to act as advocates for the disenfranchised and the black poor in the post-civil rights period, but instead became fronts for the pursuit of loans for Small Business (and other business concerns) interests within the black community. Additionally, this study poses two interesting queries: What happened to the Malcolm Xs, Martin Luther Kings, the Roy Wilkins, Elijah Muhammad's and why after nearly two generations no leader of their stature has emerged to give voice to the burgeoning frustrations of a new underclass in the post-civil rights era?

These criticisms notwithstanding, one should not overlook a salient dilemma that continues to haunt a new generation of leadership in the post-civil rights period: the problem of vision. The object of this failure was aptly explained this way:

> Their [black leadership's] failure, in brief, is one of vision. The Old Guard constantly maneuvers, responding to minor political crises, but they are hopelessly inept in projecting a constructive program to transform the larger society. They react, rather than act; they imitate rather than create; they plead

rather than demand. Theirs is a failure within a qualified and compromised success, and as the decade of the 1980s progresses, it has become obvious that the result of their limited vision has been the creation of a temporary yet quite real barrier between the immediate political agenda of the elite and the black majority. With Dubois, I must agree that many critical failures of both reconstructions were the result of black's leadership "by the blind. We fell under the leadership of those who would compromise with truth in the past in order to make peace in the present and guide policy in the future." Even though Marable saw the gap between the masses as "temporary" in the 1980s, the problem worsened, rather than improved, as the twentieth century ended (Jones, 2001).

Well into new millennia, in the minds of many scholars the predicament of a burgeoning crisis remains a major dilemma for black leadership. What accounts for this continuing dilemma and its recurrence? To put this issue in perspective, consider the following: To understand the frustrations of black scholars and the discontent within the African American community, the seeds of restlessness were well underway long before the upsurge of the aforementioned discourse. Comprehension of this discord begins with the dilemmas associated with black political development and the failure of black leadership to adjust to the post-civil rights issues and agendas of the black community (and its Diaspora) and ensuring their inclusion within the mainstream of electoral politics in the United States.

Consistent with most white ethnic groups, African Americans have completed the three stages of political development: Protest, Electoral Empowerment and Consolidation (Kilson, 1999). During the first stage, ethnic groups often clash with the dominant majority group. In this respect, African Americans were forced to pursue an altogether dissimilar strategy than their white counterparts. In the case of white ethnic groups—an instructive example is Irish-Americans—they were more fortunate in that the Protest stage and the Electoral stage occurred simultaneously, allowing this and other white groups to bypass the racism and systemic dislocation that blacks and other minority groups were forced to endure.

For African Americans, the struggle for political development sputtered under the girth of systemic racism. In an effort to level the playing field, blacks were limited to protest politics, precluding the linkage of stages one and two, thereby delaying the developmental status for blacks in the United States.

In spite of this predicament, blacks in America successfully made their way to the third stage of political development—inclusion. The success of the civil rights era leadership elevated blacks from several elected officials in the sixties to a number exceeding 10,000 today (Kilson, 1999 and The Joint Center for Political and Economic Studies, 2001). These accomplishments aside, African Americans have yet to reap the benefits that are commensurate with their political influence. Of concern to many African Americans, while achieving political development the declining results indicate all too well the failures of black leadership to translate those benefits to political power that satisfies the urgent issues of their constituents.

Structure of the Study

The book revolves around four distinct themes. Divided into four parts, the book explores interlocking problems that confront several levels of black leadership: (1) Black voting behavior and Affirmative Action (2) the dilemmas and issues challenging black leadership at the national level, (3) the legacy of black mayors, and (4) an assessment of the leadership of the Congressional Black Caucus.

Part I of the study explores the subject of **Black Voting Behavior, and Affirmative Action: Issues that Continue to Dominate Black Politics**. Historically, the issue of black voting behavior has incessantly remained a curious matter for political scientists, historians, sociologists, alike. Interestingly, if there is an agreement it is found in this statement: "in the century between the abolition of slavery and the establishment of civil rights, changes in black political behavior more or less tracked changes in the political behavior of the country as a whole" (Taranto, 2004). On the matter of affirmative action, in a conservative political culture such rights have been challenge on a regular basis. Two examples are instructive. During the Clinton administration, republicans clamored to end affirmative action. To forestall any dramatic changes Clinton came up with the policy of "mend it but don't end it", a reference to affirmative action reform that ostensibly prevented its demise. In the second example, in a more direct challenge, the administration of George W. Bush endeavored to utilize two court cases—*Gratz v. Bollinger* and *Grutter v. Bollinger*—at the University of Michigan to set a precedent that the president hoped would undermine affirmative action. The opening two chapters examine these two issues and offers unique analysis to two prominent issues in black politics.

Part II (**Critiques of Black Leadership and the Way Forward**) offers a series of critiques of Black leadership and the inability of individual leaders as well as mainstream black organizations to operate in the post-civil rights era. Indeed, the issue of black leadership continues as the single-most prominent and problematic subject in the discourse among leading African-American scholars. In a seminal effort, Robert Smith produced a controversial study titled *We Have No Leaders*. Smith's polemical thesis posits that black leadership in the post-civil rights era remains unwilling and continues to be ill prepared to participate effectively in institutional politics to the extent that it is primed to suggest broad-based structural changes that assist in the uplift of the underclass in the United States (Smith, 1996). Thus, as American politics remains continues to be dominated by burgeoning partisanship, the absence of influential black leaders able to exert influence on institutional politics continues to illustrate the frustrations, dilemmas, and disappointments associated with black leadership. In short, if it is the case that inadequate leadership diminishes the African

American voice, the point remains, what are the issues that confront black leadership? By pursuing a cross-sectional examination of black leadership, this section endeavors to elicit several of the major issues that confront African American leaders (and the black community), to offer perspectives behind this leadership inadequacy, and to provide a prospective on the success and prospects of alternative leadership.

The three essays presented in this section provide diverse perspectives on past leadership accomplishments, the failure to replicate those accomplishments (and the needed skill set for future black leaders) in the contemporary partisan political environment, and assesses the efficacy of black leadership and long serving organizations such as NAACP, SCLC and, et al, in the 21st century.

Part III examines an altogether dissimilar aspect of black leadership— **Black Mayors in America: Reassessing the Legacy**. Each and every time a black mayor is elected across America it is indeed an historic achievement. After a century of promise, a major area of black leadership envisages declining political power. Much of this decline is due to a natural phenomenon—minority assimilation.[1] Second, dilemmas associated with this decline are linked to burgeoning voter apathy within the black community that threatens to dramatically alter a major area of black leadership. Finally, as William E. Nelson, Jr. warned, black mayors face fundamentally different problems than their white counterparts:

> They must contend with constraints on their capacity for leadership not common to big city mayors generally. The heart of their dilemma is that they are, on the one hand, pressured by expectations of high performance, but on the other, handicapped in their ability to live up to these expectations by social, economic, and political factors that rob them of the resources and power they need to be successful in their roles (Nelson, 1978).

Nonetheless, indifferent to these indicators black mayors were elected in major American cities across the United States (i.e., David Dinkins in New York and Willie Brown in San Francisco). This accomplishment aside, scholarship in this area remains in a state of flux. While discourse remains at a premium, focus on the legacies of black mayors (JCPS Staff 1977, Kleppner, 1985 and Rich, 1996), and the impending decline of black leadership remains disorganized (Daggnet, 2002). This section represents an effort to refocus the debate and demonstrate why Black Mayors have proven to be a highly profitable arena of black leadership. To accomplish this, the study addresses the legacies of selected black mayors and their strategies to govern major American cities. In addition, this study explores the significance of black leadership at the mayoral level and addresses its prospects for replication in the twenty-first century. Put another way, Georgia Persons argues historically there have been six electoral mayoral waves (Persons, 1993). At issue, is the wave an end? If so, what does this portend for black leadership?

Part VI concentrates on **The Congressional Black Caucus: The Disappearing Voice?** The Congressional Black Caucus was founded with the vision "to promote the public welfare through legislation designed to meet the needs of millions of neglected citizens." To illustrate the success of the CBC, the organization boasts that their annual alternative budget is listed as a major accomplishment. However, absent public discourse concerns the degree to which elements of those budgets have been adopted by the congress and the executive branch (Singh, 1997). Put another way, in the post-civil rights era how effective is the CBC in representing black concerns, whether in the domestic or international arenas? These issues are critical to understanding the role and influence of this institutional level example of black leadership.[2] In this fourth section, we address this issue from the legislative and organizational perspective. Specifically, this study examines caucus strategy on mandatory minimums on Cocaine, attitudes towards the Congressional Black Caucus and alternatives to its leadership and the CBC strategy and politics and efforts to influence U.S. foreign policy in the post-Cold War world.

Endnotes

1. That is, as the Latino and Asian political clout increases, the phases/stages of development invariably leads to the assertion of political clout. On the road to the exercise of this newfound clout, ethnic groups seek elected office as a demonstration of their influence. For minorities, the office of mayor represents the Aberdeen proving grounds, offering a visible and accessible perch from which to view power and leadership. Thus as minority groups compete for major political offices, particularly the Office of Mayor, the theory holds that as a result, the number of black mayors will invariably decline.
2. While clearly and important issue, this is by far in the way one of the most under-researched areas of black leadership. To date, two volumes (Singh, Sinclair, 1997 and Bositis, 1994) provide a sense of the significance of this body of black leadership, but neither study effectively explores the problems of CBC leadership.

References

Barnett, Marguerite Ross. 1982. "The Congressional Black Caucus: Illusions and Realities of Power." In Michael Preston, et al. *The New Black Politics.* New York: Longman.

Bositis, David A. 1994. *The Congressional Black Caucus in the 103rd Congress.* New York: University Press of America.

Browne, Vincent J. 1949. *The Control of the Public Budget.* Washington, DC: Public Affairs Press.

Bunche, Ralph. 1968. The Ralph Bunche Oral History (Robert Martin Interviewee). Moorland Spingarn. Howard University, Washington, DC.

Cruse, Harold. 1967. *The Crisis of the Negro Intellectual.* New York: William & Company.

Dorsey, Emmett. 1961. "The American Negro and His Government—1961." *The Crisis.* October: 469-478.

Haskins, Ethelbert. 1988. *The Crisis in Afro-American Leadership.* New York: Prometheus.

Henry, Charles, ed. 2000. *Foreign Policy and the Black (Inter) National Interest.* Albany, NY: State University of New York Press.

_____.1995. "Abram Harris, E. Franklin Frazier, and Ralph Bunche: The Howard School of Thought on the Problems of Race." *National Political Science Review.*

Holloway, Jonathon Scott. 2002. *Confronting the Veil: Abram Harris, jr., E. Franklin Frazier, and Ralph Bunche, 1919-1941* North Carolina: University of North Carolina Press.

Hutchinson, Earl Ofari. 2000. *The Disappearance of Black Leadership.* Middle Passage Press.

Gomes, Ralph C. and Linda F. Williams. 1995. *From Exclusion to Inclusion.* New York: Greenwood Press.

Joint Center for Political and Economic Studies, 2001. Joint Center for Political Studies Staff. *Profiles of Black Mayors in America.* Washington, DC: Johnson Publishing.

Jones, Mack. 1971. "The Responsibility of the Black College to the Black Community: The and Now." *Proceedings of the American Academy of Arts and Sciences*, Vol. 100, No. 3: 732-44.

Jones, Ricky. 2001. "Permanent American Hegemony: Liberalism, Domination, and the Continuing Crisis of Black Leadership." *Black Scholar.* Summer: 38-47.

Kilson, Martin L., Jr. 1999. "The State of African American Politics." *The New Crisis.* Jan/Feb.: 10-12.

Kleppner, Paul. 1985. *Chicago Divided: The Making of a Black Mayor.* Chicago: Northern Illinois University Press.

McClain, Paula, ed. 1989. *Agenda Setting, Public Policy, and Minority Group Influence.* Policy Studies Organization.

Morris, Lorenzo. 1979 *Elusive Equality: The Status of Black Americans in Higher Education.* DC: Howard University Press.

_____. 1978. *Chit'Lin Controversy: Race and Public Policy in America.* New York: University Press of America.

Nelson, William E., Jr. 1978. "Black Mayors As Urban Managers." *The Annals of the American Academy of Political and Social Science: Urban Politics.*

Nelson, William Edward and Phillip J. Meranto. 1977. *Electing Black Mayors: Political Action in the Black Community.* Ohio: Ohio State University.

Persons, Georgia, ed. 2001. "Politics of the Black Nation: A Twenty-Five Year Retrospective." *The National Political Science Review*, Volume 8.

_____. 1994. *Dilemmas of Black Politics.* New York: Longman.

Reed, Jr., Adolf. 1994. "Black Leadership in Crisis." *Progressive.* Oct.: 16-18.

Rich, Wilbur C. 1996. *Black Mayors and School Politics: The Failure of Reform in Detroit, Gary, and Newark.* Garland Publishing.

Singh, Robert. 1997. *The Congressional Black Caucus: Racial Politics in the U.S. Congress.* New York: Sage.

Smith, Robert. 1996. *We Have No Leaders.* Albany, NY: State University of New York Press.

_____. 1995. *Racism in the Post-Civil Rights Era.* Albany, NY: State University of New York Press.

Walters, Ronald. 1995. *Pan Africanism in the African Diaspora: An Analysis of Modern Afrocentric Movements.* Indiana: Wayne State University.

_____. 1987. *Black Presidential Politics in America: A Strategic Approach.* Albany, NY: State University of New York Press.

Walters, Ronald and Robert Smith. 1999. *African American Leadership.* Albany, N.Y.: State University of New York Press.

Walton, jr., Hanes. 1997. *African American Power and Politics: The Political Context*

_____. 1994. *Black Politics and Black Political Behavior: A Linkage Analysis.* Connecticut: Greenwood.

White, John. 1991. *Black Leadership in America: From Booker T. Washington to Jesse Jackson,* 2nd ed. New York: Longman.

Wielhouwer, Peter. 2000. "White Cities Electing Black Mayors? Challenging Preconceived Notions of Racial Voting Patterns." Unpublished Paper. Prepared for Presentation at the Annual Meeting of the Southern Political Science Association, November 8-11, 2000, Atlanta Georgia.

Woodard, Maurice, C. 1977. *Blacks and Political Science.* Washington, DC: The American Political Science Association.

Internet

Chairpersons Statement: 64.225.79.49/ChairStatement.htm

The Civil Rights Project, Harvard University. Mission Statement.
www.law.hardvard.edu/groups/civilrights/mission.html

Dagget, Liz. "Mayors Meet to Discuss Future of Political Power." *The Daily Helmsman on line.* March 20, 2002.
www.dailyhelmsan.com/vnews/display.v/ART/2002/03/3c98a07bf385

PART I

BLACK VOTING BEHAVIOR, AND AFFIRMATIVE ACTION:

ISSUES THAT CONTINUE TO DOMINATE BLACK POLITICS

Chapter 1

Black Voting Behavior in Presidential Elections: A View From the South

Frank Pryor, Georgia Persons and Hanes Walton, Jr.

The African American millennium voter evinces a voting behavior which challenges and is at odds with explanatory variables at the epicenter of the standard psychological model of voting so dominant in the political science literature since the advent of *The American Voter* (Campbell, et al, 1960) and its sequel, *The New American Voter* (Miller and Shanks, 1996). There was far more to African American voting behavior in the first presidential election of the new century than the hegemonic variables of (1) partisanship, (2) candidates, and (3) issues, can fully describe and explain. Collectively, these variables neglect something about the African American voter.

Historian and presidential scholar, Allan Lichtman, declares in his work that political scientists have been wrong and wrongheaded all along. He demonstrates that historically-based logic of presidential elections... runs counter to the widely held assumptions of political analysts, consultants, pollsters, journalists, and politicians... [and this]..., explains why so much election commentary is so often wrong (Lichtman and DeCell, 1990: *iii*).

> Contrary to the assumptions of the pollsters, the pundits, and the political experts who track presidential campaigns, over quadrennial contests for executive power are no contests at all. They do not put one candidate's popularity, leadership ability, positions on the issues, or vision against another. They do not turn on the party loyalties of voters, their devotion to liberal or conservative ideologies, or their perception of which candidate is closer to the center of the political spectrum. Nor does the electorate simply vote its pocketbook, retaining the party in power in good times and throwing the rascals out in bad. And elections certainly are not horse races... (Ibid.).

As Lichtman sees it, presidential elections are primarily referenda on the performance and to some extent, the luck of the incumbent administration during the previous four years (Ibid). Thus, voter behavior is pegged to, if not tied to, presidential performance. Therefore, if we move from the explanatory voting model offered by political scientists, to the one provided by Lichtman, where three new variables, inherent in the performance model dominate (1) political, (2) performance, and, 3) personality (i.e., charisma, factors). The issue is whether collectively we will fully describe and explain the African American millennium voter (Ibid.)? Our answer is a simple one. This latest and newest model, rising in another discipline, is just as deficient and limited, as the one found in our discipline, but it is far more suggestive.

Data and Methodology

If the African American millennium voter evinced a voting behavior motivated by new variables, the issue is how can we discern and discover this different array of independent variables. Resorting to the academic and/or media pre-or post-election polls and surveys leads us essentially back to the dominant variable central to the standard psychological model, i.e., partisanship, candidates and issues. Such questions, with some exceptions, reoccur continually so that trends can be discerned and patterned behavior can be captured. The polls and surveys offer few new leads beyond the standard markers.

This is not to say that specific events and salient issue do not appear on the 2000 pre-election polls and surveys. The research suggests that it does but this current event data does not establish new variables. Each presidential election has it own mix of issues, personalities, and strategies as well as new and different parties. But these new elements are simply subsumed under the standard labels and categories with no allowances, intellectually or conceptually are made for contextual variables embedded in the African American community.

Thus, with limited, weak and flawed pre-election polling and survey data, one must therefore turn to aggregate election data and develop some empirically based inferential propositions. This we did using the African American voter in Atlanta, Georgia in the mid-term 1998 and 1994 elections (Walton, et al, 2001). This proved to be quite insightful as had earlier studies of African American voting behavior in that city using aggregate election data (Rooks, 1970 and Jennings and Ziegler, 1966: 128-32).

One of the earlier precinct studies of African American voting behavior (in the city that is usually overlooked except in the most well versed studies) is credited to the Jack Walker study of 1964. The essential reason that the Walker study is crucial is that it analyzes African American voting behavior on the very eve of the civil rights movement prior to the 1964 Civil Rights Act, and the 1965 Voting Rights Act, and the new wave of Black elected officials. During the era of segregation, African American voters were not only voting for the lesser of the two evils, they were voting for a brand new day. Hence, Walker's often overlooked study provided a portrait and dimensional view into racial voting behavior that was circumscribed and delimited by white segregation (Walker, 1944: 380-381). In such a political and social context, Walker's precinct study informs us that in the three mayoral races in the city of Atlanta in 1953, 1957 and 1961, the same coalition of Negro voters and Liberal elements in the white community joined to elect William B. Hartsfield, (and Ivan Allen)... as mayor.

Both Allen and Hartsfield hold moderate views on the issue of racial discrimination... (Ibid.: 381) In these mayoral elections, the African American electorate emerged as anti-segregationist voters. And since the candidates and the issue were joined, as Morris Fiorna has shown, the issue voting of the African American community was merged with candidate voting in non-partisan elections (Ibid and Fiorna, 1981:72). This remains a major moral concern inside the community.

In the 1961 mayoral election there were also alderman races, and three African Americans ran for office. Of these three candidates, a well known businessman, Q. V. Williamson, got the endorsement of *The Atlanta Constitution, The Atlanta Journal* and the Atlanta Negro Voters League, but the coalition of upper-income whites and Negroes which elected Ivan Allen did not materialize for Williamson (Ibid.: 385). In all of the precincts, the upper income white precincts, the lower-income white precincts and in the African American precincts, there was a sharp voter drop-off. The greatest drop-off was of course in the white community and especially in the lower-income area.

To explain this drop-off factor, Walker says: In an effort to attract the white voter he needed to build a majority. Williamson refrained from sharp attacks on his white opponent or compassionate appeals for an end to segregation (Ibid: 386). Thus, this campaign strategy failed to instill the Negro registrants with the enthusiasm necessary to motivate them to vote for him, even after they had taken the trouble to go to the polls (Ibid: 386-387). Here is a clue to the fact that the African American electorate was not completely sympathetic to any candidates unable to take a powerful and uncompromising stand against segregation. It was simply not enough for the African American candidate to merely list his own qualification for office and call attention to the many endorsements he had received from the cities leading newspapers and white civic organizations (Ibid: 386), particularly when he had no strong civil rights record and/or background.[1] And such a modest and non-threatening stance did get overwhelming support from the southern liberal white community at this moment. Such liberal white voter support suggests that this segment of the electorate was not completely willing to help empower the African American community in this era of segregation. They were much more willing to let the African American voter empower them and they indirectly assisted the community. This amounted to white paternalism.

Nevertheless, the reality here is that in these three early elections, the precinct analysis illustrates that an issue vote stance in the African American electorate coalesced around a moderate white candidate but not around an African American candidate. His refusal to demand an end to segregation cost him the election. Thus, embedded in this African American voter behavior is a sense of morality, notion of both equality and justice.

Beside Walker's precinct study, another model examines non-partisan election in the city, partisans at the presidential and congressional level, referenda and Democratic primary at the congressional and gubernatorial levels (Jennings and Ziegler, 1966: 391-392). Although the chapter relies in part on the percentage of the Negro in the city for its correlation analysis (simple and partial) of its four partisan elections as well as for its five Democratic primary contests and the two non-partisan mayoralty elections and the three referenda, it does make use of precinct return data in the referenda analysis and its overall interpretative findings.[2]

From the data, the chapter tells us that the African American voting behavior in the city was moving at the partisan level from the realignment with the Republican Party to one with the Democratic Party. The authors argue: between 1956 and 1964, Negroes moved to a position of support for the more Liberal national party, a movement producing greater congruity with their liberal and progressive local voting (Ibid: 405).

In referenda voting, their precinct data revealed that in terms of local legislation, the African American electorate supported in an overwhelming fashion progressive legislation, school and civic bond issues as well as potential business opportunity bonds like legal liquor licenses in a state where prohibition held sway. This led to illegal liquor and crime. What emerged was issue voting with a strong moral underpinning in their referenda voting behavior.

Finally, this study found that the moderate-progressive electoral coalition on local elections has its sequel in the Democratic primaries and the electoral tendency of Negro and upper class white voters has produced a dominant ruling coalition in the city of Atlanta (Ibid: 403-404). In another article, these authors demonstrate that this support for moderate white candidates in the city continued in congressional electors in 1962 and 1964 (Jennings and Ziegler, 1964: 595-603).

Drawing from these articles written on data taken from the era of segregation in the city of Atlanta, one finds that the voting behavior of the African American electorate in the city shifted from Republican partisanship to Democratic partisanship and from the support of moderate white candidate and limited support of moderate African American candidates and support of progressive legislation to African American political empowerment by 1969 (Rooks, 1969) to voting for African American empowerment at the state level in 1998 and values with concern for the political system in that mid-term election (Walton, et al, 2001). Therefore, a return to the precinct analysis of the electorate in this city offered additional insights about the nature and significance of African American voting behavior at the start of a new millennium in this nation-state.

To discern African American voting behavior in the 2000 presidential election, we have chosen 44 precincts inside the city of Atlanta where African American registered voters are more than 90% or more of the registered voters in these precincts (Ibid). Hence, our n=44 for this study. Additionally, we need to put the 2000 vote in comparative perspective. Therefore, we will trace back through time and used them in the 1992 and 1996 presidential elections. Thus, over the course of three elections we traced voting patterns from the democratically elected president in 1992 through the attempt for his successful reelection in 1996 through the effort to elect his vice president in the year 2000.

For additional comparative purposes, we will use another urban area in the state, Savannah, Georgia, and employ three African American County Commissioner districts. The Chatham County Board of Election Office reports its result out by aggregating all the precincts in each of the eight county commission districts and reported the results from commission districts. Hence, these districts will give us the relevant voting behavior data for the 1992, 1996 and 2000 African American voter.[3] Beside these two urban areas in Georgia, we will also make use of election return data from a rural area of the state, Hancock County. Like, Atlanta, electoral return data from this county on the African American electorate goes back in time and revealed some interesting voting patterns and trends (Walton, 1994). It has also been explored for African American voting patterns in gubernatorial and presidential elections (Walton, 1992). Hence, it will be used here for comparison purposes in terms of the 1992, 1996 and 2000 elections. The African American vote there will provide a rural perspective.

Moving out the state of Georgia, this analysis will examine African American voting behavior in Florida by analyzing the vote in a county where African Americans are the population majority (60% black and 40% white). In Gadsden County, Florida, it is possible to explore voting in this county over time exploring the 1992, 1996 and 2000 elections. The results of this vote in Florida provided us with some perspective of the problem in the state in the recent presidential election. Collectively, the empirical analysis from the states of Georgia and Florida provide us with a perspective of the southern African American vote in the 2000 election and suggest some meaning behind the African American vote at the millennium elections.

The aggregate election return data provides the informational sources for this study. The statistical methodology that will be used to analyze and evaluate this raw election data is bivariate regression. This technique permitted the authors to assess the relationship between the 1992, 1996 and the 2000 vote. Thereafter, scatterplots were generated from the correlation of these three elections enabled us to determine the degree of linearity between these elections and will therefore tell us something about the nature, scope, and significance of the electoral coalitions in these elections.

Finally, r^2 allows us to predict the nature of the role of partisanship in each election and the percentage left to non-partisan factors in each of these elections. It is the unexplained variance that is not explained by partisanship that will give us clues to the new variables in the 2000 presidential elections which is the goal of the research.

Before closing this section on the data and the methodology for this work, we would like to provide the reader with a sense of the relationship of each of the 44 precincts in each of the elections to each other and the relationship of these same precincts to each other over time. This will provide the reader with a sense of the comparability of the data to each election as well as to the white voter.

Table 1 offered insight by showing that the African American electorate in this predominately African American voting district had a very close and similar vote over three presidential elections. While the 1992 vote was clearly the high point, it declined in 1996 and then rose almost to 1992 vote levels. The fluctuation in this vote suggests that the promise of the Clinton presidency did not live up to the expectation in the African American community, nor did it justify the initial African American support. The performance of the Clinton administration mattered to this electorate. Such performance over four years clearly failed to remobilize the electorate.

Table 1
The Total Vote Parameters in the 44 African American Atlanta Precincts: 1992, 1996 & 2000

Parameters	The Total Vote		
	1992	**1996**	**2000**
Mean	742.3	658.1	727.2
Medium	655	580.5	697
Mode	--	--	801 (2)*
Minimum Vote	136	126	225
Maximum Vote	2,100	1,925	1,785
Total Vote	32,661	28,957	31,998

Source: Fulton County General Election November 3, 1992 Statement of Vote, pp. 1-4; Fulton County General Election November 5, 1996 Statement of Vote, pp. 2-5; Fulton County General and Special Election November 7, 2000 Statement of Vote, pp. 3-7; *Two of the 44 percent in the 2000 election had the same vote total of 801 votes.

Second, the parameters of the African American electorate suggested that presidential candidate Al Gore did not engender as much support from the community as did Clinton. Hence, candidate performance was important to this electorate, but comparatively speaking the support level is drawn slightly from that of the initial Clinton election. Nevertheless, the African American electorate does not penalize the Gore candidacy in any significant way for being Clinton's vice president over eight years. All the political parties in 2000 stimulated this electorate to return to the polls with only a 663 vote drop-off. In terms of mobilization, the millennium election saw only a two percent decline in the political participation level that began with the 1992 elections. Hence, the vote parameters in these Atlanta precincts offered a short time series instead of the regular cross-sectional analysis.

Besides this Atlanta data, there will be the Savannah and Hancock data in Georgia and the Tallahassee and Gadsden County data in Florida; each provided this time dimension so we can see both stability and change. Additionally, the nature of these forces produced a rise of new variables.

The African American Vote in the 2000 Democratic Primaries

Table 1 offers quite interesting information about the nature of the African American voter in the millennium. In the Democratic presidential primaries, when faced with candidate options and their issue stance and public policy options, the African American electorate, while choosing an electable candidate, will diversify their vote and support among the Democratic candidates. This has occurred in both of the states and in both the urban and rural areas.

This pattern and trend repeats and reasserts itself in the 2000 presidential primaries. Vice President Al Gore was an overwhelmingly favorite to win the election. This is more pronounced in the urban areas than in the rural areas, but the pattern in both areas is quite similar. The difference is more in the degrees of support than in the kind of candidate support. There is closeness particularly as the 2000 presidential season commenced. The vice president had significant support and backing within the African American electorate, but the question we want to raise is whether this support is based purely on Democratic partisanship and there are other concerns and wishes within the African American electorate as they entered the polling booths. And perhaps more importantly, will or did the Gore campaign pick up on these other new variables or did they simply rely solely upon the old partisan loyalties and attachments?

This is what we shall provide in our analysis of the African American vote in two states looking at their vote in both urban and rural areas of these states. Thus, the central question is did the preconceived notion of African American partisanship shape the outreach strategies of the nominated candidate, vice president Al Gore? To discern this in empirical terms we now need to turn to the vote of the African American electorate.

African American Voting Behavior at the Millennium: The 2000 Presidential Election in the South

To gain southern perspective on African American voting behavior at the millennium presidential election we did not simply select Atlanta because of the large amount of research data available on African American voting behavior there or because these extensive studies covered so many different types of elections: (1) presidential, (2) congressional, and (3) mayoral nor the longitudinal coverage from 1953 thru 1998 but because it could offer so many precincts (n-44) i.e., number of cases so that we would perform an extensive statistical analysis. Second, Atlanta resides in the state of Georgia and we needed at least two states from the South for a holistic and systematic southern portrait.

Simply put, because the contextual variable is so prevalent in this election, we needed one state where it existed and one state where it did not exist. Georgia provided the state where the central contextual variable did not exist. Pausing for a moment, we need to indicate to the reader that the central contextual variable in the 2000 election in the South was Florida's Republican

Governor, Jeb Bush's attack on and removal of the Affirmative Action legislation in the state that had been fostered in part by African American neo-conservative, Ward Connerly. The removal of Affirmative Action protection energized and mobilized the African American electorate in this state like no other force. Hence, Florida is the state with this critical contextual variable and the Georgia African American electorate did not force such a blatant attack upon their civil and political rights. Thus, Georgia and Florida were selected because one carried this variable and the other did not.[4] Tallahassee, Florida does not have as many African American precincts as Atlanta because the latter city is predominately African American, but the urban area and rural area in both states permits comparison of the two electorates in this century beginning election.

Beginning with the initial step of African American voting behavior in this election as Table 2 demonstrates that in the urban areas African American turnout at the end of the Reagan Administration was quite high with almost two-thirds of the registered electorate going to the polls. However, the Clinton Administration did live up to its initial promise and great expectations from the African American community particularly in terms of civil rights enforcement so that in the urban area there was a significant decline in the urban areas for Clinton's reelection (Walton and Smith, 2000). But in the millennium election the African American electorate once again turned out for Vice-President Al Gore and this turnout was just below the 1992 level.

In the rural areas, there is a difference between the turnout in Florida and in Georgia; however, in both counties the turnout rose from Clinton between 1992 and 1996. The rural African American electorate was quite willing to increase their support for Clinton's reelection efforts. [5] However, this higher support for Clinton's reelection did not translate to an even higher support for vice president Gore in the millennium election. In the rural eras, African Americans did not turnout in record numbers, but nevertheless, gave similar support for Gore as had the urban areas. In this millennium election, the African American urban and rural electorates in both states have converged to mobilize two-thirds of their registered voters to participate in this election. Hence, the unique feature of this election is the similar degree of convergence in turnout trends and patterns.

To gain further insights into this unique turnout pattern, a correlational analysis of Atlanta's 44 precincts demonstrates that the association between turnout in 1992 and 1996 is $r=.85$ and the association between turnout in 1996 and 2000 is $r=.91$; the numbers represent extremely high levels of association. Thus, using the r^2 measurement suggests that 73% of the African Americans who turned out in 1992 came back in 1996 and that 82% of these that turned out in 1996 came back in 2000. Hence, Clinton's reelection efforts brought 27% more people out in 1996, and Al Gore brought out some 18% more people in 2000.

Moving from the turnout picture to the number of total votes cast in this election one finds in Table 4 that in the urban areas the general trend starts with the largest vote in 1992, where the table indicate a decline in the total vote for Clinton's reelection effort and a major rise in 2000 but not back to the 1992 levels. The exception to this trend is Savannah where the 2000 vote does not rise but simply declines over the 1996 vote.

Surprisingly the rural areas mimic the urban areas; 1992 is the year of the highest vote, 1996 sees a decline and the 2000 vote rebounds, but not to the 1992 high point. Simply put, Al Gore and George W. Bush and two thirds of the parties brought out more voters to the polls in this millennium election everywhere except in Savannah, Georgia.

Table 2
The African American Democratic Presidential Primary Vote Percentage in the Urban & Rural Areas of Florida & Georgia: 1992, 1996 & 2000

Candidates	URBAN		
	Atlanta	Savannah	Tallahassee
1992			
Clinton	72.7	65.8	*
Tsongas	14.3	14.9	*
Brown	6.5	10.0	*
Others	6.4	9.3	*
1996			
Clinton	100.0	100.0	*
2000			
Al Gore	95.1	*	*
Bill Bradley	4.9	*	*

Candidates	RURAL	
	1992	
	Hancock County	Gadson County
Clinton	68.0	61.8
Tsongas	13.6	15.0
Brown	10.2	20.0
Others	7.3	3.3
1996		
Clinton	100.0	None Held
2000		
Al Gore	87.4	*
Bill Bradley	12.6	*

Source: Fulton County Presidential Preference Primary March 3, 1992, Fulton County Presidential Preference Primary March 5, 1996 Statement of Vote; Fulton County Presidential Reference Primary March 7, 2000 Statement of Vote; Chatham County Board of Electors Consolidated Returns Democratic Presidential Preference Primary March 3, 1992; Chatham *County Board of Election Consolidated Returns Presidential Preference Primary and Special Election March 5, 1996; Chatham County Statement of*

Votes Cast Presidential Preference Primary. Secretary of State, Consolidated Vote State Democratic and Republican Presidential Primary, March 3, 1992; Secretary of State, Consolidated Vote State Democratic and Republican Primary, March 5, 1996; Secretary of State, Consolidated Vote State Democratic and Republic Primary March 30, 2000; The Leon County data was taken directly from the web.

Table 3
The Mean Turnout Percentage in African American Urban and Rural Areas of Georgia & Florida: 1992, 1996 & 2000 Presidential Election

Mean Turnout	1992	1996	2000
URBAN AREAS			
Atlanta	64.8	55.1	63.5
Savannah		58.2	64.5*
Tallahassee	67.4	51.9	64.6
Mean		55.1	64.2
RURAL AREAS			
Gadsden County	59.0	66.3	71.7
Hancock County	78.0	80.7	64.0
Mean	67.3	75.5	65.4

Source: *Fulton County Presidential General Election November 3, 1992 Statement of Vote; Fulton County General Election November 5, 1996 Statement of Vote; Fulton County General and Special Election November 7, 2000 Statement of Vote; Chatham County General Election, November 3, 1992; Chatham County General Election November 5, 1996; Chatham County Statement of Votes Cast General Election November 7, 2000; Secretary of State; General Election November 3, 1992; Secretary of State General Election November 5,1996; Secretary of State, General Election November 7, 2000;* The Leon County data was taken directly from the web. All calculations conducted by the authors.

Thus, African Americans were simply not motivated to come out in large numbers than in 1996.

    If this is the turnout portrait in the African American electorate in the millennium election, how does this turnout translate into party voting behavior? Table 5 indicates that at the percentage level that the African American electorate had an overwhelming preference for the Democratic Party. Although the specific percentage varies in all five areas, the basic trend is democratic. Likewise, there is modest support for the Republican Party. By contrast, less than one in five voters cast a ballot for the Republican president.

Table 4

The Total Votes Cast in African American Urban and Rural Areas of Florida & Georgia: 1992, 1996 & 2000

Precincts &Counties	1992	1996	2000
URBAN			
Atlanta	32,661	28,957	31,998
Savannah	15,196	19,312	18,135
Tallahassee	*	2,671	3,956
RURAL			
Gadsden	14,394	14,199	14,721
Hancock	3,157	2,646	3,082

Source: Fulton County Presidential General Election November 3, 1992 Statement of Vote; Fulton County General Election November 5, 1996 Statement of Vote; Fulton County General and Special Election November 7, 2000 Statement of Vote; Chatham County General Election, November 3, 1992; Chatham County General Election November 5, 1996; Chatham County Statement of Votes Cast General Election November 7, 2000; Secretary of State; General Election November 3, 1992; Secretary of State General Election November 5,1996; Secretary of State, General Election November 7, 2000; The Leon County data was taken directly from the web.
Calculations by the authors.

In both Atlanta and Tallahassee, the vote for the Democratic Party has steadily increased over the decade of the nineties, with the millennium election getting the absolute strongest support. However, in Savannah, the strength of the support for the Democratic Party has declined over this time period. In fact, this slight decline could be explained in part to the whites in these county commission districts that voted for the Bush-led Republican Party (a Southerner in this case). At the rural level, the support for the Democratic Party is less than in the urban areas and the trend over time indicate a slow increase until the millennium election where there is a decline. But does this percentage portrait mask some of the dimensions?

The collective portrait at the total vote level is that in most of the five African American areas under analysis, the majority shows a rebound of the African American vote for the Democratic Party and a decline in the vote for the Republican Party indicating there is no uniform consistency here in this decade-long voting behavior. Additional insights can be had if we return to the Democratic partisanship percentage in the Atlanta precincts and employ a correlational analysis. The 1992-1996 elections are poorly related given that the r=.34 and the 1996-2000 vote is a bit stronger with an r=.66 and the relationship of the 1992-2000 election have an r=.31. Thus, the 1996-2000 elections are moderately associated with each other but not strongly so. In qualitative terms, the African American voters in Atlanta saw each election in a separate and different manner and not related even though the 1992 and 1996 elections had the same candidate, and the 2000 election had the vice presidential candidate of the 1992 and 1996 years. Seemingly, the African American voter discovered different things in each of these elections in terms of what interested and concerned them. Despite the fact that this analysis centers on the democratic partisanship of the African American electorate in each case, some different set or combination of variables drove their voting behavior in each presidential election. Clearly it was not democratic loyalties.

Table 5
The Mean Major Party Percentages in African American
Urban and Rural Areas of Georgia & Florida: 1992, 1996 & 2000

Precincts/	1992		1996		2000		
Counties	% Dem.	% Rep.	% Dem	% Rep.	%Dem	%	Rep.
URBAN							
Atlanta	93.3	3.8	96.3	2.3	96.9		2.7
Savannah			84.6	12.7	76.4		14.1
Tallahassee	**	**	89.2	6.3	90.0		1.8
Mean			90.0	7.1	87.8		6.2
RURAL							
Gadsden County	59.0	27.6	66.3	26.9	66.1		32.4
Hancock County	78.0	16.0	80.7	16.6	78.3		21.5
Mean	68.5	21.8	73.5	21.8	82.6		13.1

Source: *Fulton County Presidential General Election November 3, 1992 Statement of Vote; Fulton County General Election November 5, 1996 Statement of Vote; Fulton County General and Special Election November 7, 2000 Statement of Vote; Chatham County General Election, November 3, 1992; Chatham County General Election November 5, 1996; Chatham County Statement of Votes Cast General Election November 7, 2000; Secretary of State; General Election November 3, 1992; Secretary of State General Election November 5,1996; Secretary of State, General Election November 7, 2000; The Leon County data was taken directly from the web. Calculations by the* authors. *The percentages in this Table do not add up to 100 in each year simply because the minor party vote and percentage was left out of the calculations. **The vote and percentage for Tallahassee was not available on the web for 1992.

Table 6
The Votes Cast for the Major Political Parties in African American
Urban and Rural Areas of Florida & Georgia: 1992, 1996 & 2000

Precincts/	1992		1996		2000	
Counties	Dem.	Rep.	Dem	Rep.	Dem	Rep.
URBAN						
Atlanta	30,470	1,258	27,838	689	30,965	864
Savannah			16,345	2,432	15,772	2,284
Tallahassee	**	**	2,424	139	2,388	51
RURAL						
Gadsden County	8,486	3,975	9,407	3,817	4,735	4,767
Hancock County	2,461	506	2,135	438	2,414	662

Source: *Fulton County Presidential General Election November 3, 1992 Statement of Vote; Fulton County General Election November 5, 1996 Statement of Vote; Fulton County General and Special Election November 7, 2000 Statement of Vote; Chatham County General Election, November 3, 1992; Chatham County General Election November 5, 1996; Chatham County Statement of Votes Cast General Election November 7, 2000; Secretary of State; General Election November 3, 1992; Secretary of State General Election November 5,1996; Secretary of State, General Election November 7, 2000*; The Leon County data was taken directly from the web. Calculations by the authors. *This information was not available on the web.

The 2000 African American Presidential Vote: An Analysis

What can one discern about the primary, general election data and analysis concerning the African American presidential vote at the millennium? First, we learned that the Gore candidacy tended to increase turnout among African American democrats, it did not raise the turnout level beyond that in 1992. Total votes cast tend to follow this trend. This suggests that the Gore candidacy did not mobilize the African American Democrat as much as did the Clinton candidacy. This might be due in part to the Reagan legacy (Tate, 1994: 191-192).

Second, at the millennium, the Democratic partisanship of the African American electorate is still very pronounced, but it started to slip slightly from its decade peak in 1992. The Gore candidacy did not stimulate the African American electorate as much as it could have. Maybe the Clinton-Gore fatigue was starting to impact the Gore African American voters. Clearly, expectations in the African American electorate had not been fully filled and slippage was noticeable. The Democratic Party's sole reliance upon African American democratic partisan identification was certainly not enough in and of itself consistent; indeed there is a disconnect. Third, the critical issue of Governor Jeb Bush's destruction of the state Affirmative Action policies increased the turnout and mobilization efforts in the state, but there is not that much noticeable difference except at the level of the vote for the Republican Party. The minuscule vote for the Republican Party in the African American areas is not overwhelming. Thus, other factors inhibited the mobilization of the African American electorate and its influence. Contextual variables mediate this outburst. This mobilization simply did not translate into great numbers and output in Florida's presidential election.

Lastly, our measurement technique, bivariate regression, allowed us to take the 44 cases from Atlanta and use the r^2=predict values to make some interpretive reflections about new variables possibly shaping the millennium votes beside partisans Figure 1 takes the r^2 data for the three presidential elections based on the correlational analysis of the Democratic presidential vote in 1992, 1996 and 2000 and the finding from an earlier correctional analysis of the mid-term congressional election of 1994 and 1998 and combined them in a time series as presented in Figure 1 as the percentage of the African American Democratic vote not determined by partisanship. In the 1992-1996 election, 88 percent of the African American vote was driven by other considerations. Numerous issues and political matters drove the African American vote. The impact of the Reagan-Bush years, coupled with the slanting and limited outreach of the Clinton-Gore views, shaped the vote. And between the 1992 and the 2000 elections, variables like candidates, issues and community needs account for 91 percent of the African American vote. However, faced with a Democratic vice

Figure 1
The Percentage of the African American Vote
Not Determined by Democratic Partisanship

		% explained by Democratic Partisanship	% unexplained by Democratic Partisanship
1992-1996		12%	88%
1992-2000		9%	91%
1996-2000		44%	66%
YEARS	1992-1996	1992-2000	1996-2000

Source: Correlation based on the Democratic percentage of the vote in the 44 precincts. Calculations prepared by the authors.

president that has no real performance record, merely campaign promises, 66 percent of African American voting behavior at the millennium was shaped by factors other than Democratic partisanship. As we have seen, the Al Gore campaign did not really tap into these factors or identify these new variables that drove African Americans to the polls. And it goes without saying that these new variables are embedded in both contextual and systemic variables. They must have been both economic and issue based but not having identified them and the Gore campaign never reached the achievements of Clinton.

At the millennium, Democratic partisanship does not describe or begin to explain or characterize African American presidential voting behavior. It never did. As the empirical analysis revealed, it is at times not even a persuasive guide as to why the African American voters vote democratic. And even this guide overlooks the fact that at the millennium African American voting for third parties and the Republican Party remains minuscule. In fact, the very best that can be said about the Democratic partisanship of the African American voter is that it is a brilliant commentary on party behavior in America at the presidential and sub-presidential levels.

Endnotes

1. One of the authors of this study was in Atlanta during the Williamson campaign and noticed that Williamson did not even quietly assure the community about where he stood.
2. For the percentage of data see Table 1, pages 395-396 and for the precinct information, see pages 399-401, and 404-405.
3. For an earlier use of this data see Hanes Walton, Jr., *Invisible Politics* (Albany: State University of New York Press, 1988); For a use of this data to understand African American voting behavior in Savannah's mayoral elections see Hanes Walton, Jr., et. Al., "The African American Republican Vote in a Southern Mayoral Election," in Hanes Walton, Jr., *African American Power and Politics: The Political Context Variable* (New York: Columbia University Press, 1997), pp. 192-207; for a most recent use of this data for the 1996 Presidential Election see, Hanes Walton, Jr., & Robert Smith, *American Politics and the African American Quest for Universal Freedom* (New York: Longman, 2000), p. 144, Table 9.6.
4. Another major contextual factor in the South during the period just before the millennium vote was the flag issue in South Carolina. But the issue was taken care of in the South Carolina gubernatorial election in 1998 when the state African American electorate returned a Republican governor that favored the Rebel flag and the Democratic candidate called for a return of that flag. African Americans put the Democratic governor in office. Although George W. Bush in the presidential primary supported the Rebel flag, this issue subsided two years later in the presidential election, nor was it raised again in the campaign.
5. This had happened in Hancock County to President Jimmy Carter during his reelection efforts. It increased while the urban vote went down. See Hanes Walton, Jr., *The Native-Son Presidential Candidate: The Carter Vote in Georgia* (New York: Praeger, 1992), pp. 113-114.

References

Campbell, Angus, Philip Converse, Warren Miller and Donald Stokes. 1960. *The American Voter*. New York: John Wiley.

Fiorna, Morris. 1981. *Retrospective Voting in American National Elections*. New Haven: Yale University Press.

Jennings, M. Kent and L. Harmon Ziegler. 1996. "Electoral Strategies and Voting Patterns in a Southern Congressional District." M. Kent Jennings and L. Harmon Ziegler (eds.). *The Electoral Process*. Englewood Cliffs, NJ: Prentice Hall.

_____. 1966. "Class, Party, and Race in Four Types of Elections: The Case of Atlanta." *Journal of Politics*, (May).

_____. 1964. "A Moderate Victory in a Southern Congressional District." *Public Opinion Quarterly*, (Winter), Vol. 28.

Lichtman, Allan and Ken DeCell. 1990. *The 13 Keys to the Presidency: Predictions Without Polls*. Lanham: Madison Books.

Miller, Warren. 1996. *The New American Voter*. Cambridge: Harvard University Press.

Rooks, Charles. 1970. *The Atlanta Election of 1969*. Atlanta: Voting Education.

Walker, Jack. 1944. "Negro Voting in Atlanta: 1953-1961." *Phylon* (Winter), Vol. 24.

Walton, Jr., Hanes. 1994. "Black Voting Behavior in the Segregationists Era." In Hanes Walton, Jr., *Black Political Behavior: A Linkage Analysis*. Westport: Praeger.

_____. 1992. *The Native-Son Presidential Candidate: The Carter Vote in Georgia*. Westport: Praeger.

_____. 1988. *Invisible Politics*. Albany, NY: SUNY Press of New York.

Walton, Jr., Hanes, Lester Spence, Maxie Foster and Thomas N. Walton. 2001. "African American Voting Behavior, President Clinton's Scandal and the 1998 Election: The Search for the New Variables." *National Political Science Review*, Vol. 8.

Walton, Jr., Hanes and Robert Smith. 2000. *American Politics and the African American Quest for Universal Freedom*. New York: Longman.

Walton, Jr., Hanes, 1997. "The African American Republican Vote in a Southern Mayoral Election." In Hanes Walton, Jr., *African American Power and Politics: The Political Context Variable*. New York: Columbia University Press.

Chapter 2

Affirmative Action:
What is the Question?

Mack H. Jones

At this point in American history, the most widely discussed question in the area of race and public policy is: Should individuals be given special consideration in seeking access to jobs, educational institutions, and other coveted societal positions because of their race? That was the question debated by the U.S. Supreme Court in the landmark affirmative action cases of *Richmond* v. *Croson* (1989), *Miller* v. *Johnson* (1995), and by the Circuit Court in *Haywood* v. *Texas* (1996), and that was how the issue was defined in the Calilornia referendum on Proposition 209. The issue was framed in a similar fashion in 1997, when the Michigan legislatttre called for an investigation of its flagship university for discriminating against "better qualified" whites while admitting "lesser qualified" black students. To ask whether one should be given special consideration merely because of race is to guarantee that the answer will be no. No intelligent proponent of democracy would argue that special consideration should be given to any individttal or grottp merely because of their race. But in the context of the struggle for racial justice in America, that is not the appropriate question to raise nosy, nor has it ever been the question. The pertinent question is: Should special consideration be given to individuals who belong to a group that was singled out for unequal treatment by the Constitution of the United States and by statutory law at all levels of American government—national, state, and local—and whose unequal treatment was sanctioned by social custom and reinforced by the use of terror and economic intimidation and who, as a result of that government mandated and culturally sanctioned oppression, lag behind white Americans on practically every indicator of socioeconomic well-being? The question is: Should members of that oppressed group receive special consideration until such time that the gap between them and the dominant group on these indicators of well-being is eliminated?

That is the question that history and ordinary logic would lead us to raise. And if that were the question posed for the public policy debate, the dialogue would certainly be different. But that is not how the question is phrased, because the ordinary rules of logic are rarely, if ever, followed in the discussion of race and public policy in America. Questions about race are almost always raised in such a way as to deny the reality and severity of racial oppression as a fundamental force in American life and culture. To understand the contemporary debate about affirmative action and other so-called race-specific remedies, it is necessary to understand how this came to be. To do so we must go back to the very founding of the country.

On matters involving relations between European and other peoples of the world, the United States was founded on a fundamental contradiction. The Declaration of Independence, and the Constitution that was adopted subsequently to bring about the new state envisaged in the Declaration, spoke of the rights of man as the major pillar of human society. Yet the framers of these documents were slave holders in a slave holding society that owed its very existence as an economically viable state to the then ongoing genocide of the native inhabitants and to the unrequited labor of millions of enslaved Africans. As a slave holding, multi-ethnic, and multiracial society founded on the principle of white supremacy, America evolved a uniquely racist culture that made qualitative distinctions not only among the different socially constructed racial groups but also among the various ethnic communities within the different racial groups. Europeans were placed at the apex of the racial hierarchy, followed by Asians, Native Americans, and Africans, in that order. Within the European group, Aryan-featured Europeans received top billing, with their more swarthy, central and southern European compatriots occupying the lower rungs. The hierarchy among the ethnic groups in the Asian and African communities (i.e., Chinese versus Koreans, West Indians versus North American born blacks, etc.), was more fluid depending upon white interests at any given historical moment.

The idea of white supremacy and its corollary, the notion of black inferiority, provided the ideological justification for this pernicious rank ordering of humanity. It created and sustained ideologies that justified the most inhumane treatment of people of color. At the same time, the basic documents of the country that proclaimed belief in the equality of all humanity were cleverly written to disguise the racists principles imbedded in them. For example, those who drafted the Declaration of Independence managed to call for the creation of a new political system dedicated to the proposition that all men were created equal and had the inalienable right to life, liberty, and property—while at the same time enslaving millions of African people and holding countless thousands of their white compatriots as indentured servants. Following their successful war of independence, these self-proclaimed democrats drafted a constitution that retained the legitimacy of slavery, forbade the new government from legislating on the matter for at least 20 years, and obligated the National government to use its powers to return those who managed to escape enslavement to their erstwhile slave masters. The framers put all of this in the Constitution without ever mentioning the words slavery, African people, or anything else that would indicate the real nature of the society they had built and were trying to maintain.

Hence, since its inception, the United States has been a thorough going racist society, but one in deep denial and one in which everything is done to maintain white supremacy and domination at home and abroad while denying that racism and racial oppression are major elements of American political culture and practice. Indeed, the principle documents of American history raise self-deception to the level of an art form. One of the results of this charade in self-deception has been the development of a cultore in which the normal rules of logic are often suspended when the subject is race and racial oppression. Concepts and conceptual frameworks are developed to facilitate public policy discussions of the reality of racial oppression while at the same time denying that it exists. I have in mind concepts such as minorities, the disadvantaged, inner cities, individuals at risk, multiculturalism, and diversity, to name just a few.

The development of such concepts and their use in generating propositions about the nature of American life and the place of black folk in it defy the rules ordinarily used in developing empirically useful concepts and making logical inferences about experience. Instead, we get discussions that are more non-logical or illogical than logical. At the same time, however, those of us who are grounded in the American conceptualization of sttch matters are conditioned to accept this illogical discussion of race as if it makes sense. This spastic dance of self-deception is joined by practically every segment of American life, without regard to race, class, gender, creed, or color. Indeed, an interplanetary visitor from Mars who observed America at work and play and saw the great racial divide manifested in these activities and then listened to the public discussion about it would certainly find it incredulous.

There is, however, a transcendental logic to this illogical dance. The transcendental logic is that it serves to maintain and reinforce the system of white supremacy and black subordination while, to borrow a term from a different but related area of inquiry, leaving space for plausible denial by those who have a need to do so.

Nowhere is this more apparent than in contemtporary discussions of race and public policy, particularly discussions about affirmative action and other so-called race-specific remedies. When the question is stated as "should individuals be given special consideration because of race," it camouflages the historical reality and the systemic character of black oppression. And even more perniciously, by asserting that the pertinent category is race rather than oppression and that the question is should special consideration be given because of race, it equates the lived experiences of the various racial groups as theoretically and historically coordinate and prepares the public to accept the argument that what is done or not done for one should be done or not done for all others.

But the theoretical, historical, and empirically useful category that gives rise to affirmative action as an intervention strategy is oppression, and not race or minority status. Special consideration is being sought for members of a group that occupies a subordinate position in society, not because of their race or their minority status, but because of an empirically demonstrable, specific pattern of historical and contemporary oppression. This concept of oppression, as inferred in the opening paragraph of this essay, can be easily and scientifically operationalized. No other group falls into this category. To be sure, other groups have suffered oppression in America, but none was the subject of slavery and constitutionally mandated oppression and none suffered through centuries of violence and terror. The matter of terror and violence is especially important because, more than anything else, it is this that prevented blacks from accumulating wealth during the early days of primitive accumulation in the republic; as Oliver and Shapiro have demonstrated, this lack of wealth is perhaps the major factor that guarantees the continued subordination of black Americans.

To reinforce this point, many have forgotten and perhaps even more never knew that for almost a full century, lynching was used as a primary tactic to maintain black subordination. The practice was so widespread that, beginning in 1881, Tuskegee University began issuing annual reports on the lynching of black Americans. It was not until 1952, 71 years later, that it reported no lynchings had been brought to its attention *(World Almanac,* 88). It was through violence and terror that the southern planter class reimposed its dominance on the emancipated black nation and sowed the seeds for the enduring "race problem." However, the ideology was so strong that Congress repeatedly refused to make lynching a federal crime.

Rather than acknowledge the reality of oppression and use it as the triggering mechanism for remedial legislation, policy makers prefer to use terms such as "minority" and "diversity" to justify affirmative action initiatives. Taken together, such terms paint a rather benign and self-serving portrait of the problem while reinforcing the image of the United States as a racially and ethnically diverse society in which some groups are overwhelmed because of their smaller numbers and, as a result, are underrepresented in various societal institutions. To compensate for this and because they believe that there is some special virtue in diversity, this portrait implies, dominant whites develop programs to increase the number of minorities in these institutions. Affirmative action becomes an act of majority benevolence rather than one of reparation to atone for past and continuing crimes against humanity.

But if we put the question of affirmative action and other so-called race-specific remedies in proper historical context, we begin with a quite different set of questions, and a decidedly different and more useful discussion unfolds. We begin by asking how and why did blacks get so far behind white Americans on practically all indicators of socioeconomic well-being. The answer, of course, is to be found in slavery and the century of state mandated and culturally sanctioned oppression that followed emancipation. The angry white males and their sympathizers would prefer not to hear this. For them, slavery and its aftermath were merely an accident of history that has no connection to contemporary problems and shottld be forgotten. To insist on the salience of slavery as an important catisal factor in the current unequal position of blacks is decried as whining victimization.

However, while we may will that slavery and its aftermath be forgotten. their social and systemic consequences have proven to be more stubborn. How else can we explain that none of the pressing societal problems of the current age—

deteriorating inner cities, public welfare, the urban underclass, inadequate public schools, crime, poverty, structural unemployment, drugs, and the militia movement, to name a few—can be understood apart from the issue of race and racism in society?

At the time of emancipation, as even the most unenlightened cannot deny blacks lagged behind whites on all measures of socioeconomic wellbeing; after Sherman's aborted experiment in the sea islands, nothing was done to promote socioeconomic equality. Instead, states passed laws requiring segregation and discrimination, and the national government, through its own policies, reinforced the discrimination and oppression mandated by the states. This was true in education, in government service, in corporations and labor unions, in sports, in the church, and in the military. These oppressive policies were culturally sanctioned and enforced by terror and violence. As a result, from the beginning of their freedom blacks had higher unemployment rates, a higher incidence of poverty, lower educational attainment, higher infant mortality rates, lower incomes, and lower life expectancy (see U.S. Bureau of the Census, *The Social and Economic Status of the Black Population in the United States, 1790-1978)*. The gap between blacks and whites that existed following emancipation never svent away. An elementary nile of causal analysis says that the cause must exist prior to the effect. Since the gap dates back to emancipation, more recent contemporary effects cannot be its cause.

When the civil rights movement erupted in the 1960s, these inequalities that initially developed during slavery and its aftermath still characterized black life. In spite of remedial laws and court decisions, the gap between black and white wellbeing remained substantial. It was the realization that changing laws would not necessarily change the material conditions that led to the push for what came to be known as affirmative action.

Affirmative action as an intervention strategy to reduce the gap between blacks and whites grew out of a particular understanding of the nature of the American political economy—an understanding that viewed the economy as analogous to a big gun that fires a shot and at the same time recoils. Out of one end it produces advantages, such as employment, good jobs, wealth, advanced education and training, comfortable housing, enviable health care, safe neighborhoods, and a host of other desirable outcomes. Simultaneously, out of the other end comes the debilities: unemployment, poverty-level jobs, substandard education, poor and limited health care, and a litany of other undesirable outcomes. The important thing to understand here is that both the advantages and debilities, the good things and the bad, are all routine outcomes of the American political economy. Low-paying jobs are not created by the people who hold them. Both high and low-paying jobs are systemic creations. The relative mix of high-paying and low-paying jobs at any given historical moment is a function of the dynamics of politico-economic processes. We see this in the current reduction of the number of high-paying industrial jobs and the concomitant rise in the volume of lesser-paying service sector positions. And we see it when increases in unemployment follow decisions of the federal reserve system to raise interests rates to temper inflation.

The compelling question in this regard is: What forces determine who will get the advantages routinely produced by the system and who must settle for the debilities? How will the disadvantages be allocated? American political thought says that individual inilialive determines who gets ahead, but experiential reality is much more complex. As even the casual observer knows, individual initiative is exercised within a framework structured by major systemic forces. Thus, the critical questions are: What forces structure the environment within which individuals strive? And how does this structure impact the allocation of advantages and debilities?

The law is one major force. For a long time in America, the law guaranteed that whites would get more than their fair share of the advantages and, correspondingly, that blacks would get more than their fair share of the debilities. Laws limiting black access were put in place to regulate the ltves of free blacks during the slave epoch and were carried over and elaborated upon following emancipation. For example, when the law denied blacks the right to enter the only state school that offered degrees in, say, engineering, medicine, or law, it ensured that whites would get more than their fair share of the advantages and, conversely, that blacks would get more than their fair share of the debilities. Even when blacks managed to obtain such training in spite of the law, other social forces operated to ensure their subordination. The advantages for whites were cumulative and transgenerational, as the sorts and daughters of the graduates of such professional programs accumufated wealth that guaranteed that their children would start with even greater advantages over the sons and daughters of blacks whose opportunities had been constrained by the law. The systemic impact of such laws was recognized by the Supreme Court in *Sweat* v. *Painter* (1950).

But it was not only the law that guaranteed this inequality. The social, financial, cultural, educational, and economic systems functioned interdependently to ensure that whites, particularly white men, got more of the advantages and less than their fair share of the debilities, We should keep in mind that in the decades immediately following emancipation, the preponderance of blacks lived in the southern states where they constituted substantial proportions of the population, in some areas approaching majority status. This meant that in the then-racist, patriarchal, class-based society, white men of means had to compete only with themselves for the most coveted societal positions. Perhaps that should be designated as the first era of affirmative action. Under current conditions, the competition is much keener, and perhaps, hence white men's anger.

Oliver and Shapiro captured the systemic character of deprivation when they asserted the following:

> Our examination ... shows that tinequal background and social conditions result in unequal resources. Whether it be a matter of education, occupation. family status, or other characteristics positively correlated with income wealth. Blacks are most likely to come out on the short end of the stick.. We argue furthermore, that the racialization of the welfare state and institutional discrimination are fundamental

reasons for the persistent wealth-disparities we obsersved. Government policies that have paved the way for whites to amass wealth have simultaneously discriminated against blacks in their quest for economic security. From the era of slavery on through the failure of the freedman to gain land and the Jim Crow laws that restricted black entrepreneurs, opportunity for asset accumulation rewarded whites and penalized blacks. (1997, 174)

To return to the argument of systemic deprivation and to demonstrate how the various systems working interdependently reproduced and continue to produce racial inequalities, we might reflect on the plight of the child of a low income Black family living in inner city America and compare it with that of a white child in suburbia. To make the comparison we might ask how the financial system and the labor market impact their respective chances for living in a safe and commodious neighborhood. How do the political and educational systems determine the quality of elementary and secondary schools each will attend, and, in turn, how do these systems influence their respective scores on college admission tests; on devices used for screening applicants for professional schools, such as law and medicine; and on their financial ability to matriculate at such an institution? *To raise these questions is to dramatize the extent to which individual initiative is constrained by systematic forces that predict group outcomes.*

Here, the phrase *group outcomes* is important because opponents of affirmative action are quick to point out that countless Black individuals from such neighborhoods have siteceeded and that their success is evidence that individual initiative rather than systemic conditions determines outcomes. However, the question, or at least the one that interests me, is not about individual success but about why there is such a wide gap in well-being between *blacks and whites as groups* and how the gap can be reduced. The argument being advanced here is that sustained intervention in the various systems reinforced by supportive changes in other societal institutions would change the systems themselves and eventually produce different group outcomes. Greater numbers of Blacks would receive the advantages and fewer would get the debilities. Eventually, more Blacks would occupy pivotal positions in these systems and, in turn, the systems would begin to produce different and more equitable outcomes.

Systems, of course, are resistant to change and can easily coop limited and short-term interventions, but they can be transformed through concerted action. The hiring of a few black loan officers, for example, would not necessarily change lending policies, but the presence of significant numbers of Black bank directors and bank officers committed to policy changes could, over a long period of time, change how the system works. Indeed, the changing racial complexion of American institutions of higher education is evidence of the impact that sustained intervention may have and the deliberately deceptive debate over so-called political correctness and the present anti-affirmative action hysteria dramatize the resistance that it may generate.

Let me close this essay by commenting on the arguments of some of the critics of affirmative action and other so-called race specific remedies. A popular argument among some whites is the lament that while affirmative action may have been necessary early on, it is no longer the case since racial discrimination is a thing of the past (Cohen. 1996). It is interesting to note that those making this argument vehemently opposed efforts to end state-mandated segregation and discrimination in the 1950s. In response to the Supreme Cottrt ruling *Brown* v. *Board of Education* (1954), these opponents argued that segregation (and by inference, racism) was a valuable and enduring aspect of American culture and that cultures could not be transformed by legislative, judicial, or other political acts. Cultures, they argued further, could be transformed only through gradual, self-initiated change. Political actions, they continued, would only heighten tensions between the races and make things worse.

However, a few decades later, after fighting tooth and nail against all efforts to overturn the racist order, these erstwhile proponents of state-mandated segregation declared that racism had indeed ended and that the question of race and oppression should no longer be a public concern. The inequities and inequalities that were carried over from the era of statemandated discrimination are declared to be functions of individual and/or group failures. Indeed, some go as far as to argue that affirmative action and other so-called race-specific remedies are the cause of current inequalities. As alluded to above, such assertions contravene the elementary principles of causal inference.

There are other criticisms, particularly those coming from conservative black intellectuals that merit consideration. Some argue that affirmative action only benefits the black middle class and, as such, its social divisiveness outweighs whatever benefits it may bring (Loury, 1984). Two responses to that criticism come quickly to mind. The first is that the validity of the claim has not been established. It is true that affirmative action and set-aside programs do not target low-income jobs, but no intervention strategy was necessary to give blacks access to low-paying, dead-end jobs. The important question is: Who are the people moving into the middle-income positions and university spaces made available through affirmative action? I am unaware of any systematic studies designed to answer such questions. I do know, however, scores of persons from poor families, myself included, who have achieved middle-class status with the assistance of such efforts.

The other response to the claim that affirmative action benefits the black middle class disproportionately is that the United States is a class-based society and that in such societies all public policies are biased in favor of the more well-to-do. All of the other government intervention programs favor those who are better off. This is true of the farm programs, the various housing/mortgage programs, programs offering assistance to businesses, and programs focusing on international trade, to name only a few. Even programs established expressly to assist poor individuals invariably do more for privileged classes than they do for the poor. So even if it is trite that affirmative action has a class bias that is no different from any other government-sponsored intervention program. Thus, the criticism is more of an indictment of America as a class-based society than an indictment of affirmative action as an intervention strategy.

The class issue, however, is central to any enlightened discussion of the controversy over affirmative action and other so-called race-specific remedies, and it should be confronted head-on. To the extent that these programs benefit middle—income blacks, working—class whites with lesser incomes and material privileges may justifiably feel aggrieved. After all, they are being taxed in one way or another to assist those whose material conditions may already be greater than their own. But that is trite for all of the government intervention programs mentioned. The fact that the class bias of affirmative action and other race specific remedies are recognized and opposed while the similar bias of other intervention programs are cheerhitily indulged cries out for explanation. Those who oppose affirmative action because of its class bias, especially black intellectuals, should broaden their opposition to include all class privileges. In doing so they would fulfill the role of enlightened dissenters called for by Martin Luther King, Jr.

On the other hand, noderlying the argument for affirmative action and set-aside programs (though rarely clearly stated) was the commitment, however tepid, to create a class structure within the black community that mirrored that of the broader American society. That was the focus of the vartotts government and privately sponsored Black capitalism schemes, including efforts to have franchises for capital intensive operations, such as automobile dealerships and television stations, awarded to prosperous blacks and to award multimillion-dollar contracts to Black construction firms. If properly structured, the debate over the class bias of affirmative action and set-asides could be used to educate all Americans about the systemic implications of the class character of American society and make white working class people more conscious of their own self interest.

Another anti-affirmative action argument advanced within the black community is the assertion that it is detrimental to black self-esteem, because affirmative hires do not command the respect of their white colleagues (Carter, 1991). In response to this assertion, at the risk of sounding flippant, one could argue that the lack of white approbation may be a small price to pay for group advancement. I know of scores of black men and women who hold advanced degrees from prestigious universities, earn a comfortable living, and are in positions to advance the cause of racial justice as a result of the boost provided by affirmative action. Indeed some of these critics would not have had access to the very forums from which they launch their criticisms were it not for affirmative action. This is especially true for the growing number of conservative black commentators in both the print and electronic media. They are hired and promoted because they are black (Jones, 1997). Yet their self esteem seems intact. On the matter of affirmative action and self esteem, whites held negative stereotypical attitudes toward blacks long before affirmative action. Indeed it is instructive to remember that even an intellectual giant such as Dr. W. E. B. DuBois, who earned a Ph.D. at Harvard in the 1890s in the very shadow of slavery, never had the respect of his white peers. He was offered no positions commensurate with his training and talents. To further clarify the issue of self esteem and inter-community approbation, it is worth noting that historically when whites achieved enviable status without having to cotnpete with blacks, it did not cost them any self esteem or loss of public approbation. Babe Ruth, the baseball hero, for example, was not ashamed of his home rito record, even though he did it without having to compete against Satchel Paige, the fabled black pitcher of his era. Nor has it tarnished his image among contemporary whites. Instead, we know that Hank Aaron was censored by sonic for daring to challenge Ruth's record.

Finally, there are those who argtte that affirmative action is unnecessary because so many blacks have excelled without it and that their performance is sufficient evidence that any individual, no matter their color or previous condition of servitude, can do so if they put their mind to it. Suffice it to say that during slavery some enslaved Africans were so industrious that they were able to not only buy their freedom and that of other loved ones but became wealthy freepersons whose material conditions outstripped that of many of their white neighbors (Berlin, 1974). However, individual successes, no matter how spectacular, do not change the reality of group oppression. Within every group the law of random distribution ensures that there will be high and low achievers. The problem addressed by affirmative action is the negatively skewed distribution within the oppressed community. Affirmative action and other so-called race-specific remedies are intervention strategies designed to correct that maldistribution.

Affirmative action, the critics should understand, is really a weak remedy designed to address an intractable problem, a problem that can be adequately resolved only through comprehensive reparations. However, as long as American culture remains in denial about the crimes for which reparations are due, affirmative action may be all that we can get. The struggle should be to expand it rather than end it.

References

Berlin, Ira. 1974. *Slaves without Masters: The Free Negro in the Antebellum South.* New York: The New Press.

Cancr, Stephen. 1991. *Reflections of an Affirmative Action Baby.* New York: Basic Books.

Cohen, Carl. 1996. *Naked Racial Preference: The Case against Affirmative Action.* Madison. Wt: Madison Books.

Jones, Mack H. 1987. "The Political Thought of the New Black Conservatives: Analysis, Explanation, and Interpretation." In *Anterican Political Issues,* ed. Franklin Jones and Michael Adams. Dubuque:Kendall/Hunt.

Loury, Glenn. 1984. "A New American Dilemma." *The New Republic* 184 (December 31).

Oliver, Melvin. and Thomas Shapiro. 1997. *Black Wealth/ White Wealth: A New Perspective on Racial Inequality.* New York: Routledge.

U.S. Bureau ot the Census. 1979. *The Social and Economic Status of the Black Population in the United States: An Historical Overview. 1790-1979. Washington, DC: Government Printing* Office.

World Almanac. 1992. *Words That Set US Free.* New York: Pharos Books.

PART II

CRITIQUES OF BLACK LEADERSHIP

AND THE WAY FORWARD

Chapter 3

From Incorporation Toward Irrelevance: The Afro-American Freedom Struggle in the 21st Century

Robert Smith

Preface to Chapter

On January 9, 2001 William Raspberry, the African American columnist, wrote an essay in the *Washington Post* titled "The Incredible Shrinking Black Agenda." In it he discussed how the Congressional Black Caucus (CBC) and other black leaders and organizations had abandoned the comprehensive reform agendas of the 1970s and 1980s. These agendas dealt with full employment, comprehensive urban and anti-poverty policies and programs of ghetto reconstruction and development. By contrast in 2000 the priority items on the CBC agenda were an accurate census and the appointment of an African American to the Fourth Circuit Court of Appeals.

In May 2003 Bill Cosby, the entertainer and philanthropist, at a black tie-celebration of the 50th anniversary of *Brown vs. Board of Education* lashed out at lower class blacks, saying they were not living up to the legacy of *Brown* and the Civil Rights Movements. Referring to poor blacks as "those people," Cosby said they lacked "family values." The parents he said were unwilling or unable to speak English correctly preferring to spend $500 on sneakers rather than $200 on Hooked on Phonics. He even denigrated the names of black children, apparently preferring Bill and Jessica to Jamal and Lakisha.

The Raspberry column and Cosby's comments illustrate the continuing relevance of the conclusions reached in *We Have No Leaders: African Americans in the Post-Civil Rights Era*. Raspberry's column speaks to the fact that even more so than when the book was published nearly a decade ago African Americans have no leaders. They have no leaders because persons in leadership positions still have no plan, no program of action and no organizations to mobilize or lead blacks in directions that would ameliorate their communal problems. Cosby's remarks illustrate that the core black community, segregated and impoverished, is still criminalized and denigrated. The marginalization and denigration of poor blacks used to be the work of conservatives, racists, and white supremacists. Cosby, however, is an icon and patron of the liberal black leadership establishment.

This chapter provides dismal, detailed evidence of the irrelevancy of black politics in producing in the last twenty-five years benefits for most blacks, especially the imperative to reconstruct and integrate the ghettos into the mainstream of American society. The problem is multifaceted. First the political culture and system in the United States is, historically, stubbornly resistant to social change and reform, but especially when such change and reform involves race.[1] Indeed, without a systemic crisis of some sort the American political system has *never* responded to citizen demands for fundamental change in its class or racial hierarchies.[2] Second, American political institutions in the last twenty-five years have become increasingly weak and fragmented, as a consequence of the decline in the party system and the presidency, the ever-increasing influence of ever narrower, special interest groups and the growth in power of political pollsters, consultants and assorted hucksters, and of a trivia and sensation seeking media. It is very difficult therefore for the government to produce coherent public policies in the public interest, and the public, knowing this, does not trust it to do so. Third, the white establishment or power elite in the last twenty-five years has essentially rejected the idea that the federal government has a role to play in dealing with the problems of the ghetto poor, arguing that blacks are to blame for their own conditions. Finally, the leadership of black America instead of pursuing the leadership, organization and mobilization of its core community has instead pursued integration into systemic institutions and processes in the classic top-down hierarchical tradition of middle-class liberal reformers.

In this chapter I summarize the results of this study in terms of these four facets of the problem and note what I take to be the implications for the future of Afro-American society, and racial politics and democracy in the United States.

In the post-civil rights era virtually all of the talent and resource of the leadership of black America has been devoted to integration or corporation into the institutions of the American society and polity. Meanwhile the core community that they would purport to lead has; become increasingly segregated and isolated, and its society, economy, culture and institutions of internal uplift and governance have decayed. There is a systemic or structural logic to these processes, one that was probably inevitable and is perhaps irreversible.

The logic of the civil rights movement was systemic integration. Thus, as opportunities for entry and advancement in the institutions of the larger society became available, those blacks with the talent, resources or luck necessary to take advantage of them did so. This process, without a comprehensive plan of ghetto reconstruction along the lines proposed by the Urban League in its domestic Marshall Plan, would necessarily leave substantial numbers of persons behind, even if racism as an active force in American society disappeared. That is, the historical consequences of racism, even in an open society, would mean that a substantial number of blacks for a substantial period of time would lack the skills and resources necessary to effectively integrate into the system. If racism lingered, as it almost surely would, then the situation would be exacerbated.[3] This is essentially what has occurred in the last twenty-five years; all in some senses predictable and predicted.

This predictable bifurcation of black leadership and community has been made worse by ongoing changes in the economy and culture of the larger society that matured at roughly the same time as the civil rights revolution. The economic changes involved, first, a decline in the nation's manufacturing base, resulting in a loss of low-skilled, well-paid employment. Related to this was a fairly systematic and ongoing relocation of employment opportunities beyond the core black community. The cultural changes, communicated and shaped by an increasingly pervasive mass media, involved a loosening of traditional or communal constraints—with respect to family, sex, children, education, violence and drugs—that in the past tended to hold together communities in the face of adversity.[4] The result is a crisis in the black community and leadership of unprecedented magnitude.

At a lecture at Prairie View A & M University in 1989, in response to a question asking him to evaluate black leaders, Harold Cruse responded, "What leaders? We have no leaders." The puzzled student questioner responded by listing the familiar names of the heads of the civil rights organizations, members of Congress and big city mayors. Cruse, responding with evident irritation, said that those persons were not leaders because they had no plan, no program of action and no organization to mobilize or lead blacks in a direction that would deal with their communal problems. This *study* documents the acuity of Cruse's observation.[5] The civil rights organizations are moribund and largely irrelevant, operating more as relics of the past than instruments for action in the present or future. The black mayors, congresspersons, cabinet officers and the rest are unable to deliver on promises and programs to meliorate conditions in the communities, and increasingly even consider themselves leaders of American institutions who just happen to be black.[6] Even Jesse Jackson, the preeminent "black leader" of the post-civil rights era, subordinated his campaigns for president to the needs of the Democratic Party and the Washington establishment rather than those of blacks. Compared to the experience of other ethnic groups in the United States this situation is near unprecedented. The integration or incorporation of Irish, Jewish, Polish and Italian American leaders into the institutions of the society and polity roughly paralleled the integration of their communities as a whole. In contrast, black leaders are integrated but their core community is segregated, impoverished and increasingly in the post-civil rights era marginalized, denigrated and criminalized.

Again, this situation was a logical outcome of the civil rights movement's integrationist impulse and the system's cooptative response to social movement pressures. As Cruse argues, the only possibility of dealing with this logic was for post-civil rights era black leadership to confront what he calls the "plural" nature of blacks in American society and developed a consensus program for the internal organization and consolidation of blacks as a separate and distinct group in the United States.[7] At the outset of the post-civil rights era most leaders of

Black America recognize this throughout the 1970s and attempted to act on it. They failed; and since the 1980s blacks have fell under an institutionalized leadership that seems incapable of dealing honestly and realistically with the situation of its constituency internally or in its relationship to the larger society. Rather, as in the post-Reconstruction era it appears that once again "we are blind and led by the blind," with a leadership more interested in the trappings and symbols of power than in internal communal development and mobilization.

There is also a logic and predictability to the failure of internal black leadership organization and mobilization in the post-civil rights era. Twice before, such efforts to build and sustain what the Reverend Lewis Woodson in 1830 called a "national institution . . . that would unite and harmonize the distant and discordant parts of our population" were attempted, and twice before they failed. The previous attempts and the 1970 effort failed for essentially the same reason: the discordant parts of the black community probably cannot be brought together in a single national institution because the discordances—institutional and ideological—are unbridgeable. First, because the middle class leadership establishment is wedded ideologically, institutionally and economically to white structures of power and is therefore adverse to independent or radical thought and action, having as one of its foremost concerns quiescence in the black community and stability in American society. The material conditions in the black community, however, necessarily give rise to radical and nationalistic thought and action, which in turn makes race group solidarity and action all but impossible. This is especially so since the traditions of radicalism and nationalism in black America tend often toward the apocalyptic and the utopian. This historical dilemma in black political life is exacerbated today, since unlike in the 1830s and 1930s, black leaders have responsibilities for managing the institutions of American society as well as looking out for the interests of black people as a whole.

Three consequences flow from the post-civil rights era leadership's inability to act. First, in spite of—indeed in a sense because of—a bewildering variety of organized groups, old and new, the black community today remains largely unorganized. Second, blacks remain dependent on a decaying party (and party system) that attempts to maintain itself in power by ignoring black policy interests and symbolically distancing itself from black people altogether, although blacks provide the party a fifth of its national vote. Third, as a result in part of a lack of effective organization and dependency on the Democratic Party, blacks have been unable to develop the requisite pressures to get the system to respond to its most pressing post-civil rights era demand: the need for employment in the context of some kind of overall program of internal ghetto reconstruction and development. The result is a core black community, euphemistically referred to as the inner city that is increasingly poor, dispossessed and alienated.[8] Meanwhile the leaders of white America respond with neglect, contemptuously suggesting that unless there is a change in the "values" of African Americans, nothing can be done about the deterioration of their communities.

The civil rights revolution generated a sense of optimism about the prospects for equality, integration and acceptance in American society. Twenty-five years later, blacks now increasingly experience a sense of alarm, a turning back of the clock, a renewed sense of apartness, of being outsiders in a hostile world. Alexis de Tocqueville, that most acute observer of American democracy, did not believe that blacks and whites would ever live together in America on the basis of equality. Instead, he saw inequality and violent conflict between the races as more or less inevitable. Tocqueville saw this problem as inherent in American democracy. He wrote:

> I do not imagine that the white and black races will ever live in any country upon an equal footing. But I believe the difficulty to be still greater in the United States than elsewhere. A despot who should subject the Americans and their former slaves to the same yoke, might perhaps succeed in commingling the races; but as long as the American democracy remains at the head of affairs, no one will undertake so difficult a task; and it may be foreseen that the freer the white population of the United States becomes, the more isolated will it remain.[9]

Twenty-five years after the great civil rights revolution and as American democracy approaches its third century, it is still not possible to conclude that Tocqueville got it wrong.

Endnotes

1. The political culture is resistant to change because of the absence of a tradition of cross-ethnic working class solidarity and organization; racism and the ideology of white supremacy; an individualistic, anti-statist, commercial ethos; and the tendency among the people toward apathy and ignorance regarding politics. The political system is resistant to change because of federalism, the separation of powers, the separate and staggered terms of the executive and the Congress, the anti-majoritarian character of the Senate in terms of its constituency and its rules and procedures, and the "winner take all" provision in the allocation of House Seats and Electoral College votes.
2. Reflecting on these systemic and cultural obstacles to change as well as the "privileged position of business" in shaping government decisions, an eminent student of American democracy concludes "it may be true that our best, yet dismal, hope for structural change is through a transitory catastrophe." See Charles Lindbloom, "Comment On Manley," *American Political Science Review* 77 (1983): 368-83. Implicit in Lindbloom's notion is that a crisis or system catastrophe will result in structural changes that are progressive in character, as has been the case historically in the United States. However, theoretically at least, such a crisis might result in regressive social policies and political repression.
3. On the persistence of racism and white supremacist attitudes in the last twenty-five years see Robert C. Smith, *Racism in the Post Civil Rights Era: Now You See It, Now You Don't* (Albany: SUNY Press, 1995). See also Joe Feagin, "A Slavery Unwilling to Die," *Journal of Black Studies 18* (1988): 415-69 and Feagin and Heman Vera, *White Racism: The Basics* (New York: Routledge, 1995).
4. The economic changes in general and with respect to the black community in terms of their consequences have been thoroughly researched and are by now well known. The

cultural changes in general or with respect to blacks in particular are less thoroughly researched or understood. The best treatment, in my view, of the general problem of cultural changes in the 1960s and their consequences is Christopher Lasch, *The Culture of Narcissism: American Life in An Age of Diminishing Expectations* (New York: W.W. Norton, 1978) and his *Haven in a Heartless World: The Family Besieged* (New York: Basic Books, 1973). There is no good book-length treatment of the race-specific component or consequences of these broader cultural changes.

5. Harold Cruse, "New Black Leadership Required," *New Politics* 2 (1990): 39-49. See also Mack Jones, "The Increasing Irrelevancy of Black Leadership" (paper prepared for presentation at the 1981 Annual Meeting of the National Conference of Black Political Scientists, Baltimore).

6. See Huey Perry (ed.), "A Mini-symposium Exploring the Meaning and Implications of Deracialization in African American Politics," *Urban Affairs Quarterly* 27(1991): 198-226 and Perry (ed.), "Black Electoral Success in 1989," *PS* 23(1990): 141-60. See also Georgia Persons (ed.), *Dilemmas of Black Politics: Issues of Leadership and Strategy* (New York: Harper/Collins, 1993).

7. Harold Cruse, Plural But Equal: Blacks and Minorities in America's Plural Society (New York: William Morrow, 1987). Cruse did not systematically develop the idea of black plurality but compared to the other ethnic racial minorities (Latinos and Asian Americans) the African American community is much more of a plural or distinct society. Politically, it is much more ideologically distinct; socially its members face far higher levels of discrimination in housing, employment and education than other ethnic racial minorities; and African Americans tend to be more conscious of their separate and subordinate status than the various Latino and Asian American minority communities. The concept of a plural society was first advanced by M. G. Smith in his *The Plural Society of British West Indies* (Berkeley: University of California Press, 1965). See also Ira Katznelson, "Comparative Studies of Race and Ethnicity: Plural Analysis and Beyond," Comparative Politics 1(1972): 135-54. Although she does not use the concept or idea of black plurality (preferring instead the legal term "insular group") it is central to the line of analysis pursued by Lani Guinier in her law review articles. Finally, see the recent paper by David Sears, Jack Citrin and Colettee Van Laar, "Black Exceptionalism in Multicultural Society" (presented at the 1995 Annual Meeting of the American Political Science Association, Chicago).

8. Poor blacks are not only alienated from mainstream American politics and leaders but also increasingly from black establishment leadership and politics. While generally supportive of the liberal policy initiatives of the black establishment, poor blacks are also more nationalist in outlook, disengaged from traditional black organizations and in general feel that no leaders or organizations represent their interests or concerns in national politics. These generalizations are documented quite effectively in a fine case study of Detroit's inner city black community. See Cathy Cohen and Michael Dawson, "Neighborhood Poverty and African American Politics," *American Political Science Review* 87 (1993): 298-99.

9. Alexis de Tocqueville, Democracy in America (Garden City, N.J.: Doubleday, 1848; 1969): 356. The extraordinarily high incidence of violent crime committed by blacks; and the society's increasingly violent, almost it seems near militaristic response to it, while less dramatic than open rebellions like the 1992 Los Angeles riots are probably the best indicator of the violent polarization of the races, although most of these acts of violence are intra-racial. The ill advised war on drugs, which in effect and implementation, has

become a war on poor blacks, only exacerbates the overall violence associated with the war on crime.

Chapter 4

Learning for Leaders: Notes on a Pedagogy for the Praxis Of Black Political Leadership

Donn G. Davis

Introduction

African American political leadership, both individually and as a class, has always reflected the socio-political context in which it was molded and from which it emerged. Within this context, or at least it's parameters, African-American leadership underwent three distinctive changes during the twentieth century: a late nineteenth to mid-Twentieth Century stage, during which the only accepted and effective leadership was accommodationist, in the manner of Booker T. Washington, (although W.E.B. DuBois and others protested and struggled for full democratic rights and participation). Then, in the middle of the twentieth century, accommodation gave way to more aggressive, non-violent direct action, militant, and often confrontational, protest against all forms of de jure social segregation and political exclusion based on race. Led primarily by a broad collective of informal leaders and groups, the seminal victories of this stage of black struggle were the Civil Rights Act of 1964 and the Voting Rights Act of 1965, both of which opened pathways for the emergence of a new class of black leaders.

Finally, at the close of the tumultuous 1960s, rightly or wrongly, the mass black public, encouraged by an enhanced legal status and the greatest access to political participation since reconstruction, began to formalize their leadership by voting into public office what would become a record number of black public officials, from local to state and federal offices. At the outset of this new trend in the selection of leaders, a large number of those chosen came from the ranks of "the movement." Increasingly, since the middle 1970s, these new formal leaders have come from non-movement affiliations and/or lower offices or political party (usually Democratic) connections. In the case of both lower and non-prior officeholders, there is a great likelihood that the new (higher officeholder) will confront a mélange of elaborate bargaining and decision-making processes not previously encountered. As the process becomes more complex at the more elevated level and division of the spoils finer and more difficult to garner, the need for trained skills and knowledge also increases. Even more importantly, procedural aspects, which dominate the new terrain, are often torturously complicated if not outright arcane.

This chapter suggests and urges acceptance of the idea that much of what may be confronted by the most recent wave of formal black leaders can be taught and learned, as much of what is involved are political skills and informed methods of assessing gains and losses and the merits of trading various political assets and liabilities. The study also offers the suggestion that leadership training programs for young professionals—especially those who are interested in politics—are a valuable asset worthy of organizational and collective group investment, and that the collective, as a race, has not supported such endeavors to the fullness of its capability.

Leaders in Historical Perspective

Every historical epoch, however, characterized by historians, is generally associated with either individual *leaders* or a *leadership class* of one persuasion or another. Even Marxist historians, who eschew popular notions of the individual as historical catalyst and champion the idea that all history is made by the masses, are unable to separate individual actors (or leading *classes*) from major developments in the historical process. It is one of those points at which present reality almost invariably departs from theory. It is virtually impossible, for example, to separate the deeds and influence of, say, for example, Luther, Cromwell, Ataturk, Garabaldi, Lenin, Mao, Gandhi, Stalin, Churchill, Roosevelt or Martin Luther King, Jr., from the monumental social and political changes with which they are indelibly associated (Lenin, 1992; Marx & Engel, 1947; Burns, 1978:51-53). Indeed, the historical process appears, in these and numerous other instances, to have been critically effected by the articulated will of the individual, theoretically running head-on into the Marxian dictum that it is the masses that make history, not individuals. As one of several intellectual postulates that attempts to address the question of historical causation, this particular cornerstone of Marxist thought is not easily dismissed, as it is difficult to refute the relatively well-established fact that major historical changes, particularly those that register in human consciousness as epochical, appear to arrive on a shifted wave of collective consciousness and action. At the same time, it is virtually impossible to separate these waves of change from individuals who rationalized and articulated the perceived need for change.

For Season and Reason the Title of 'Leader' Persists

While theorists and academics that research and write on this subject rarely agree on its exact nature, the concept and the *praxis of leadership* endure. That is, some acts and patterns of behavior that are generally regarded as influential, if not determinative, continue to be carried out by individuals with an impact that may be consequential for the many. Elected officials, organization heads, bureaucrats, and informal leaders are regularly engaged in decision making which directs and impacts large numbers of people.

To be certain, the masses have played a huge and indispensable role in the making of history, but more often than not, their actions have been less spontaneous than orchestrated by persons recognized as leaders. This observation is not intended to diminish or downplay the very considerable importance of spontaneity and mass behavior in the historical process, for they have historically been the key factor in eclipsing a number of social orders (Hobsbawm, 1959; Rude, 1964)

Recognizing Leadership Characteristics and Assets

While there is, at present, no promising prospect of resolving the definitional issues surrounding leaderships; no real hope, that is, of anything approaching a universal consensus on the variables and components most essential to the phenomenon of human leadership (See Heifetz, 1994). There are, nevertheless, some generally acknowledged characteristics and functions associated with the ability of some (or several) human beings possessing the unique capability of being able to successfully motivate large numbers of their fellow human beings to follow them, and at critical junctures, to take one course as opposed to another. Individual and/or group rewards may figure prominently, they are not, however, sufficient explanations of behavioral choices, as the course of action extolled by the leader may, and often does, present a greater challenge, higher risks, and uncertain rewards. Thus, there are major and oftentimes intangible and inexplicable variables surrounding the phenomenon of leadership, without which the concept not only rings hollow, but also suggests that, at best, we are likely to experience limits to our ability to understand the operational components most essential to the success factor that is endemic to the function of leadership (See Kotter, 1993: 26-35)

Stated differently, there are some attributes and capabilities essential to the most commonly accepted definitions of leadership, and the requirement of efficaciousness is ordinarily regarded as perhaps the most seminal aspect of the overall concept. In addition to effective exhortation, if leaders cannot, or do not analyze, organize, plan, prioritize, administer, etc., the leadership role may become marginalized to the point that its effective exercise will likely be questioned. While these functions have not eclipsed popular perceptions of leaders as charismatic and visionary figures, the emergence of these critically necessary skills, for effective decision-making in the highly bureaucratized and complex processes of post-industrial society, have placed them squarely among the competencies required for any present-day leader to have any chance at all of succeeding (Cronin, 1993)

'Know How' and Skills That are Essentials for Leaders

The fundamental alteration of this change in the imperatives associated with leadership roles is that it introduced the need for skills that are generally regarded as conducive to an organized pedagogy. An integrated approach of study—combined with planned exposure to problematic and challenging conditions—may be expected to inform and enhance leadership capabilities that are both identifiable and subject to measurement and evaluation by ordinary and commonly accepted standards. The operative assumption underlying this conclusion is that demonstrated interest, involvement, well-honed and tested knowledge, the ability to accurately assess facts and findings, and a degree of maturity and commitment, may not only be discerned and evaluated, but enhanced by programs designed to nurture and develop these capabilities.

Learning to Lead

The idea that various aspects of leadership may be taught is, of course, not new. Near the end of the 15th Century, Niccolo Machiavelli turned this idea into a branch of political science (Abbot, 1973:125-174). In explaining the importance that he attached to *The Prince* and other works, he quoted Dante: "Knowledge doth come of learning well retained, unfruitful else" (Abbot, 1973: 126).

Unlike the virtual catalogue of *ascriptive* characteristics of leadership (e.g., the need to be *intelligent; charismatic; persuasive; attractive; charming; courageous, commanding, and enduring,* etc.)—all qualities over which the individual has little control—the advice here is *prescriptive* and suggests, unlike the former, that something might be done to improve the leader's success in his vocation, or his art, if that is one's perspective of what leaders do. Ultimately, however, it is efficaciousness in general, or the ability to be effective in situations of particular importance; those that rely upon the use of skills and influence unique to the individual, that selects and sets the leader apart from others and validates not only his or her the right to lead, but also their perceived ability to do so.

The possibility that individuals may *learn,* or be *taught,* much of what is required of leaders is more promising than questionable. As important as the differences may be, resolving the continuing debate over the psycho-biological and/or enviro-behavioral determinants of leadership development, it is ultimately less important than the prospect that those who may be opportune to make decisions that impact the lives of others may be taught many of the essentials relative to such decision-making. Those aspects of an individual's make-up that are purely endogenous, i.e., (the individual's internal "constitution") are, at present, beyond the practical and ethical reach of society's ability to examine are alter them. To the extent that social, as well as medical and religious ethics, deny this possibility, society must hope and wait for leaders to be *born.*

The alternative, and far more promising possibility, is that a number of exogenous factors related to the development of leaders can not only be reached by society, but may be manipulated for the benefit of society. Among these factors, the *learning* process is both the most accessible and potentially the most rewarding:

Most theories ignore or underplay the force that may be the most important in shaping most Leaders: *learning*. Learning from experience, learning from people, learning from successes and failures, learning from leaders and followers: personality is formed in these reactions to stimuli in social environments (Burns, 1979:63)

James MacGregor Burns (1979) cites Albert Bandura and Richard Walters work in (Kagan & Havemann, 1968) as having shown that "Behavior is learned not only by conditioning but also by imitating persons with whom the learner identifies and whom he takes as models" (Burns, 1979:20).

Beyond the Mythical Foundation of Leadership

Since popular culture will most likely continue to extol common-sense notions regarding the merits of being led by the "talented" and the "gifted"—however lacking in such attributes those who eventually arrive at the top may be—the idea of training leaders may need considerable encouragement. The need, however, and the potential benefits of increasing learning opportunities for present and future leaders are undeniable for several major reasons. The African American Civil Rights Movement provides a number of clear examples of this claim.

Status is One Thing; Leadership is Another

To begin with, the early years of the movement rode an enormous crescendo of mass emotional energy and commitment, which was directed primarily by associated cadres of *informal* leadership, meaning that, for the most part, they were not usually the representatives of any *official* or authoritative entity of the state. Rather, they stood distinctly apart from such bodies and generally challenged the manner in which they did or did not exercise their authority. The collective character of this leadership was what Burns has called *transforming,* which to him means that this particular form (or phase) of leadership challenge has a crucial moral dimension, and that such leadership serves as the catalyst for "[raising] the level of human conduct and ethical aspiration of both leader and the led" (Burns, 1979: 20). This definitional paradigm—owing far more to victory than defeat—neither defines the character nor explains the function of the black political leadership class that has emerged in the post civil right period.

What Kind Of Leaders and Whose Side Are They On?

Another leadership type, defined by Burns as *transactional,* (Burns, 1979: 19) more accurately describes the character, function and purposes of the leadership *class* that succeeded the *transforming* leadership *collective* of the civil rights years. *Transactional* leadership, according to Burns:

> Occurs when one person takes the initiative in making contact with others for the purpose of an exchange of valued things. The exchange could be economic or political or psychological in nature: a swap of goods or of one good for money; a trading of votes between candidate and citizen or between legislators; hospitality to another person in exchange for willingness to listen to one's troubles. Each party to the bargain is conscious of the power resources and attitudes of the other. [Moreover] The bargainers have no enduring purpose that holds them together; hence they may go their separate ways. A leadership act took place, but it was not one that binds leader and follower together in a mutual and continuing pursuit of a higher purpose (Burns, 1979: 19-20).

This description of *transactional* leadership varies in only the least significant details from the overall character, motivation and behavior of the post-civil rights leadership class, especially as it may be applied to black political leadership. It is possible that race, remaining as it unfortunately does, the most compelling determinant of outcomes in American economic, social and political life, may lessen somewhat the detached certainty and predictability of the exchanges described here by Burns, and it may well have kept intact some of the rapidly dissolving "mutual support for common purpose" aspects of the relationship between leaders and followers, (Burns, 1979: 20) since it has thus far prevented the emergence of anything resembling a completely race-neutral political process, let alone a color-free meritocracy. Nevertheless, without rendering a value judgment, it may be fairly said that Burns' description of transactional leadership clearly provides a better picture of the interaction between post-civil rights leaders, their followers and others with whom they must bargain for favorable exchanges.

As suggested earlier, these significant changes emerge in the behavior of the new class of leaders occurs as a direct result of successes wrought by the group's *transformational* predecessors. A previously closed political process, (Branch, 1988; Bunche, 1973; Franklin & Moss, 1988; Logan, 1965; Myrdal, Sterner and Rose, 1944; Silver, 1966; Williams, 1965; and Zinn, 1985) forced to be more open and accessible by the collective of *transformational leadership,* led to both greater opportunities and greater competition, and this enlarged (and more intense) competition has since led to increased bargaining on every level. That is, increased bargaining not only between leaders and followers, but also between leaders, influential sectors and interested brokers external to their base constituencies. The attention of leaders' can (and does) sometimes become diffused. The faithful find it hard to bear (and they should) when the horses that they nourished on small plots become less attentive and sometimes run wild when gates open onto large pastures. But the new terrain suddenly opened to them is rarely, if ever, flat and straight.

It is a place of many mountains and valleys and crooked turns that must be negotiated with skill and deftness. The contention made here is that some of the problems encountered at this juncture may be addressed by acquired skills and knowledge, assuming the willingness to address them at all. Let us look at some of these changes and problems from our present vantage point in time, which allows us not only to assess them more objectively, but also to propose measures that could lead to constructive solutions.

Major changes began to take place in African American leadership at the end of the 1960s when both black voting and the number of black elected officials increased dramatically (Tate, 1993). While still seriously under-represented nationally as a percentage of all elected officials, the total number of black elected officials climbed from fewer 500 in 1965 to over 10,000 at the outset of the year 2000. The membership of the Congressional Black Caucus (CBC), which remained near twenty throughout most of the 1980s, nearly doubled as it reached thirty-nine (39) in 1992 (Tate, 1993). This trend contributed to the rapid *formalization* of black leadership, such that it is now fair to say that most black leadership is now *formalized, routinized,* and/or *bureaucratized* (Weber, 1947) Thus, the need for systemic knowledge and sophisticated skills within the black leadership class is now greater than ever before.

While there was a time in the past when relatively simple instructions—or rousing rhetoric—would effectively motivate and mobilize oppressed outsiders to address social injustices and intransigent authority, but the complex and sometimes intractable nature of contemporary issues demand more trained study, skillful analysis and astute direction. This need is all the more urgent in a political context where well-organized, well-funded and sophisticated opponents are challenging hard won gains (Stefanie, 1996).

Battles to Be Fought and Choices to Be Made

There has always been a need for informed and keen analysis on the part of groups and their leaders who find themselves locked outside the overlapping and interlocking circles of the American power structure, if they have any hope of ever having any say regarding their plight in American society. Over the course of the twentieth century, American society became increasingly complex and compartmentalized, first with the accelerated process of industrialization, and in more recent years with the advent of the Information Age. Combined, these developments spawned hundreds, if not thousands, of converging and often conflicting interests and organizations, both public and private. And the decision and policymaking processes of both government and the private sector, of necessity, have followed the same course (see Truman, 1981; Horowitz, 1963 and Mills, 1996). They have developed complex, labyrinthine processes for making decisions—and subsequently policies—the course of which, more often than not, can be effectively navigated only with considerable knowledge and sophisticated skills. For the seasoned leader who has been on the water before, these processes are *rapids,* but for the novice they may be deadly *undertow.* In either case, however, the key to survival is a sound analysis of the conditions. This is both critical and essential, but regrettably the problems of the leader do not end here.

Thereafter the challenge emerges to deal with the (sometimes arcane) institutional rules, regulations, policies and procedures of various branches of the system of American government. The system of American government, like the American Constitution—before it was altered by a single amendment—was not designed for the use of everyone, and so is the case with government, as we know it today. It is both safe and fair to say that it will only serve those who force it to do so, which some will argue is fair, there is (or should be) however, a caveat, and it should be that this rule applies only if and when one has sufficient knowledge and the resources to forge such a reckoning. But of course the game is not played that way. On the other hand, the *resource* qualification is a point that should be granted, since the most casual observer and most participants clearly recognize that the Founders dealt from a stacked deck, and gave no cards at all to far too many would-be *citizens.*

Knowledge to Be Acquired and Resources to be Utilized

Our concern here, however, is with another matter, and is based on the conclusion that any fighting chance for rectitude must rely on the power of knowledge that is skillfully applied, and that it is possible to *acquire* much of the most beneficial knowledge prior to the need for its use. This would appear to be especially true in regards to the need for sound analyses, which is all too often taken for granted, when in fact it is sorely lacking in all too many instances, visa-via the American policymaking process. This is a very critical shortcoming, because the lack of an accurate analysis of any given situation means that no effective organization can be forged to address that particular situation or others.

Here then is not one, but two problems confronting leaders (and their followers) that could diminish their efforts to impact the complicated policymaking process in the arena of conventional American politics. Without a sound analysis, there can be no sure guidelines for developing either general purpose or specialized *ad hoc* organizations. Critical issues may subsequently go un-addressed, or they may be mishandled or glossed-over because there is no well-honed apparatus with which to deal with them. As suggested, however, this outcome can and should be avoided. We have said that the key to avoiding this problem is *learning,* and that learning (or knowledge) is a critical component of the axis of effective leadership. For the good that it may do, however, the learning has to take place *before* the need for it.

If we look again at our example, post-civil rights era black political leadership, we see that this problem has persisted, at least in part, because of the extremely limited effort to construct programs and organizations designed to collapse the 'need for knowledge curve.' Throughout the entire country there continues to be only one major, well-funded think tank with a research agenda devoted exclusively to the study of issues affecting African Americans, The Joint Center for Political and Economic Studies in Washington, D.C. This center plays a major role in fact-finding, studying and analyzing issues of paramount concern to African Americans, but it is not an advocacy organization, and therefore cannot be to black leadership what, say, The Heritage Foundation may be to conservative Republican thought and leadership.

In the same context, the Congressional Black Caucus Foundation (CBCF) *does* train and expose a number of young people to the legislative environment through the annual College Internship and Graduate Fellows Programs, and it also provides invaluable issue and program assistance to the members of the Congressional Black Caucus (CBC). Yet, is not the complement of a CATO Institute. This is as much or more a resource problem as it is any other kind, but not entirely excusable as such. Not only does the capital that flows through African American communities exceed or rival the GNP of a number of moderate size nations, (See *Ebony* Magazine, February 1999 issue) the income of one class, alone that of black athletes dwarfs the GNP of a host of small African and Latin American nations. Thus it can be concluded that both the knowledge and learning base of African American political leadership suffers in equal parts from lack of organization, under-funding and general neglect. The first step to overcoming this problem is to recognize that going to the polls and electing a black leader, and then going home assuming no further need for commitment or action, is much like leaving one's new-born infant at the hospital and assuming no further need for involvement.

Nascent leadership of any kind requires nourishing and training, and this is all the more true when such leadership is expected to advance and defend its interest in an environment not only complex, but equally hostile. These circumstances dictate the need to place a very high priority on leadership training and development. They also dictate that this imperative take precedent over all but the most urgent endeavors in the process of resource allocation, which is often not the case, since the greatest dividend lies in the future and may not be seen in the present.

Programming for Success

The CBCF's College Internship Program and their Graduate Fellow's Program are outstanding prototypes of the kind of leadership training and development programs that are likely to make a future difference in the capability and quality of future leaders. Both programs combine direct participant exposure with and academic component that provides the opportunity to review and examine their experiences through a prism of existing theoretical and empirical knowledge. These programs further develop and contribute to leadership skills and capability by requiring participants to make live presentations (usually with Members of Congress present) and draft issue and policy papers requiring both primary and secondary research. The policy paper required of Graduate Program Fellows must be on a topic of immediate currency and legislative relevance, i.e., issues surrounding policy initiatives with great importance to the African Diaspora in general and African Americans in particular, and also likely to be acted on in the immediate or near future. There is also the expectation that one of more members of the CBC should be able to make use of the findings contained in these papers.

Of equal if not greater importance, the young professionals who participate in this program are usually well qualified to assist decision-makers and work effectively within the decision-making environment.[1] In recent years, the same young people have been placed in executive agencies (for a period of six to eight weeks) to allow them to gain insight into the process of interpreting and administering laws and policies that have come out of the legislative branch. This expansion of the experience of the learner came about primarily because, not infrequently, members of the legislative branch become significant decision-makers in the executive branch of government.[2] There is only one problem with this kind of program: there are not enough of them. African American decision-makers, especially Members of Congress, have made a significant effort to promote and assist in the effort to expose young people to the legislative and decision-making environment, usually as congressional office interns and fellows. This work provides valuable experience and would be far more difficult to obtain but not for the black and other minority Members of Congress, since the non-minority Members of this body have not shown a strong commitment to diversity, a fact that is less applicable to the black Members of Congress, who to some observers appear to be over-committed to the concept.[3] A more serious problem however, as regards not only Congress, but political officialdom in general, has been the inability to get minorities into top-level decision-making positions where their ability to shape outcomes could be considerable, but this is the topic of another discussion.[4]

Between 1993 and 1995, Howard University, in Washington, D.C., was host to a Leadership, Education, and Development Program (LEAD) sponsored by the U.S. Department of Education. Over the short life of the program, fifty-two, Howard University upper-classmen were placed in public and private sector agencies and organizations where they worked directly with a mentor for 15 hours per week. Appointments ranged from the White House to Congress to organizations such as The Children's Defense Fund and the American Civil Liberties Union (ACLU). The program was an outstanding success, introducing bright young people to the internal processes of critical decision-making and raising their awareness of how the policy process is influenced by variables that may or may not be controlled (See Donn Davis, 1995) Significantly, well over half of these young people went on to graduate and professional schools, and a number of them are now employed in public and private sector roles which they began with a useful degree of knowledge and familiarity, further testimony to the benefit of learning aspects of the leadership role prior to actual engagement.

In conclusion, any commitment to preparing and assisting African American leadership through organized learning, the dissemination of information and the utilization of existing knowledge, should take account of the phenomenal growth and present availability of a large pool of black intellectual capital and special expertise. This is a much-underutilized resource, despite its breadth and depth. There is at present a clear disconnect between black political decision-makers and a very substantial number of black academics with skills and knowledge that cover the range of issues and problems facing black decision-makers. Black political scientists, economists, sociologists, policy analysts and a host of legal specialists, all exist today in greater numbers than ever before.[5]

There are critical *ascriptive* aspects of leadership, which, regrettably, cannot be taught. *Loyalty, integrity, commitment and courage* are among these. On the other hand, critical *prescriptive* aspects of what is required of today's leaders could and probably should be the subjects of a pedagogy that could significantly enhance the effectiveness of those who accept the challenge of leading and representing others.

Endnotes

1. The need for Black professional skills and trained expertise was made painfully clear when former South African President Nelson Mandela first visited the United States in 1994. In one speech, he explained, with some pain and embarrassment that his entourage was composed of mainly White South Africans because too few blacks South Africans possessed the skills and expertise necessary to manage the issues and problems, logistically and otherwise, associated with the travel and various engagements arrangements.

2 It is not uncommon to have Members of Congress named to high-level executive branch positions. Former Congressman Andrew Young and Mike Espy are but two examples.

3. This issue is the subject of present and future research into congressional hiring and promotion practices. It might be noted, however, that the Library of Congress has been the subject of major hiring and promotion discrimination lawsuits for more than two decades. On the other hand, Congress itself, at least until 1996, had no legally codified rules or regulations for hiring and promotion. The entire process was totally discretionary with the individual Member of Congress making his or her own independent decisions in such matters.

4. This issue is part of the above noted ongoing and future research.

5. Exact numbers are somewhat difficult to obtain, since the most reliable sources, the professional membership organizations to which a number of these individuals belong, can only report numbers for paid members. However, the total exceeds 2,000 if only paid members of the American Political Science Association, the National Conference of Black Political Scientists, and the National Bar Association are counted. This leaves out several other professional membership organizations whose membership also represents an assortment of expertise. Organizations and associations of professional economists, for example, would be but one of many others. All such resources and wells of specialized knowledge must be utilized to the maximum extent possible if black expect to make

58 *Donn G. Davis*

meaningful strides on behalf of the extremely marginalized population that they represent.

References

Abbot, L. S. (1973). *Masterworks of Government*, Vol.1. (New York: McGraw-Hill)

Bennis, W. & Nanus, B. (1986). *Leaders: The strategies for taking charge.* New York: Harper & Row Publishers, Inc

Branch, T. (1988). *Parting the Waters· America in the Kings Years, 1954-63*, New York: Simon and Schuster.

Bunche, R. J. (1973). *The Political Status of the Negro in the Age of FDR*, Chicago: Chicago University Press.

Burns, J. M., (1979). *Leadership* New York: Harper and Row Press.

Cronin, T.E. (1993). Reflections on leadership. In W.E. Rosenback and R. L. Taylor (Eds.), *Contemporary Issues in Leadership*. Boulder, Colorado: Westview Press, 7-25.

Davis, D. G. (1995). *Government and Politics*, Presented at the 1995 Howard University's Eisenhower Leadership Program: Preparing the Young to Lead, Department of Political Science, Howard University.

Chappell, Kevin. "Apostle of Economics." *Ebony Magazine* (February 1999).

Franklin, J. H. & Moss, A.A. (1988) (ed.) *From Slavery to Freedom*, New York: Knopf.

Heifetz, R. (1994) *Leadership Without Easy Answers*. Cambridge: Harvard University Press.

Horowitz, I. L. (1963). *Power, Politics and People: The Collected Essays of C. Wright Mills*. New York: Oxford University Press.

Hobsbawn, E. J. (1959) *Primitive Rebels: Studies in Archaic Forms of Social Movements in the 19th and 20th Centuries*. New York: W.W. Norton & Company.

Kotter, P. J (19930. "What Leaders Really Do," In W.E. Rosenback and R. L. Taylor (Eds.), *Contemporary Issues in Leadership*. Boulder, Colorado: Westview Press, 26-35.

Lenin, V. I. (1992). *What is to be Done?* New York: International Publishers.

Logan, R. W. (1997). *The Betrayal of the Negro, From Rutherford B. Hayes to Woodrow Wilson*. Da Capo Press.

Marx, K., & Engel, F. (1947). *The German Ideology*, New York: International Publisher.

Myrdal, G., Sterner, R. & Rose, A. (1944). *An American Dilemma*, Vol. II New York: Harper and Brothers.

Olesek, W. ed. (1996). *Congressional Procedures and the Policy Process*, Washington: Congressional Quarterly Press.

Rude, G. (1964). *The Crowd in History, New* York: John Wiley and Sons.

Silver, J. W. (1966). *Mississippi: The Closed Society*, New York: Harcourt, Brace and World.

Stefanie, J. (1996). *No Mercy: How Conservative Think Tanks and Foundations Changed America's Social Agenda*, Philadelphia: Temple University Press.

Tate, K. (1993). *From Protest to Politics*, Cambridge: Harvard University Press.

Truman, D. (1981). *The Governmental Process: Political Interest and Public Opinion*. Westport: Greenwood Press.

Weber, M. (1947). *Theory of Social and Economic Organization*, New York: Oxford University Press.

Williams, J. (1987). *Eyes on the Prizes: America's Civil Rights Years, 1954-1965*, New York: Penguin Books.

Zinn, H. (1985). *SNCC, The New Abolitionists*. Westport: Greenwood Press.

Chapter 5

Black Leadership: Toward a Twenty-First Century Perspective

Ronald Walters and Robert Smith

In concluding this work returns to a fundamental premise, which is that Black leadership emanates from the Black community in the sense that the individuals who present themselves for leadership have their origin in that community and its culture and that they should reflect the needs and aspirations of that community.

We interpret community in an "essentialist" fashion. That is, to us it is self-evident that there is a Black community; a historically constructed community of shared history and memory; with distinctive cultural, political, and economic interests; and with a geographic or spatial anchor in the nation's urban centers and the heavily populated Black belt counties of the rural South. We are concerned in this chapter with the actual behavior of men and women, as leaders, who attempt to mobilize power resources in pursuit of that community's interests.[1] To assume otherwise—that the idea of the Black community and a Black leader is itself problematic—would be to engage in a project of theoretical fantasy that ignores facts and evidence in pursuit of the researcher's vision of reality rather than the reality envisioned by Blacks themselves.[2] And while our major objectives in this study were to summarize the existing research on Black leadership make a critical analysis of the theory and practice of leadership, and thereby contribute to the parameters of the field of study, an underlying premise is the legitimacy and integrity of the post-civil rights era Black community.

The Stability of Black Leadership

When one considers the breath of the research on Black leadership over the last sixty years, one is struck by the degree of stability of the issues raised over time and by the continued usefulness of the analytical categories used to describe this complex phenomenon. While the studies published in the last decade do not make explicit use of these categories, we note that the analytic categories developed earlier—power structure, social background, organization, and leadership styles—find consistent support over time.

Community Power and Its Structure

With respect to community power, we reconfirm our view that the community, either local or national, is not only the wellspring for Black leadership but the most critical element of its outcome-based performance. Therefore, the view of the community with respect to the performance outcomes of its leadership is the most legitimate source of evaluation. However, this legitimacy will always be contested by forces internal to the community and by forces in the dominant society.

This has much to do with the relative power of the Black community in relation to the dominant society. The ideas advanced earlier concerning clientage linkages between the Black power structure and the dominant White community is crucial to understanding Black leadership behavior. It posits a vertical set of relations in which Black leaders interact and connect with Whites and a set of horizontal structures and activities that connects Black leaders with other Blacks. In other words, Black leadership is characterized by a dynamic internal conflict over values, resources, and legitimacy as well as a simultaneous conflict with the dominant community, a dominant community that is frequently involved in a patron-client relationship with leadership factions within the community.

Social Background

While Black leaders are still drawn disproportionately from the middle class, we believe that the color of Black leaders, as a reflection of proximity to Whites, is less of a problem today than in earlier times. This is in part because the focus on "Blackness" as an ideology of group culture and pride has helped to lessen, though not to obliterate, such distinctions altogether. What we see today is the residual effects of the earlier "mulatto aristocracy" written about Myrdal, E. Franklin Frazier, and others: that is, the persistence of Blacks with lighter skins in positions of leadership through the consistency of familial ties, as well as the emergence of new formations of multiracial families among middle-class Blacks and Whites who have access to each other within elite social situations.

Otherwise, it is a matter of our subjective impressions that the mediation of opportunities available to Blacks has generally not occurred with respect to the color hierarchy, since the opening of access to institutions of higher education have been afforded to most Blacks, thus persons of all colors are able to assume positions of leadership. It is also our subjective impression—supported by some evidence—that skin color does not affect leadership ideologies or styles (Seltzer and Smith 1991).

Organization

Since the 1930s there has been remarkable stability in the structure of Black organizations, at the local level in particular, this is of course important to any community's leadership. These organizations, whether civil rights, civic, religious, or professional, have traditionally contributed to the leadership class of the Black community at the local level. Moreover, the national organizational structure has been remarkably stable, with a core group of civil rights, religious, political, and professional groups.

In the first instance, our task is to understand what has been responsible for this consistency, and then account for changes in growth or decay of this structure. And although we have not attempted in this work to do more than outline a suggestive agenda of research, it is clearly one of the more important tasks that lay ahead in Black leadership studies. Clearly one direction to explore is that which suggests that the condition of the Black middle class is important to organizational growth. In sociological terms, it is the knowledge that resource mobilization is facilitated by the strength or weakness of this class.

This brings into relief the necessity to consider those factors responsible for the viability and health of community organizations, such as the opportunities for middle-class Blacks to exercise social mobility by moving into the broader environment of organizations. It would be logical to suggest that factors such as the withdrawal of economic resources by business, government and the philanthropic community from urban areas during the last two decades has caused a weakening of community life and therefore of its institutions and organizations. In addition, factors such as the outward migration of the middle class from cities and the upsurge in crime and social disorganization have exacerbated the problem. How have these factors affected organizational health, especially those agenda-setting and community-activism groups at the local level? Is there a reflection of growth or decay of these organizations at the national level?

A second challenge is to understand what factors are responsible for the cycle of growth and decay of organizations that arise on the stage of history in response to a given crisis, only to wither away not long after the crisis has receded. Thus, if one examines the 1960s in terms of the civil rights movement, the popular uprisings in the ghettos, and the Black power and Pan African movements that followed, a diverse array of organizations came into existence but they lasted only for a decade or less. Did the relevant factors have to do with the waning of the crisis, the weakness of the organizations, the maladaptation of leadership strategies and tactics, the inadequacy of organizational recruitment, or simply the process of struggle itself?

These issues are important, but we will not be able to answer them except to suggest that the acknowledged decline in the membership of organizations such as the NAACP may be due more fundamentally to the factors we cite, rather than to the lack of programmatic effectiveness. Or perhaps it is some combination of these factors.

Leadership Styles

Black community objectives are defined by a diffuse and often very abstract or generalized set of ideas such as "freedom," "justice," and "equality." These abstractions are then elaborated by more concrete policy objectives such as affirmative action, education reform, welfare reform, or employment policies. These policy objectives are then mediated by different styles of leadership behavior. Do we then confuse the various style differences with the objectives or their policy manifestations? The question suggests that there is a systemic relationship between the policy demands, the arenas in which the demands are processed, and leadership styles.

Thus while it is relatively unimportant to determine stylistic manifestations of leaders with respect to the abstract objectives, it is critically important to understand leadership styles in terms of concrete policy issues. Obviously, in the situations dealing with mass protest mobilization, we have a style of leadership fitted to levying pressure for change in employment practices and contracting. However, how are we to evaluate the leadership style of Congressional Black Caucus Chair Maxine Waters when in December 1997 she organized a mass mobilization to protest a House Sub-Committee hearing intended to pass legislation eliminating affirmative action (the hearing was successfully disrupted and forced to adjourn)? And how are we to evaluate Rev. Jesse Jackson's opening an office on Wall Street, meeting with the nation's economic policymakers and financial leaders and the use of tactics such as buying stock in fifty major corporations in order to have access to stockholder meetings to press the case for equity? And what is the style involved in the NAACP's Kwesi Mfume's negotiation of what he described as a "Reciprocal Economic Empowerment Initiative," to encourage and monitor selective buying by Blacks at hotels with poor records of employing and contracting with Blacks? All of these tactical stylistic thrusts are contrary to the post-civil rights era presumption that large complex institutions no longer respond to mass protests, and as such Black leaders must abandon those styles of leadership.

Perhaps what is meant by this presumption is that far more influence can now be exercised by Blacks when they act as managers of economic development, bank executives, corporate board members, or others who have the ability to directly influence the allocation of economic resources. However, realism requires evaluation first of the extent to which Blacks in such positions will have the range of capabilities to allocate such resources toward the Black community. And second, to what extent might reinforcing styles of internal influence along with external pressures constitute a more effective strategic formulation.

Historical Transformations in Leadership Styles

The 1930s marked the advent of modern Black leadership. It was also noted that much of the contemporary research lacks an appreciation of the historiography of the emergence of the modern Black leadership class and how it has been transformed in the last several decades. Powerful social and demographic forces have played important roles in these transformations. For example, the consolidation of the Black urban leadership class in the 1930s in the North and West was a direct response to Black migration out of the South during this period. Leadership arose in the process of the adjustments of Black populations to the challenges of becoming socialized to new conditions, whether in the industrial cities of the Northeast and Midwest or in the rough terrain of the West, where Blacks built new settlements or contributed to existing settlements such as those in Texas and California.

The issue of class, however, must be seen as a major force in the early diversification of the Black leadership group from its base among preachers, teachers, and small businesspeople. One of the most important manifestations of this diversification was the Harlem Renaissance (which existed in other cities as well), which foretold the emergence of a new post-Reconstruction intellectual class. The growth of this class, fueled by such institutional factors as Black colleges and universities, Black churches, and White philanthropy, was an important factor in the aggressive mobilizations that would start in the 1940s and reach their peak in the 1960s.

The class factor has had the most important impact on the nature of Black leadership during the 1980s and 1990s, in that the continued growth and diversification of the Black middle class has resulted in its occupying new, elite positions in government, business, the academy, and the nonprofit sector, thus increasingly complicating what one means by "Black leader."

The historical transformations of the Black middle class and its impact on the changing character of Black leadership may be related to the problem of "strategy shifts" from one historical period to another. Black leadership has the onerous task of accurately determining, within any given historical context, what problems with what strategies can be addressed that give promise of positive outcomes. While this task of historical assessment is important, it should not result in the complete elimination of any set of strategies but rather experimentation with the entire arsenal of approaches that historically have demonstrated viability. The basis of this suggestion is that minority groups and their leaders possess relatively fewer power resources and therefore need to be alert to the use of strategies that may not, at first glance, appear likely to be successful. Such is the historical logic of the Selma to Montgomery March in 1965, the anti-apartheid demonstrations in the 1980s, or the marches and rallies that helped to mobilize support for the Martin Luther King Jr. Holiday Act.

Reflections On Leadership Praxis

Having commented on some of the more salient features of the studies on leadership with an emphasis on their theoretical aspects, we turn our attention to some summary comments on the nature of changes in leadership practice. These issues of practice compliment those raised earlier but include other factors such as leadership beliefs (ideologies), gender, unity and diversity, and protest and accommodation.

Ideology, we think, is a dynamic determinant in both the historical development of leadership and a problem in leadership unity. Although the belief system within the Black community is diverse, the range of critical policy differences is relatively small. So, for example, while most members of the Congressional Black Caucus are liberal in public policy preferences, these ideological labels may mean different things within the Black community because these ideological constructs are defined by the dominant group.

For example, in the last decade of the twentieth century what might be considered "moderate" policies may be defined by Blacks as radical conservatism to the extent that they detrimentally alter the structures of opportunity. Accordingly, Blacks who are defined as liberal should be understood to be so only in respect to dominant group attitudes on issues of race and social justice. In the larger framework of Black politics, however, dominant group liberalism has been in tension with self-determination as was illustrated by its conflict with the Black power movement of the 1960s.[3]

These differences notwithstanding, the belief system within the Black community is extraordinarily diverse encompassing various varieties of Black nationalism, liberal, and conservative integrationists, as well as radical Marxists and democratic socialists (Smith 1992). However, as we suggested above there is a relatively clear set of consensus positions on a number of issues that constitute a "Black mainstream." Nevertheless, some differences in policy preferences are so critical as to be internally and publicly divisive, and this allows for the exploitation of the collective power of the group.

An important example of this is the role of Black conservative leaders. With regard to the internal politics of the Black community, the NAACP is a relatively conservative organization that is squarely within—in fact, helps to define—the mainstream of Black politics. Black conservatives, while within the dominant group mainstream, are clearly outside of the Black mainstream. What Black conservatism therefore represents is the dynamic tension between the Black perspective and the attempt by Whites to impose the dominant group perspective on the minority.

Black and White conservatives share a consistency of views on such issues as the values of patriotism, Christianity, the traditional family, school prayer, the death penalty, public school choice, and relatively lower taxes and spending on social programs. And of course they share in the negation of mainstream Black leadership.

While mainstream Black leaders and Black mass opinion share conservative values on some of these issues, the fault line for Black conservatives in the Black community is their deference to White conservatism's narrow view of race, which renders them, in the eyes of the Black majority, a minority without autonomy or legitimacy. However, since the dominant group accords them extraordinary visibility, they appear to have legitimacy and thus they are a source of disunity.

Unity and Diversity

Obviously, the changing nature of the community and its historical diversification creates new challenges to unity. The emergence of Black conservatives as a putative leadership group in the wake of the election of Ronald Reagan is an obvious example. However, the collective response of Black leaders to the Texaco case is also revealing. The National Urban League was consciously absent in this response. The rationale for the league's absence was explained by its president, Hugh Price, in an interview with *Emerge* magazine:

> **Price.** Not every organization can do the same thing; you don't do that. If every organization does the same thing, then when you've accomplished that [and] you've got to do the next thing that follows from it, you don't have an organization there that can do that. You have no victory. You've won, but you don't have the ability to deliver on it. We are bridge-builders. We maintain the bridges between corporate America and the African American community, between the media and the African American community. It is our strategic niche to say we'll be in the advocacy mode, but we'll work with these companies to try to create those hiring policies that bring young people into the contracting policies, etc.
> **Emerge.** But, what if these corporations don't do as they promise, in terms of minority hiring, and refuse to work with you? What do you do? Do you boycott them?
> **Price.** Other organizations can do that. I mean, that's again, why you have to have in a civil rights movement, different kinds of organizations that play different roles. We had breakfast meetings, we had midnight conference calls. And we were all of the same mind about what Texaco had to do. And we were all supportive of the direct action that was taken even though not all of us engaged in direct action. You have to have a variety of people who play different roles at different points of time. ("Price Fixing" 1986:38)

These sentiments by Price show the further complexity of the quest for unity. Even when there is basic belief system agreement and unity of objectives, Black organizations because of their role perceptions and differential linkages to dominant group powers may have less leverage to engage in strategies of protest.

A final example is the relationship between Black Nationalist Minister Louis Farrakhan and the Reverend Jesse Jackson. Putting aside basic differences in belief systems, when Minister Farrakhan returned to the United States from a fifty-two nation world tour in February of 1998, he strongly criticized Reverend Jackson—on moral grounds—for Jackson's silence in the face of President Clinton's preparations for war with Iraq (Fletcher 1998: A9). This suggests that while on some issues—the basis of group identity and legitimacy—there may be room for agreement, on others there may be inevitable conflict. A critical factor in this particular incident is that Jackson was at the time a presidential envoy to Africa and thus his ability to exercise independent leverage in the Iraq crisis was constrained, while Farrakhan was free to behave as he wished.

Perhaps, then, a realistic view of the issue of unity among Black leaders must take into consideration the diversification of Black leadership roles in the post-civil rights era, a situation that creates both opportunities and constraints. When there exists leaders such as Reverend Jackson, Minister Farrakhan, General Powell, as well as others, who command large followings in separate and overlapping domains and have access to powerful dominant group leaders, national and international (although, paradoxically, they are often excluded from other power centers and often treated as "Negroes" in the most debased meaning of that term), the prospects for unity inevitably ebbs and flows. For these leaders must react to issues and circumstances contingent on the legitimate needs of the Black community as well as the legitimacy of dominant group communities. So, unity of action is not always an option.

Gender

The most important social fact that will influence the composition of Black leadership in the future is the changing role of Black women. Women have been a part of the struggle for freedom since the abolitionist movement (Richardson 1987). Nevertheless, the growing predominance of Black females in colleges and universities suggests that Black women will play increasingly important leadership roles. This too may create problems for unity, to the extent that men refuse to yield power and status. A larger proportion of Black women relatively to Black men are graduating from college, obtaining graduate and professional training, and moving into professional, executive, and managerial positions, as well as elective office (40% of all Blacks in state legislatures are women).

Protest or Accommodation

Protest has ebbed as a major strategy of Black leadership, as more moderate approaches have come to dominate in the post-civil rights era. This strategic shift toward accommodation is in part a result of the incorporation of middle-class Blacks into mainstream institutions and civic organizations. The argument might be advanced that since in the past protest politics produced more then accommodation, the relatively small degree of incorporation into mainstream institutions and processes and its accommodationist imperatives is not warranted given the distance Blacks have to go to achieve equality in the United States. So, while a case is made for the persistence of protest mobilization, it should be clear that this case is usually not persuasive to mainstream leaders.

Here, it is tempting to suggest that a new era of accommodationist politics is here to stay, driven not as much as in the 1950s and 1960s by the ties of religious leaders to the White power structure of localities, but by the rise of the new middle class and the reluctance of the leaders of that class, in each of the institutional arenas in which they operate, to put those relationships at risk for more radical strategies of Black advancement.[4] Whether one assesses the leadership of the new class of Black mayors in Cleveland or Detroit, the lack of protest or dissent by Black cabinet and sub-cabinet officials to the punitive public policies of the last decade (including the Clinton welfare reform legislation) or by the overall lack of demand from the middle-class Black intelligentsia for a more aggressive politics; accommodation is paramount. However, if the status of the Black community continues to deteriorate, then accommodation may turn on itself, leading to increasing alienation of ordinary Blacks from mainstream leadership. This would make it difficult for this leadership to use protest when it might seem strategically efficacious, or to lead a spontaneous popular mobilization when such mobilizations occur in the twenty-first century; Interesting observations on the theory of the practice of leadership. This writer has attended some of the sessions, the results of which will be published featuring the work of its working groups, one of which is devoted to assessing problems of leadership for the twenty-first century.

Endnotes

1. See Harold Cruse's discussion of the concept of a plural society in relationship to the idea of Black community in *Plural But Equal: A Critical Study of Blacks and Minorities in America's Plural Society* (New York: William Morrow, 1987).

2. For a radically erroneous, idiosyncratic example of this phenomenon, see Orlando Patterson, The Ordeal of Integration: Progress and Resentment in America's "Racial" Crisis (Washington, D.C.: Civitas/Counterpoint, 1997).

3. For a thoroughgoing philosophical inquiry into the built-in tensions between liberalism and the Black quest for community, see David Cochran, *The Color Freedom: Race and Contemporary American Liberalism* (Albany: State University of New York, 1999).

4. Michael Lind argues that in exchange for affirmative action and other ameliorative benefits Black leaders have made a "tacit agreement" with the elites of the dominant society not to disrupt the status quo, a status quo that benefits them. See his The Next American Nation: The New Nationalism and the Fourth American Revolution (New York: The Free Press, 1993), as quoted in Norman Kelly, "Disappearing Act: The Decline of Black Leadership," Bedford Stuyvesant *Current*, Winter 1997, 4.

PART III

BLACK MAYORS IN AMERICA:

REASSESSING THE LEGACY

Chapter 6

From Insurgency to Deracialization:
The Evolution of Black Mayoralties

Georgia Persons

Black Mayoralties As The Pivot Point Of The New Black Politics

From the vantage point of a new millennium it now seems "back in the day" when the political horizons were marked by great possibilities for and great anticipation of a host of African American candidates to major posts in state and local government. At the start of the last decade of the 20th century, the new black politics had seemingly come of age. Douglas Wilder was poised to win the governorship of Virginia, and Andrew Young was considered a fairly reasonable bet to win the governorship of the State of Georgia. Black candidates were vying for mayoralties in new territories, in predominantly white venues such as New York City; New Haven, Connecticut; and Seattle, Washington, to cite a few contests that were particularly interesting at the time.

These electoral contests were seen as reflections of a promising and perhaps new national political phenomenon, not just as routine growth in the numbers of black elected officials (beos), but rather as a deepening and extending of black political empowerment, an outcome far more important than mere increase in numbers. The traditional electoral strategies of system challenge and black insurgency which had reaped the greatest increase in the number of beo's had been significantly set aside in many of these contests, and completely abandoned in others, supplanted by a new electoral strategy of deracialization, but that was seen as being all right. The new black politics was coming of age. Bigger prizes and gains lay just ahead, or so it seemed.

By the middle of the decade of the nineties, the horizon of black politics had changed dramatically. Doug Wilder had won the Virginia governorship by a very thin margin and went on to serve a largely uneventful four-year term. Andrew Young had been handily defeated in his bid for the Georgia governorship, and Harvey Gantt had been easily defeated in his efforts to unseat Jesse Helms as U.S. Senator from North Carolina. David Dinkins served a single four-year term as mayor of New York City. New Haven's experience with black mayoral leadership was fleeting. Chicago had failed to elect a second black mayor in the aftermath of Harold Washington's death. Although many big city black mayors continued to serve into the 1990s, during the 1980s, many of the high profile black mayors across the country had left office for various reasons. In the early years 2000s, black mayoralties had clearly evolved in significant ways, and the broader, national level socio-political context within which they participated had evolved significantly as well.

One way to illuminate the evolution of the new black politics is to better understand the evolution of black mayoralties. It has been argued that the singular achievement of the new black politics has been the election of black mayors in many of the major cities of America. In 1970, 15 years after passage of the Voting Rights Act, there were only two African American mayors of big cities, Carl Stokes of Cleveland and Richard Hatcher of Gary. By 1990, that number had increased to 30 black mayors in cities with populations of 50,000 or more (See Table 7). By the year 2000, there were 47 black mayors in big cities (See Table 8). However, there had been significant turnover in their numbers. Only 14 of the cities with black mayors in 1990 still had black mayors in 2000. Generally there continues to be a disproportionate reliance on the black vote to elect a black mayor as roughly 60 percent of black mayor cities in 1990 and 2000 had at least 40 percent of the black population.

Table 7
Black Mayors of Cities with 50, 000 Population, 1990

Name	City	Population	% Black
David Dinkins	N.Y. City	7,971,000	25.0
Thomas Bradley	Los Angeles, CA	3,259,000	17.0
W. Wilson Goode	Philadelphia, PA	1,642,000	40.2
Coleman Young	Detroit, MI	1,086,000	63.1
Kurt Schmoke	Baltimore, MD	763,000	54.8
Marion Barry	Washington, D.C	626,000	70.0
Michael White	Cleveland, OH	573,000	45.0
Sidney Barthelemy	New Orleans, LA	554,000	55.3
Norman Rice	Seattle, WA	493,800	9.5
Maynard Jackson	Atlanta, GA	421,000	66.6
Lionel Wilson	Oakland, CA	356,000	46.9
Sharpe James	Newark, NJ	316,000	46.9
Richard Arrington	Birmingham, AL	277,000	55.6
Richard Dixon	Dayton, OH	181,000	37.0
Jessie Ratley	Newport, News, VA	154,000	31.5
Carrie Perry	Hartford, CT	137,000	33.9
Thomas Barnes	Gary, IN	136,000	70.8

John Daniels	New Haven, CT	129,000	31.0
Chester Jenkins	Durham, NC	110,000	47.0
Edward Vincent	Inglewood, CA	102,000	57.3
Noel Taylor	Roanoke, VA	100,000	22.0
Walter Tucker	Compton, CA	93,000	74.8
Melvin Primas	Camden, NJ	82,000	53.0
John Hatcher, Jr.	East Orange, NJ	77,000	83.6
George Livingston	Richmond, CA	77,000	47.9
Walter L. Moore	Pontiac, MI	70,000	34.2
Edna W. Summers	Evanston Township, IL	72,000	21.4
Ronald Blackwood	Mt. Vernon, NY	68,000	48.7
E. Pat Larkins	Pompano, FL	66,000	17.2
Carl E. Officer	East St. Louis, IL	51,000	95.6

Source: Joint Center For Political and Economic Studies, 1990.

Although blacks have served as CEOs of major counties have equal or greater responsibility than mayors, and have far larger budgets and many more employees to manage, big city black mayoralties have traditionally been perceived as the more coveted political prize. Perhaps this is because economically, politically, socially, and culturally, cities are the defining pillars of American society. Whatever the reasons, the election of a black mayor, particularly a big-city black mayor, has been traditionally perceived as a highly symbolic achievement, as well as highly visible evidence of the success of black strategic efforts and substantive inclusion in the political mainstream. Black mayoralties have been seen as the embodiment of the major developments and constraints of the new black politics. Hence a focus on black mayoralties particularly affords illumination of the evolution of the new black politics from its early manifestation as an insurgent movement to its seeming "maturation" as a variant of politics as usual in which the significance of traditional racial appeals and social reform efforts have substantially diminished overtime.

The objectives of this chapter are two-fold: To recapitulate a narrative account of the evolution of black mayoralties, with particular focus on, and second, to offer a detailed discussion of the dynamics of the early period of black mayoralties. This emphasis has been chosen for two reasons. First, the early period encompasses a very rich historical moment in the black political struggle. Indeed, history may well judge this period to have been a critically defining moment. Secondly, by looking backwards, we are able to see that the seeds for the dynamics and situation regarding black mayoralties in the years 2000s were planted in that early period of the late sixties through the early eighties A second objective of this chapter is to suggest a new analytical framework for understanding the evolution of black mayoralties which seeks to

Table 8

Black Mayors of Cities with 50, 000 Population, 2001

City	Pop. Total	% Black	Name	Term Expiration
Houston, TX	1,953,631	25.3	Lee Brown	12/01
Philadelphia, PA	1,517,550	43.2	John Street	12/03
Dallas, TX	1,188,580	25.9	Ron Kirk	06/03
Detroit, MI	951,270	81.6	Dennis Archer	12/01
San Francisco, CA	776,733	7.8	Willie Brown	12/03
Columbus, OH	711,470	24.5	Michael B. Coleman	12/03
Memphis, TN	650,100	61.4	Willie Herenton	10/03
Washington, DC	572,059	60.0	Anthony Williams	12/02
Denver, CO	554, 636	11.1	William Webb	06/05
New Orleans, LA	484, 674	67.3	Marc Morial	05/02
Cleveland, OH	478, 403	51.0	Michael White	12/01
Atlanta, GA	416, 474	61.4	Bill Campbell	12/01
Minneapolis, MN	322,969	13.7	Elzie Odom	05/03
Newark, NJ	273, 546	53.5	James Sharp	06/02
Birmingham, AL	240, 055	73.5	Bernard Kincard	12/01
Jersey City, NJ	219,773	28.3	G. Cunningham	06/05
Rochester, NY	219, 773	38.5	William Johnson	12/01

Chesapeake, VA	199, 184	28.3	William Ward	06/04
Des Moines, IA	198,682	8.1	P.A. Daniels	12/03
Richmond, VA	197,790	57.2	R. McCollum,	07/02
Jackson, MS	184,256	70.6	Harvey Johnson	06/05
Oceanside, CA	161,029	6.3	Terry Johnson	12/04
Patterson, NJ	149, 222	32.9	Martin Barnes	06/02
Hampton, VA	146, 437	44.7	Mame Locke	06/04
Savanna, GA	131,510	57.1	Floyd Adams	12/03
Flint, MI	124,943	53.3	Woodrow Stanle	12/03
Beaumont, TX	113,866	45.8	David Moore	05/02
Inglewood, CA	112,580	47.1	Roosevelt Dorn	12/02
Portsmouth, VA	100,565	50.6	James Holley	06/04
Compton, CA	93,493	40.3	Eric Perrodin	06/05
Carson, CA	89,730	25.4	Daryl Sweeney	03/05
Trenton, NJ	85,403	52.1	Douglas Palmer	06/02
Camden, NJ	79,904	53.3	G. Faison	06/05
Kalamazoo, MI	74,239	22.5	Lorraine Morton	04/05
Wilmington, DE	72,664	56.4	James Baker	12/04
East Orange, NJ	69,824	89.5	Robert Bowser	12/01

Source: Joint Center for Political and Economic Studies, 2000.

specify a set of critical variables which link past developments to present-day conditions of black mayoralties. This framework should also serve as the basis for forging new directions in research and analysis. Data for this chapter were drawn from extant studies of black mayoralties and the author's own research on black mayoralties in Atlanta, Washington, D.C., Gary, Newark, and other cities.[1]

The Institutionalization of Black Mayoralties
and a Changing Political Order

In examining the collective experience of big-city black mayoralties, three somewhat simultaneous and overlapping developmental paths are apparent. These paths and/or phases overlap both in terms of temporal occurrences, and in terms of defining characteristics. In other words, as we will in the discussions below, at different periods in time, there have been several political and strategic pageants playing out at the same time in regard to black mayoralties.

1. *A pattern of insurgency* characterized by challenges to the prevailing political order, embracing of a social reform agenda, and utilization of a pattern of racial appeals to mobilize a primary support base of black voters;

2. *A pattern of racial reconciliation* where in some cases, black candidates wooed white voters by simply diminishing, avoiding, or perverting racial appeals, while in other situations, black candidates exploited the images of insurgent style candidates to enhance by contrast their own appeal as racial moderates. In both instances, black candidates expected to reap the benefits of racial symbolism and concomitant black voter support in a black-on-white contest.

3. *A Pattern on deracialization* in which the transition that had begun with racial reconciliation was completed. Black candidates deemphasize issues that may be viewed in explicitly racial terms; use of race-neutral issues that would appeal to broad segments of the electorate across racial lines. With deracialization black candidates still reap the benefits of racial symbolism and resulting racial solidarity and continue to reap the benefits of solid black voter support.

We have traditionally spoken of black mayors as a collectivity. There are good reasons for that. They initially emerged during a very specific point in time and they emerged from a common socio-political movement. The initial successes of the first wave of black mayors were attributable to the mobilization of the black voter base and the dynamics of racial bloc voting where blacks held a population majority or near majority. So it has been logically and theoretically useful to speak of black mayors as a holistic political genre. However, there has always been much diversity among black mayors, and after some four decades of black mayoralties that diversity has grown immensely, especially in terms of key variables such as place, time, electoral dynamics and other contextual circumstances.

In regards to big-city (population 150,000 and above) black mayors, there have been roughly six electoral waves. The first wave occurred with the election of black mayors in Cleveland and Gary in 1967, and Newark in 1970. Cleveland lost its first black mayoralty in an unsuccessful effort to elect a second black mayor in 1972. The second wave occurred with the election of black mayors in Detroit, Atlanta, and Los Angeles in 1973, and the District of Columbia in 1974.[2] The third wave brought black mayors to New Orleans and Oakland in 1977, and Birmingham in 1979. The fourth wave occurred in 1983 with the election of Harold Washington in Chicago, Wilson Goode in Philadelphia, and Harvey Gantt in Charlotte, North Carolina.

The black mayoralty in Chicago was lost in 1989 subsequent to the death of Harold Washington during his second term in office. In Charlotte, Harvey Gantt was defeated for reelection by a white female Republican. Baltimore was added in 1987, initially by default with the election of then Mayor Shaeffer to the state governorship, and the automatic ascendancy of the black deputy mayor to the position of mayor. Harvard-trained attorney and Rhodes scholar, Kurt Schmoke became the first elected black mayor of Baltimore in 1987. The fifth wave occurred in November 1989 with the election of black mayors in New York City, New Haven, Seattle, Durham, North Carolina, and again in Cleveland, Ohio. And then the music largely stopped in the sense that both media and scholarly attention to the election of black mayors waned, and their election no longer captured the imagination and hopes of the black electorate in quite the same way as in earlier years.

The sixth wave in the election of black mayors began around the mid-1990s with the election of black mayors in cities such as Houston, San Francisco, Memphis, Denver, Savannah, Columbus, Ohio, Dallas, (and many smaller cities) and continues to the present time. The six electoral waves to date embody a developmental path of insurgency, racial reconciliation, and deracialization. In many instances specific black mayoral cities have evolved along this continuum. Some cities have embarked on black mayoralties at different points along this continuum, not all having necessarily begun at the insurgency stage.

Institutionalization as a Political and Social Process

Social scientists use the concept of institutionalization to capture a dynamic in the processes of socio-political development when political leadership, governmental bodies, the rules and procedures of governance and general methods of politics become accepted and widely supported by the polity (Polsby, 1968). Institutionalization is assumed to have occurred when methods of political and institutional processes and political leadership reach a significant level of stability as characterized by orderly, predictable, and infrequent changes, and in some cases, obtain a presumed permanent status. Institutionalization is characterized by predictability in patterns of recruitment of political leadership, professionalization of personnel and standards within governmental bureaucracies, infrequent and orderly change, and adaptability of political processes and institutions to change. The factors that are crucial to the success institutionalization are broad-based public support and acceptance, stability of functions, procedures, and political leadership resulting in a stable leadership corps.

The concept of institutionalization has been used explicitly as an analytical framework in studies of the U.S. Congress which is said to have institutionalized over time as turnover in its membership declined, and as members served longer terms; as representation became more stable (Polsby, 1968) The concept has also been used extensively in the study of developing societies, particularly in reference to the process of political development in post-colonial regimes as the procedures and institutions of representative democracy have taken hold (Nordlinger, 1971). Thus institutionalization is a useful concept for understanding the interplay of social and political dynamics pertinent to the realization of politically defined objectives. The concept of institutionalization is particularly useful in observing and understanding the processes of social change underlying the incorporation and representation of diverse interests in a political system.

In the heady days of the early nineties when the number of big-city black mayors was increasing along with other breakthroughs in the new black politics, analysts dared to envision a process of the institutionalization of black mayors that was suggestive of their permanent presence in America's largest cities. It is now quite clear that the mere election of a large number of black mayors is not tantamount to institutionalization. Indeed, the situation which prevailed so briefly in 1990 (See Table 8) when African Americans held the mayoralties in more than a dozen of America's largest cities effectively masked an enormous complexity which in turn harbored substantial political instability. A decade or more later, a level of institutionalization has occurred, but not according to earlier expectations. However, in reviewing the early period of black mayoralties we are able to see the actual processes and foundational substance of the institutionalization of black mayoralties.

The Early Period of Black Mayoralties: Insurgency As Strategy And Style

In the early period of the new black politics, insurgency served as the predominant campaign strategy for black mayoral aspirants and later served as a style of leadership for many elected mayors. Generally, insurgency as a strategy was associated with the initial election of a black mayor in a given locale, and as a leadership style was adopted and retained by many first black mayors throughout their tenure in office. Insurgency was characterized by direct challenges to the prevailing white dominated political order and encompassed explicit criticisms of incumbents, institutional processes, civic leadership structures, and the resulting mobilization of interests and bias in local political contexts.

As a tactical strategy, insurgency was driven by imperatives of time and place, and the prevailing demographics. The nature of the times was such that blacks were not only systematically excluded from elected positions and other posts within local political establishments, but their exclusion was also supported by a prevailing ethos which rendered their desires and efforts to obtain access to the political process to be illegitimate demands on the political order. Prevailing patterns of voting behavior were such that a black candidate could not expect to receive more than a very small percentage of white votes, thus dictating an almost exclusive reliance on black voters. Many black voters were not registered or were generally unaccustomed to participating in politics, especially politics that deliberately threatened the prevailing political order. Given this convergence of conditions and circumstances, evening the absence of advocacy of specific social reform issues, insurgent black candidates were perceived as social reformers.

The early pattern of insurgency pitted a black candidate against a white candidate in a racially charged contest (Nelson and Meranto, 1977; Nelson, 1982). The basic pattern has been one of mobilization based on racial appeals with the successful black candidate garnering a solid black bloc vote, supplemented with the crossover of a small percentage (rarely exceeding 20 percent) of white voters (Bullock, 1984). Thus, the overwhelming majority of early black mayors were elected in cities with a majority or near-majority black population. In most cases of the initial election of a black mayor, either substantive issues were subordinated to overt racial appeals (frequently by both black and white candidates), or positions espoused by black candidates were of a social reform nature, racially exhortatory, and clearly directed towards black voters. White candidates in these races resorted to "save our city" racial appeals or adopted a newly "race-neutral" position of desiring to "represent all of the people" (Hahn et al, 1976; Pettigrew, 1976).

As a strategy, insurgency promoted black political mobilization and provoked white resistance. The result in most locales was that, subsequent to the election of a black mayor, the initial period of transition and white displacement was characterized by severe racial polarization (Levine, 1974; Eisinger, 1980s). Racial polarization subsided over time, but in many locales remained sufficiently ingrained to make for a tendency among whites and blacks to define most issues within a racial context (Persons, 1985). However, severe racial conflict has not been a constant attendant to the election of first black mayors, although reasons for this significant deviation are not clear. The case of Atlanta, which became severely racially polarized, disputes a theory of the mediating effects of a previously prevailing biracial coalition (Persons, 1985). The racially polarized 1983 election in Chicago, almost 20 years after the nation's first election of a big-city black mayor, disputes temporal factors as an explanation, as does the contrast of the Philadelphia election of 1983 in which racial polarization did not occur. A highly plausible explanation may rest on whether the black mayoral contender espoused an explicitly social reform agenda or otherwise made strong and explicit appeals to the black community, thereby clearly challenging the prevailing political order.

In the case of Chicago, much more was at stake than a comparatively simple political and racial displacement. Harold Washington ran against the white ethnic-dominated political machine, which had variously dominated Chicago politics for almost half a century, and the prospect of his election carried a particularly severe threat (Akalimat and Gills, 1984). Moreover, by many observers, Chicago had long held a reputation for a particularly invidious form of racial tensions, in no small part attributable to the organizing tactics of the old line political machine that was founded and sustained by drawing on heightened ethnic appeals, making exclusion and oppression of blacks both politically expedient and socially acceptable. Thus the dynamics of the local socio-political context in Chicago in 1983 were very similar in nature and effect to those that prevailed in many cities some two decades earlier.

The early black mayoral elections signaled a potentially significant level of social reform. These elections meant major change in the most important and visible local leadership corps. They also meant the representation and entry of new claimants to local political arenas. Most early black mayors explicitly articulated a social reform agenda in their campaigns, emphasizing such issues as police brutality, the hiring of blacks in municipal jobs, increased contracting to minority vendors, improved low-income housing choices, improved and equitable delivery of public services, and a more open government relative to groups formerly shut out of the local governing process. While strong social reform agendas clearly caused concern among white voters, such an explicitly articulated agenda was not always necessary for mobilizing the black vote. In most initial black mayoral elections, for most black voters, the symbolic significance of the significance of the potential to elect a black mayor tended to override concerns for the specifics of issue positions. Moreover, in most black-versus-white mayoral contests, most black voters have somewhat understandably automatically associated descriptive representation (electing a representative who mirrored their racial and general social characteristics with substantive representation (the support for and advocacy of issues and interests of greatest concern to them). Well beyond the early stages of insurgency politics, some black mayoral candidates and candidates for other offices as well have factored the significance of this symbolism into their strategies and, discounting the importance of explicitly stated substantive issues for black voters, have directed issue-specific appeals almost exclusively to white voters (Ransom, 1987; Keiser, 1990).

After the initial election of a first-black mayor, the crucial next step in the process of institutionalization is reelection. This is a particularly critical step for insurgent black mayors if social change and reform efforts are to be established and continued. Some new dynamics emerge at this electoral juncture, which in many cases presented something of a strategic dilemma for incumbents. However, perhaps the most interesting development is that at the stage of reelection there were startling manifestations of the many faces of the coin of race and its varied uses in politics. Reelection efforts of insurgents have been characterized by the continued resistance of a significant number of white voters to black mayoral rule, manifested in efforts to develop more effective strategies against a second black electoral victory (Watson, 1984). This occurred in Atlanta in 1978 and Chicago in 1987. In both instances, overtly racist campaigns were launched by white challengers to "save our city" from continued black governance. Moreover, there is the added problem of maintaining the monolithic clout of a well-mobilized black community in the face of major white and black challengers. First black mayors know well the dynamics of a black versus white contest, having experienced this in their initial elections, and having benefited from having a "white ogre" as an opponent. One might thus conclude that the dynamics of a reelection contest involving a strong black challenger might require an adjustment in strategy.

The pairing of two black contenders in a multi-candidate race suggests a need to create a distinction between the two while preserving the monolithic black vote in support of a single black candidate. This leads to a highly tenuous situation for black candidates, as a split in the black vote may result in a loss of the mayoralty to a white candidate. The black challenger may, of course, seek to build a pivotal base of support among white voters with a smaller supplement of black votes. Such a strategy by a black challenger would simply reverse the conventional first-black-mayor strategy.

Coleman Young of Detroit faced this situation in his first reelection bid in 1977. Young's black opponent sought to make Young the issue: his frequently abrasive political style; his lifestyle, and his frequent use of rough language was labeled as inappropriate for the leadership of Detroit. Young's strategy was to describe his black opponent as a "black, white hope." Young's black challenger had received only five percent of the black vote in the primary, but had forced Young into a runoff on the strength of his white support (Rich, 1989). The appellation of "black, white hope" embodied the message which many incumbent black mayors, at one time or another, have sought to convey: competition is a threat to the tenuous political hold of black mayoralties and may result in a major setback to the black community—the loss of the newly won mayoralty to a white contender. The strategy of Young's challenger also has become a familiar one as the appeal of the mayoralty became a means of fulfilling the personal and political ambitions of many black aspirants. In the Detroit case of 1977, racial appeals of essentially the same type as were used in the initial election continued to serve the incumbent despite the change to a black-versus-black contest. For strategic purposes the black challenger was depicted as the surrogate "white ogre," an interesting turn of the coin of race, and an interesting means of sustaining insurgency.

Insurgency And Long-Term Incumbency

In many locales, structural factors such as the absence of statutory limits on the number of consecutive terms a mayor may serve have played a major role in institutionalizing insurgency through facilitating long term incumbencies of first black mayors as well as other mayors who have run on an insurgency strategy. The result has been that some first black mayors and others have succeeded in institutionalizing their individual presence in office. This was the case in Detroit and Los Angeles where incumbent black mayors were elected for five consecutive four-year terms (although it is arguable whether Los Angeles is correctly characterized as an insurgency mayoralty). Similar situations prevailed in Gary and Newark until both first black mayor incumbents were defeated in 1986 and 1987 respectively. However the pattern has repeated itself in Newark with the long-term incumbency of Sharpe James, one of the last remaining insurgent style black mayors.

It is reasonable to assume that long-term black mayoral incumbency might provide insights into the experiences of black mayoralties beyond the immediacy of the racially charged, initial transition and displacement to a period of normalcy, when the routine issues of governance come to dominate the local political agenda in a less racial context. Based on a study of the Young mayoralty in Detroit (Rich, 1986), one can identify two major, though somewhat distinct dynamics of long-term incumbency. First, there is the continuation of racial appeals in mobilizing the black community with the use a kind of racial ostracism in efforts to differentiate the incumbent from his black challengers. Concomitantly, there is the continuation of clear, racial divisions in voting patters regardless of the race of the challenger. In other words, the insurgent incurs the wrath of many white voters and that collective attitude prevails indefinitely.

Second, there is a distinct change over time in the type of issues that dominate the local political agenda, with a shift away from general social reform issues to basic issues concerning the overall economy of the city and its fiscal stability. However, despite successful mayoral efforts in garnering the active support of white economic elites in responding to these issues, and despite the fact that the white business community belatedly provided very strong support for the Young mayoralty, the majority of the mass-level white electorate remained generally unsupportive. For example, a crucial vote on a tax increase to save the city of Detroit from insolvency in 1981 was supported by white business elites, but won exclusively in the black wards of the city.

For the primary support group of black voters who sustain long-term insurgencies, the full range of advantages remained unclear. Long-term insurgencies may assist the large process of institutionalization by transcending the difficult period of initial transition and displacement to firmly establish a new, more exclusive political order. On the other hand, long-term incumbencies may well discourage or otherwise eliminate viable black successors. The long-term dominance of a single black mayor may serve to stymie the development of an independent black leadership corps, resulting in a decline in the number and efficacy of black activists who seek to monitor local government and help to keep it accountable and inclusive. Thus, by adversely impacting the local black leadership structure, the longevity of a single black mayor may serve to obstruct democratization and accountability, and may thereby hinder the move towards institutionalization of substantive black interests and participation.

There are also indications that the institutionalization of a single black mayor may otherwise have transforming effects on the local political arena. The District of Columbia is a case in point. Both scholarly and lay observers have pointed to the existence of a machine-style politics attendant to the three-term mayoralty of Marion Barry, crediting Barry with influencing political and electoral processes across the board, including city council and school board elections for nearly decades until his departure from political office in 1998. The Barry machine repeatedly undermined viable black mayoral successors by arousing mass-level black concerns about the danger of creating prime conditions for a "white takeover." Barry successfully used insurgency to build and sustain a political machine that was held together in the traditional mode of political machines: by patronage in the dispensation of city jobs and contracts, and firm control of the political mobilization, recruitment, and candidate slating processes.

The retention of insurgency as a leadership style for long-term incumbents is no doubt attributable to the reluctance of political leaders to risk an obvious change in tactics and style, or perhaps a perceived inability to relinquish this posture, given the political exigencies prevalent in a particular political context. For whatever strategic or other considerations, insurgency is a continuing use of the coin of race even when population dynamics and other factors do not afford the likelihood of a white takeover (Persons and Henderson, 1990).

Over time, we have seen that insurgency has served as a useful strategic resource in the mobilization of the black population requisite to the election of most first black mayors. In a game of low-resource electoral politics, insurgency tactics are a powerful means of creating vitally needed political resources. Having adopted the political style of an insurgent, many black mayors, in tending to their maintenance needs in office, have used the spirit of insurgency as necessary, as long as it was a winning currency. We have also seen over time that s a matter of style and image insurgency could be utilized as a way of undermining and delegitimizing all challengers, black and white, to an incumbent black mayor. However, as s strategic political tempo and leadership style, insurgency can be difficult to maintain over time. It can effectively give way, (in some cases) to the exigencies of governance, lose its social reform content, and subsequently serve merely as a rhetorical tactic for rallying necessary black electoral support. In some cases its demise was facilitated by the dynamics of black mayoral succession.

Black Mayoral Succession: The Shift To Racial Reconciliation

Black mayoral succession is of great significance in the process of institutionalization as it suggests the move towards permanency in securing the black mayoral presence in American urban politics. In the early stages of the new black politics, the longtime dominant pattern in the election of black mayors was the first time election of black mayors in what was then an increasing number of cities. Also in the early years, it appeared that the succession stage constituted the defining stage of the new black politics. The mayoralty was now clearly a realistic political and personal goal and this newly obtainable prize provoked tensions at both the intra-group level and among individual competitors. At this stage we saw a fully charged political dynamic in which the new black politics as a socio-political phenomenon had been launched and was fully in play. Thus we saw evidence of the emergence of critical contradictions internal to the black community that posed constraints to fostering of serious system challenging action. We also saw critical decisions by key players in this political game which defined new strategic tactics and which in effect helped to set the tone and thrust for much of the future practice of black politics. Some of the unique dynamics attendant to the mayoral succession stage includes the following:

1. The pairing of two blacks in the absence of a "white ogre" or a surrogate "white ogre;"
2. The move towards racial reconciliation as a strategic means of political differentiation between black competitors;
3. Situations in which white voters held the decisive swing vote even with black population majorities;
4. The emergence of nascent, class-based cleavages within the black community that resulted in the subordination of claims by low-income blacks given the imperative of solid black bloc voting;
5. Yet another face of the coin of race with the use of race as its stereotypical stigma by black candidates seeking racial reconciliation as a strategic tactic;
6. The emergence of issues other than race which are specific to the local political context such as the state of the city's economy and questions of who can best lead the city to sustainable economic recovery.

Two variants of black mayoral succession are discussed here, voluntary succession and involuntary succession. Voluntary succession occurs when an incumbent leaves office at the end of a term as set by statute or otherwise declines to seek reelection and is succeeded by another black mayor. Involuntary succession occurs when an incumbent is defeated or otherwise removed from office and is succeeded by another black mayor. A third variant, what we might call "intermittent succession" is not covered here. Intermittent succession occurs when black mayoral regimes are interrupted by the election of a white mayor (or mayors), but an African American mayor later recaptures the mayoralty. Early analysis of this development in the case of Cleveland, Ohio indicates that the black succession contest pits an insurgent style candidate against a black candidate who seeks racial reconciliation with the latter being victorious. No doubt there are other dynamics that characterize this variant of black mayoral succession.

Voluntary Mayoral Succession: Atlanta

The October 1981 election in Atlanta to succeed first black mayor Maynard Jackson was at once a serious test of the black community's ability to hold on to the mayoralty and a bitter reminder to whites of their displaced political status. For many whites the election became a last ditch effort to recapture city hall. The reported sentiment of many white elites was that the Jackson succession election was the last hope of electing a white mayor of Atlanta in the then foreseeable future. Nonetheless, in a style peculiar to Atlanta's historical political culture, the succession campaign was expected to be carried out in a manner devoid of any racial overtones. As one observer put it, "everything was racial, but nothing was racist!"

There were three major challengers in the Atlanta succession race: former Congressman Andrew Young and former Public Safety Commissioner A. Reginald Eaves, both black; and one white contender, popular state legislator Sidney Marcus. Despite the fact that the black population had reached the level of 56.6 percent, making a black victory a theoretical certainty, this situation did not preclude a white victory in the event of a severely split black vote. This possibility was enhanced by the fact that Young and Eaves appealed to different segments of the black electorate; young to solidly middle-class blacks, and Eaves to low-income and marginal middle-class blacks. This nascent class cleavage has long been intermittently evident in Atlanta's politics as many low-income blacks, excluded from the historically discriminating black social and economic elite circles, at times have sought to displace those blacks who were, relatively speaking, "to the manor born." As recent as the 2001 Atlanta mayoral election, this class split in the black community emerged with one black candidate (out of a field of three blacks) claimed to be "The People's Candidate" seeking to claim benefits for "those still locked out of city hall."[3]

In the 1981 succession race, Eaves was clearly identified with the insurgent regime of Maynard Jackson's first mayoralty and he had been the lightning rod of white ire and much discomfort among the old-line black leadership. Eaves had been appointed the "superchief" by Jackson, with authority over the police, fire, and emergency management departments in city government. This move led to prolonged racial polarization, a legal challenge to the constitutionality of the city charter, and Eaves's eventual resignation under a cloud of scandal surrounding promotional examinations for police officers. Thus an Eaves candidacy continued the political tempo of insurgency.

Interestingly, *The Atlanta Constitution* ran a major news analysis series on poverty in Atlanta during the campaign, in conjunction with an assessment of the changes that had occurred during the previous eight years of black mayoral rule. It is not clear what the motivations were for the series, but it could have served to further incite a counter-mobilization among low-income blacks, thereby enhancing the possibility of electing a white candidate. The legal requirement that a mayoral winner receive a real majority (as opposed to a plurality) of the total vote all but dictated that one of the black candidates would face the white challenger in a runoff, given the racial demographics of the city and the generally racial voting patterns that had characterized the city's politics in the past. Eaves would have been, by far, the easier black of the candidates to defeat in a runoff with a white challenger, as many middle-class blacks would likely have supported the moderate white candidate out of a sense of "voting responsibly without regard to race." However, Young was a leader in the general election with 41 percent of the vote.[4] Marcus and Eaves received 39 and 20 percent, respectively.

In the succession runoff race, Atlanta was back to mayoral politics as usual with a black-versus-white contest in which the stakes were starkly clear. Most observers agreed that there were no major issue differences between Young and Marcus, and not surprisingly, substantive issues gave way to explicitly racial overtures. In the end, Andrew Young was endorsed by *the Atlanta Constitution* and won with 55.1 percent of the vote. There was roughly a 10-15 percent crossover vote for both Young and Marcus. Otherwise, voting occurred along racial lines, giving Young a decisive advantage because of the black population majority in the city (*Atlanta Constitution* 10/29/81). The white business community had supported the white candidate, displaying a continued resistance to black control of city hall, which historically was controlled by the white business community via politically moderate white mayors who were able to garner black support against generally avowed racist opponents (This arrangement had been the basis for the infamous Atlanta bi-racial coalition that was not a genuine coalition at all.).

Despite the refusal of the white business community to support Andrew Young's bid for mayor, in a grand gesture of racial reconciliation, in the early days of his mayoralty Young informed the white business community that he could not govern without their support (Stone, 1989). Insurgency was clearly dead.

Atlanta had enjoyed an extended period of black mayoral succession. Andrew Young easily won reelection in 1985. In 1989, former first black mayor Maynard Jackson came back and won over a young black protégé, Michael Lomax. In 1993, Bill Campbell won in a contest against a prominent black female politician, April Davis, and won reelection in 1997 in a contest against a prominent black attorney and politician, Marvin Arrington. In 2001, Atlanta elected its first black female mayor, Shirley Franklin who won without a runoff over two other black candidates. Since the first succession race in Atlanta, there have been two constant themes in Atlanta's mayoral politics: a class based cleavage which has emerged intermittently with varying levels of strength and appeal; and an underlying fear of a "white takeover," either by the direct election of a white mayor or by a black surrogate. However, since that first succession race, Atlanta's mayoral politics have gradually shifted from racial reconciliation to a more full-fledged deracialized politics. However, Atlanta's mayoral contests have not had a viable white candidate since that initial succession race in 1981, and given the city's population makeup with roughly 70 percent black population, it remains somewhat untested political waters.

Involuntary Succession: Newark and Gary

Within the span of a twelve-month period in the late eighties, two of the country's longest serving first black mayors were defeated in reelection bids; Gibson in Newark in May 1986, and Hatcher in Gary in May, 1987. Both incumbents faced strong black challengers in the absence of a white challenger, and therefore were faced with a relatively new and different set of dynamics in their reelection bids. In Newark, which was roughly 47 percent black at the time. All three challengers to Gibson were black in a non-partisan contest. In Gary,

Hatcher's challengers for the Democratic nomination in a heavily Democratic city with a 78 percent black population were all blacks. In both Newark and Gary, the most important factor in these succession contests seemed to have been the absence of a "white ogre." In both cases, this missing element appeared to catalyze a different dynamic that significantly contributed to defeat and involuntary succession.

Gibson was initially elected mayor of Newark in 1970, winning with 60 percent of the vote in the heady and hopeful period (three years) following the Newark riots. He was reelected in 1974 with 55 percent of the vote in a bitter, racially charged contest against Anthony Imperiale, whom Gibson had defeated in his initial win. Gibson won again in 1978 with 68 percent of the vote. Gibson faced a black challenger in his fourth race in 1982, winning with 52 percent of the vote despite the fact that he and his major challenger were under federal indictments on charges of corruption. In 1986, the deficiencies in Gibson's record became a liability. Also, the generally continuing decline of the Newark economy had paralleled Gibson's tenure in office.

Gibson's 16 years in office provided a convenient timeframe for assessing the economic well being of the city. Between 1970 and 1985, the city had a population loss of 68,050 residents, a decline of 17.8 percent. The steel fabrication plants, breweries, and other factories, which once boosted the local economy, had closed or declined. Unemployment in Newark in 1986 was 11.2 percent overall, and triple that for some segments of the black community. During the period 1970-1986, the number of movie theaters in Newark had declined from 14 to 6; hotels from 32 to 6; bowling alleys from 15 to 0; restaurants from 937 to 246; and food stores from 377 to 184 (*The New York Times* 5/24/87). Interestingly, *The New York Times* asserted that Newark's economy had begun to rebound with a burgeoning downtown and plans for major corporate relocations from Manhattan to Newark. However, may of Newark's neighborhoods remained blighted and the real estate office boom was not expected to aid the poor.

Gibson had made clear his political ambitions over the years. He had twice, but unsuccessfully, sought the Democratic nomination for governor, in 1981 and 1985. He had achieved the stature of a nationally prominent politician in Democratic Party circles, which had been both necessary and beneficial to the city during Democratic administrations. Those ties had facilitated the rewarding the low-income black voter base so crucial in the calculus of national Democratic Party politics. However, under the Reagan regime, the city of Newark, like most major cities, had lost substantial federal funds previously provided under the Community Development Block Grant program and the Comprehensive Employment and Training Act program among others. Thus, Gibson was rendered vulnerable against a strong black challenger and was defeated by Sharpe James, who emphasized economic revitalization, improving the image of the city, increasing the housing stock, and more effectively combating crime. Ironically, in many respects, the issues resonated in Gibson's campaign of 1970. In another interesting irony, his old white opponent Anthony

Imperiale endorsed Gibson. Sharpe James carried all five of the city's wards, garnering 55 percent of the total vote to Gibson's 40 percent (*The New York Times* 5/15/86).

In 1986, there was no racist ogre to assure automatic black support for Gibson based on an obscuring of issues by the shield of racial solidarity. There are no indications that Gibson's opponent made special efforts to woo the support of the white community despite the fact that the black population comprised slightly less than 50 percent of the total population. The combined black and Hispanic population totaled 70 percent of the electorate. The white vote was not pivotal in this election. The mayoral contest thus pivoted around substantive issues regarding the future of the city, as espoused by two black contestants, with the record of the long-term incumbent used against him. Interestingly, the black challenger's campaign did not reflect a politically conservative turn, for the black incumbent was no longer perceived as radical. The challenger's theme was explicitly directed toward issues deemed critical to the needs of the black community in particular, and towards improving the image and economic vitality of the city in general; much as Gibson had promised over the years. The critical exception in 1986 was that the record of the long-term black incumbent was the standard against which blame was assessed, and the challenger was welcomed as a refreshing breath of new leadership.

In relationship to the Newark succession election of 1986, the outcome of the Gary succession election in 1987 was very much one of deja vu. Richard Hatcher, initially elected in 1987 was the longest serving black mayor in America. Like Gibson, Hatcher had the misfortune of presiding over a city that declined along with the steel industry, upon which its economy depended. Gary had also lost substantial population, 60,000 or 29 percent since 1967. The City had also lost its taxi service, movie houses, many restaurants, and many other businesses (*Indiana Crusader* 3/14/87). Hatcher, too, was indisputably a black politician of national prominence and stature, and was widely respected beyond Gary for his efforts on behalf of the national struggle for black political empowerment. Many national level black politicians campaigned on his behalf, but to no avail. Hatcher lost of a black challenger who promised to improve the functioning of the city government and the general welfare of its citizenry.

In part, Hatcher's embattled position significantly reflected the consequences of the long-standing refusal of major components of the white elite structure to accept the transition to black mayoral governance. Hatcher had never won the support of the white business community or the white ethnic-dominated Democratic Party. In the case of the business community, their split with city hall had actually preceded Hatcher as they had earlier objected to mayoral efforts in support of striking steel workers (Lane, 1979). They were, of course, not satisfied with Hatcher's initial election, and when Hatcher faced reelection in 1971, the white business community had endorsed a black moderate in a last ditch effort to forestall their political displacement. Apparently in response to the prospects of an extended period of insurgent black mayoral leadership in Gary, the business community moved to abandon the city by building a new mall in the adjacent suburb of Merrillville. Within fewer than 10 years after Hatcher's initial election, all 4 major department stores, more than 100 smaller businesses and 2 major banks had closed operation in Gary and had moved to the suburban mall (Lane, 1979).

Moreover, Gary was a classic example of a company town, originally established as the locus of a major U.S. Steel operation and company housing areas for its employees. U.S. Steel and ancillary industries dominated the economy of Gary and the Lake County region. Subsequently, the fortunes of the Gary economy waxed and waned with the fortunes of U.S. Steel. Unfortunately, the waning of the local steel-based economy in Gary paralleled many of Hatcher's later years in office. For example, during the period of 1979-1982, employment at U.S. Steel in Gary dropped from 25,000 to 8,000, and by 1987 had declined still further to 6,000 (*Post Tribune* 1/17/86). Although Hatcher had not inherited a hollow prize, as some analysts predicted that black mayors would (Feemstra, 1969), in the end, he was left to preside over one.

While black political rule had of come exclusively at the price of a loss of economic vitality (as there was no causal relationship between black political dominance and the decline of the steel industry), ironically, blacks in Gary were forced to entertain the option of trading political dominance for the prospect of improving the economic lot of the city. Thus, when the state legislature proposed a consolidation of the many separate governments in Lake County into the single political entity of Metrolake that would have subordinated Gary residents politically and racially, many blacks in Gary speculated that such consolidation was perhaps what the city needed for economic revitalization. Metrolake would have consolidated some 70 governmental entities into a single metropolitan government of 405,000, excluding Merrillville. Although the consolidation effort failed, Mayor Hatcher was able to garner only minimal support at public rallies in opposition to the consolidation (*Post Tribune* 10/28/86, 11/3/86).

Hatcher had not been able or necessarily willing to establish ties with the Republican dominated state legislature, and in early 1986, the state taxation board granted U.S. Steel of Gary a reduction of $16 million in its property tax assessments, leading to a 10 percent shortfall for the city of Gary and its school system. The state taxation board had previously refused to allow the city to raise taxes (*Post Tribune* 1/16/86). Hatcher was faulted by many for not seeking support from the state legislature until 1983, far into his mayoralty, when it was effectively too late. Despite his efforts to expand and consolidate his power base, Hatcher's primary support base of black voters had eroded considerably over the years. Hatcher had run an entire slate of black candidates for office in 1984 and they were all defeated, including then U.S. Representative Katie Hall (Caitlin, 1985). In 1987 Hatcher lost the mayoralty to Thomas Barnes with Barnes winning 56 percent of the vote and carrying all but one of the voting districts.

From Racial Reconciliation To Deracialization

The election and collective experience of black mayors have taken place within the context of broad-based socio-political change. Black mayors were first elected in the wake of the civil rights movement and the period of urban unrest that extended into the mid-sixties and early seventies. The brief and quite strident period of the black power movement also helped to give content and form to the context out of which black mayors emerged. Thus it was expected that early black mayors would be activists and strong social reform advocates. They could do no less. However, time makes for change and, in the main, the era of the insurgent black mayor passed. The first major dimension of change seemed to occur at the point of succession when a changed political dynamic significantly dictated a change in strategy and tactics. Just as insurgency could not be sustained indefinitely, neither could rancorous racial conflict be tolerated indefinitely. Thus, many black mayoral aspirants adopted racial reconciliation as a political posture as a perceived necessity for effective governance as much as for purely electoral strategy.

Collectively black mayoralties have spanned nearly four decades of broad-based socio-political change both in their specific locales and nationally. Many have experienced the declining economies of their respective cities; all have experienced and been affected by the declining fortunes of the national Democratic Party to which they were overwhelmingly wed politically. Over time, the rhetoric of social reform has given way to more generalized issues of good governance. Racially charged issues have yielded to more race-neutral issues. For the sixth wave of black mayors, deracialization is the operative norm. The new ethos is one of saving the city, as a civic duty and responsibility and as a means of benefiting the entire electorate. And perhaps as a means of proving that black leaders can indeed take on the full mantle of governance.

In summary description of what has been described herein as the general evolutionary path of black mayoralties, the election in Newark, New Jersey is instructive. During the summer 2002 mayoral election in Newark, New Jersey is startling evidence that all black mayoralties have not evolved along the same evolutionary continuum at the same pace. In a significant manner, the Newark mayoralty remains stuck in the insurgency phase. In May 2002, Incumbent Sharpe James was a veteran mayor at age 66 after having served four terms in office. James came of political age during the civil rights movement. James succeeded Newark's first black mayor, Kenneth Gibson, in 1986 when the declining state of Newark's economy had paralleled Gibson's 16-year tenure in office. The challenger to Sharpe James was Cory Booker, a 33 year-old freshman city councilman with degrees from Yale, Stanford, and Oxford, who had moved to Newark in 1996 to organize poor tenants against slumlords.

The 2002 contest drew intense national media attention and attracted extensive financial and rhetorical support for Cory Booker from individuals in liberal circles outside of Newark. Cory Booker was turned into a black ogre, "a wolf in sheep's clothing" by James and national black political leaders such as

Jesse Jackson and Al Sharpton. James was also supported by much of the leadership of the New Jersey Democratic Party establishment including the governor and both Democratic U.S. Senators who owed extensive political favors to James for delivering black voter support over the years. Over the years, James had apparently built a powerful and well-entrenched political machine (*Washington Post* 5/14/02: A1). Two days before the election, the Governor is said to have come to Newark and unveiled a proposal to fund a new stadium to be built in Newark for New Jersey's professional hockey and basketball teams; a proposal that would only go forward if Newark returned James to office. (*The New Republic*. 6/3/02: 6). James won with 53 percent of the vote to Booker's support of 47 percent.

After some 32 years of black mayoralties, Sharpe James legacy and Newark's social conditions were summed up as follows:

> In the 1990s the city lost 20 percent of its tax base—a statistic made even worse by the fact that Newark collects an abysmal 83 percent of the taxes it is owed. The city's infant mortality and unemployment rates are double the state average. Its murder rate is more than three times that of neighboring Jersey City and Patterson. Since James took office the city has destroyed more housing than it has built. Six years ago the state took over its schools. A 1999 poll ranked Newark as the worst place in the United States to raise a child. And in 1997 the mayor's chief of staff was convicted of bribery, and his police chief was found guilty of embezzlement. As one prosecutor told the *Newark Star-Ledger* in March of that year, "They should tie a yellow ribbon around City Hall and designate it as a crime scene." (*The New Republic*, 6/3/02:).

Cory Booker's approach to bringing attention to Newark's social conditions has been described thusly:

> In his brief time on the city council, he has injected a moral urgency into Newark politics that has been painfully lacking during James's tenure: He staged a ten-day hunger strike at a drug-infested housing project and lived for five months in a trailer on a notorious drug corner in an effort to shame the police into action. And Booker's agenda reads like a guide to the best practices that reform-minded mayors have developed over the last decade, from quality-of-life policing to expanded after-school programs—practices that have never even been tried in Newark. Last year, when Booker pushed through a modest increase to the city's pitifully low recreation budget, James didn't even spend the extra money. (*The New Republic*, 6/3/02: 6).

While Sharpe James cannot fairly be blamed for all of Newark's social and economic ills, it can be fairly said that James and Booker had significantly contrasting visions of black politics, Newark's future, and the ends to which black mayoral power should be directed. Sharpe James is among the last of a passing generation of black mayors. Cory Booker as staked a strong claim on the future of black politics.

A Broader Framework for Understanding The Evolution of Black Mayors

There are major theoretical and explanatory lacunae in the literature on black mayors and in our shared understanding of the political phenomena that black mayoralties represent. By far, most of the research on black mayors has not only focused on the early black mayoral victories, but also by far the greater focus of research has been on the racial dynamics of these mayoral contests. While such an analytic focus is fully understandable, it is not sufficient for illuminating questions about the legacy of black mayors, the evolution of black mayoralties, nor the maturation of the new black politics. What is needed is a broader, more comprehensive analytic framework for understanding the emergence and evolution of black mayoralties.

We might be reminded here that social science analysis frequently mimics the art of movie making in the way that sometimes sequels to movies substantially inform our understanding of the original productions. Such is the case in understanding the evolution of black mayoralties. After some four decades of black mayoralties in big cities, we can see some things in hindsight that were not fully apparent in the initial studies of black mayors. Hence what I will offer here might be seen as a prequel of sorts, substantially drawing on hindsight as well as ongoing and current observations to sketch out an analytic framework for understanding the emergence of black mayors in specific local contexts and the evolution of black mayoralties across time and across different spatial contexts. Thus what is needed is what we might call a systems based framework for understanding the emergence and evolution of black mayoralties.

What is needed is an analytic framework which links macro-level factors to micro-level dynamics, and which in turn, links these factors to individual mayoral behavior and leadership style. A systems-based framework takes into account these linkages. A systems based framework also takes into account the relationship between specific system elements. The framework which is presented below is meant to both expand our thinking about black mayoralties; to structure approaches to future research; and to invite, nay encourage, work by other analysts in further elucidating and testing what is presented here largely as theory, and of necessity, in brief and in a state of significant incompletion.

Within the context of a systems based framework, there are five major factors which are key determinants in the emergence of black mayoralties and which help to shape and define the character of black mayoralties across time and spatial contexts. These five determinants are outlined and briefly discussed below.

1. The broader, national level political context. This is what we might call the national zeitgeist; or the spirit and nature of the times. For example, it has been argued that the early period of black mayoralties was buoyed by a zeitgeist of creedal passion in which the general tempo of politics nationally was characterized by a sense of urgency in bridging the gap between the American creed for equality and justice, and the starkly contrasting conditions and status of black Americans (Persons, 1993). This period of creedal passion coexisted with and helped to sustain several social movements of the 1960s and early 1970s. These in turn spawned a general policy climate that produced major public policies, which helped to both forge and anchor major social change. For the two decades of the sixties and seventies, the Democrats were the dominant party nationally and this dominance created enhanced political currency for early black mayoralties, which were the locus of a critical electoral base for the Democratic Party. Because of an improved policy climate and Democratic dominance, early black mayors were able to reap programmatic and monetary benefits at the local level. The national political context can either create or restrict support for major socio-political change.

2. The state of the movement. Here I refer to the longstanding struggle for black empowerment of which the new black politics is the most recent manifestation. Social movements wax and wane. The period of the early black mayoralties was the "fever pitch" period of the post-civil rights/new black politics era. It appears that black mayors are generally in tune and in step with the state of the movement, its tenor, and tone. Historically, the state of the movement has set forth the larger issues and demands of Black America. At various points in time, this was a varying mix of organized protest, policy advocacy, and pursuit of public office. This mix of activities peaked between 1955 and 1985. By the start of the 1990s, in the aftermath of two presidential campaigns by Jesse Jackson (and in the midst of a Republican ascendancy), analysts were already writing about the end of civil rights and the death of black politics. With liberalism under attack and in retreat, the only acceptable statement of black demands was in the form of deracialized issues, both nationally and locally. The former robust mainline civil rights organizations had lost their sense of purpose and had ceased their traditional function of defining a national agenda for Black America. Within the context of the times, there was no longer a national level black strategic perspective with which black mayors could connect. In the early years of the 2000s, that situation continues. Quite arguably, the only strategic perspective that has significant currency within Black America is a strong and well-entrenched anti-Republicanism, hardly a sufficient basis for defining or sustaining a political strategy or a policy agenda.

3. The local socio-political context. There is an old truism in American politics that "all politics is local." This is true, despite the integral ties of local politics to state, regional and national level political dynamics. Indeed, local political contexts evolve and change at there own pace, sometimes seemingly indifferent to national level socio-political change. Historically, this has been particularly evident in the timing of black political mobilization in different cities. Similarly, the patterns of white political dominance and the structure of civic and political leadership have taken on different specific variations across cities. Different cities have experienced varying dimensions and degrees of demographic change. Some cities have experienced major growth of Hispanic and Asian populations and some cities have experienced major population losses, including substantial black flight to the suburbs. Some cities have experienced all of these changes. Cities must also be attentive to their relations with state government and their obligations as members of a region of governments less the fortunes of the city are adversely affected by these relations.

The factors cited here and others are keys to structuring the local political context and in defining and shaping the general issue-set from which mayoral contestants must draw and on which they must define their positions. Key dynamics peculiar to specific local contexts ultimately define which issue-positions are viable and which are not. The local socio-political context is the immediate environment within which black mayors must be elected and within which they must be responsive.

4. The local economy. The local economy can be likened to a political and economic "gene pool" with which a mayor is either blessed or cursed. Such factors as the local tax base, tax rates, employment base, and employment rate; quality of the public schools, quality of the local labor pool, and the general business climate; condition of core infrastructure such as streets and roads, sewer and waste treatment capacity and facilities; public works and the quality of public services; the social services burden and the quality of health care systems; the general capacity of city government and its ability to function effectively within the federal system; quality of the housing stock; recreational and cultural amenities, etc. All of these factors directly affect the vitality of a city in terms of attracting and holding businesses and residents. These factors also affect the level of confidence that citizens will hold about the future of their city. Together, these factors will comprise either a powerful resource base upon which to establish a governing regime, or these factors will post severe constraints to establishing effective leadership. Many of these elements are under the administrative control of the mayor and many are not. All affect a mayoralty, and the successful mayor must devise ways to bring all of these factors within the realm of his or her influence. The state of the local economy will frequently affect the choice of candidates that local political elites will seek to recruit for the mayoralty, and it will dictate a host of choices that a mayor can and must make while in office.

5. Individual mayoral leadership style. By leadership style we mean the choices made by an individual occupying public office; the general orientation towards the authority and responsibilities of the position; the vision which is set forth; and the ways in which the activities of governing are carried out. We know from the social science literature that "the occupant defines the office," and a host of factors affect individual leadership style. For example, the type of issues to which a leader must respond will frequently determine leadership style as some issues create resources and others restrict resources and options. It has been argued here that the broader political context, both nationally and locally, helps to structure the climate within which certain mayoral leadership approaches are viable or not. There is also a wild card component to individual mayoral leadership style, that of the personal philosophy and aspirations of the individual mayor. This is a very critical factor because there is frequently an expectation that an individual black mayor will adhere to a particular philosophical predisposition, which will govern his or her behavior in office. The reality is more likely that ultimately black mayoral behavior cannot be predicted. What does seem more the case is that the leadership style which a black mayor adopts will help to redefine the local political context, and will in the process, either reinforce or alter black voter demands and expectations? This seems particularly true for long-term black mayors.

The five factors outlined above together comprise the foundation of broad-based social change within which black mayoralties exist. Although the factors comprise an interactive system of sorts in which any particular factor changes to some degree in relationship to the others, each factor also changes in a significantly independent and uneven pattern in relationship to the others. Similarly, certain factors will tend to exert a stronger influence at certain time and a lesser influence at other times. These key factors will influence the context within a candidate seeks the mayoralty; the dynamics of particular mayoral election contests; the general and immediate environment for mayoral governance and overall efficacy; the legacy of individual mayors; and the collective legacy of successive black mayors.

Endnotes

1. An earlier version of this chapter appeared in Georgia A. Persons, ed. 1993. *Dilemmas of Black Politics: Issues of Leadership and Strategy.* New York: Harper Collins College Publishers.
2. The District of Columbia's first black mayor, Walter Washington, was initially appointed by President Lyndon Baines Johnson (who also appointed the entire city council), when the city was being governed completely by the federal government. Washington subsequently sought and won election under the 1973 Home Rule Charter. In his bid for reelection, Washington lost in a three-way race to Marion Barry, who had formerly served as President of the D.C. School Board. Prior to the (limited) Home Rule Charter of 1973, the only local elective offices open to D.C. Residents were seats on the school board.
3. In the 2001 Atlanta mayoral election, there were three black candidates. Shirley Franklin was deemed the candidate of the black social and political establishment and received the endorsement of former mayors Maynard Jackson and Andrew Young. Long-term councilman Robb Pitts was deemed the candidate of the Republican dominated local business community. Former mayor Maynard Jackson played the third party role by depicting Pitts as a proxy for white Republican controlled city hall. Gloria Tinubu, a Spelman College Economics Professor, was characterized as the peoples' candidate. Shirley Franklin won without a runoff.
4. Atlanta's mayoral elections are non-partisan. Therefore, the initial election is the general election with a runoff required by state law if no candidate receives more than 50 percent-plus 1-vote of the total votes cast.

References

Alkalimat, Abdul and Doug Gills. 1984. "Black Power v. Racism: Harold: Washington becomes Mayor." In *The New Black Vote*. Rod Bush, ed. 53-179. San Francisco: Synthesis Publications.

Bullock, Charles. 1984. "Racial Crossover Voting and the Election of Black Officials" *Journal of Politics* 46 (February): 238-51.

Caitlin, Robert. 1985. "Organizational Effectiveness and Black Political Participation: The Case of Katie Hall." *Phylon* 41(3). 179-92.

Eisinger, Peter K. 1980. *The Politics of Displacement: Racial and Ethnic Transition in Three American Cities*. New York: Academic Press.

Feemstra, L. Paul. 1969. "Black Control of Central Cities." *Journal of American Institute of Planners*. 4: 75-79.

Hahn, Harlan, David Klingman, and Harry Pachon. 1976. "Cleavages, Coalitions, and the Black Candidate: The Los Angeles Mayoralty Elections of 1969 and 1973."*Western Political Quarterly* 29 (December): 507-520.

Keiser, Richard A. 1990. "The Rise of a Biracial Coalition in Philadelphia." In *Racial Politics in American Cities*. Eds. Rufus P. Browning, et al. New York: Longman.

Lane, James. 1979. *City of the Century: Gary from 1900-1975*. Bloomington, IN: Indiana University Press.

Levine, Charles H. 1974. *Racial Politics and the American Mayor: Power, Polarization, and Performance*. Lexington, MA: Lexington Books.

Nelson, William E. 1982. "Cleveland: The Rise and Fall of the New Black Politics." In *The New Black Politics: The Search for Political Power*. First ed., eds. Michael Preston et al. 187-208. New York: Longman.

Nelson, William E. and Philip Meranto. 1977. *Electing Black Mayors: Political Action in the Black Community*. Columbus, OH: Ohio State University Press.

Nordlinger, Eric A. 1971. "Political Development: Time Sequences and Rates of Change." In *Political Development and Social Change*. 2nd ed., eds. Richard Gable, et al. New York: John Wiley & Sons.

Persons, Georgia A. 1993. "Introduction" In *Dilemmas of Black Politics: Issues of Leadership and Strategy*. Ed. New York: Harper Collins College Publishers.

Persons, Georgia A. 1985. "Reflections on Mayoral Leadership: The Impact of Changing Issues and Changing Times." *Phylon* 46(3) (September): 205-218.

Pettigrew, Thomas F. 1976. "Black Mayoralty Campaigns." In *Urban Governance and Minorities*. Ed. Herrington Bryce. New York: Praeger.

Polsby, Nelson W. 1968. "Institutionalization of the U.S. House of Representatives" *American Political Science Review* 62(1): 144-68.

Ransom, Bruce. 1987. "Black Independent Electoral Politics in Philadelphia: The Election of Mayor W. Wilson Goode." in *The New Black Politics: The Search for Political Power*. 2nd ed., eds. Michael B. Preston, et al. New York: Longman.

Rich, Wilbur. 1989. *Coleman Young and Detroit Politics: From Social Activist to Power Broker*. Detroit, MI: Wayne State University Press.

Stone, Clarence. 1989. *Regime Politics: Governing Atlanta 1946-1988*. Lawrence, KA: University Press of Kansas.

Chapter 7

The Political, Economic & Social Implications of Mayor Lee P. Brown

Kevin L. Glasper

Introduction

Houston is known for its oil and energy industries and now can be identified as the home of one of the top corporate failures due to fraud and impropriety of the 21st century: the Enron bankruptcy. Despite this negative publicity and the fact that it happened on the watch of Houston's first black mayor does not negate Mayor Lee Brown's success in making this city a thriving economic metropolis once again.

In January of 1998, when Lee P. Brown took the oath to become Houston's first black mayor, no one knew what to expect from him, nevertheless, the history of Houston and its local politics would be forever changed. This chapter examines four areas: (1) Brown's campaign strategy; (2) Brown's ability to revitalize the urban area in general and the black community in the areas of improved housing, better jobs and increased minority contracts; (3) this chapter examines Brown's strategy to improve relations between the African American community and the Houston Police Department; and (4) the study closes with an analysis of Brown's overall ability to lead the city of Houston and a discussion of the mayors legacy.

Houston's Demographics

The discussion begins with an analysis of the demographic and ethnic makeup of Houston. When Brown first entered office, like most black mayors, he inherited a city that was replete with urban economic and social decay due to poverty, crime, and an unstable economy that affected the employment rate. In addition, unlike many of the cities that blacks govern, Houston was becoming relatively diverse in its ethnic make-up. For example, the Hispanic population was steadily increasing. In addition, there was a stable black population, and an increasing Asian community on the rise. Nevertheless, the political and economic resources remain under the control of whites despite the fact that the white population in the inner city of Houston is on the decline. Houston has clearly become a model city in terms of the melting pot theory whereas many minorities with diverse backgrounds have merged in terms of geographical location. Nevertheless, there remain heavily concentrated areas of majority white or majority black and Hispanic communities that make Houston typical of most American cities.

Recent statistics show that some four to five years after Brown's first administration, the demographics have changed since 1998. According to the 2000 Census, Hispanics comprise the largest ethnic group in Houston with 37.4 percent of the population (Nissimov: *Houston Chronicle*, 2002). Anglos represent 31.5 percent of the population and blacks represent 25 percent (Ibid). The change in the ethnic make-up in Houston is significant because it indicates that Lee Brown was successful in receiving some of the white vote particularly during his first campaign.

Political and Economic Implications

In a city as large as Houston such ramifications as voter turnout and support, non-voter apathy, and being able to interact effectively with those who control the economic and political power is significant. Whites still control and maintain a majority of the political and economic power structure. Some of the political implications include the idea that the white power structure in Houston maintains a major impact on city governance in terms of influencing city ordinances. Economically, the white power structure can influence city government through business commerce. The notion of control and source of power is significant because if black mayors have to yield to the political and economic power of the white businesses and political leaders then the question becomes whether black mayors such as Brown can produce real programmatic policy solutions or merely represent symbolic agents of change.

As a result of the above indicators, black mayors often have had to lead and govern differently than their white counterparts. For instance, in most urban areas, the business community supported white candidates and displayed continued resistance to black control of city hall, which historically was controlled by the white business community via politically moderate white mayors (Persons, 1993: 52). Although the style of black mayoral personality centered leadership varies from city to city, in no metropolis has a black mayor developed a vision of urban reform centered on the urban poor or developed any ideology or organization that challenged the dominance of the business community in limiting the urban reform agenda (Walters and Smith, 1999: 73-74).

Deracialization as a Political Strategy

Deracialization "is an electoral strategy that involves the efforts of black candidates to deemphasize their race and race-related issues while emphasizing issues that appeal across racial lines in order to win elections in and represent the interests of multi-ethnic constituencies" (Walters and Smith, 1999: 74). In the view of some political scientists, "African American as well as Whites, applaud the emergence of a transracial or deracialized category of African American leadership, several have cautioned that this development may bode ill for the future of black group progress" (Ibid). This is particularly true for black local politics because the majority of blacks have obtained office on the local level either by holding the office of mayor or city council. Second, most blacks still participate in the electoral process on a large scale at the local and national levels and since some blacks have grown disappointed in national politics with the last two elections of 2000 and 2004, the resurgence of the black vote could return to the local level, thereby causing a reduction in the potential use of deracialization strategies particularly if the constituency is a majority African American population.

In 1997, Brown's campaign slogan, "a mayor for all of Houston," symbolized his desire to neutralize the issues from being race specific. As a result of this strategy, Brown appealed to a broader voter constituency that captured a significant share of white votes. By using this strategy, Mayor Brown was not only able to appeal to a broader number of voters, but was able to conduct a race-neutral campaign strategy by choosing to isolate the race issue within his message for all racial groups in Houston. Black mayoral candidates and many black candidates for legislative offices have appealed to and often attracted some white support by emphasizing transracial issues and coalitions (Ibid: 75). This is an important notion to consider particularly during periods where black voter turnout may be at a lower percentage than is necessary to win an election.

This may be due to both voter apathy and decreasing numbers in black voter registration. Under these circumstances, blacks were forced to find alternative ways to appeal to other voters to ensure victory. Traditionally, black mayors usually do not develop a plan that centers solely on the urban poor because they risk losing the necessary support from middle class whites and the business community. For example, even in cities where there are large cities populated by blacks, such as in Detroit, Washington, D.C., and Chicago, in order to be effective, black mayors have had to exercise tremendous negotiating and bargaining skills. These bargaining and negotiating skills must appeal to the group that controls and wields the political and economic power in the city. In most cases that includes the business community and middle class whites. In addition, black mayors must maintain a loyal commitment to the black community. By contrast, white mayors already represent an integral part of the internal political system and thus rarely have to bargain and negotiate at the level of black mayors. Thus, white mayors remain loyal to their community without sacrificing their cultural identity or jeopardizing support from the business and other governmental entities. Black mayors often have to work their way into the inner circles of the political system of local politics long after they are elected.

The deracialization strategy must be well planned and takes time to develop to be an effective campaign strategy. However, some political scientists and other scholars have warned that deracialization may actually detract from the black group progress as a whole. In an instructive example, Starks writes that this leadership strategy detracts from the substance of black politics (Starks, 1991:216). It may appear to the black community that once the black mayor is elected and able to penetrate the inner political system that he or she may have been co-opted and is now apart of the establishment or government that is designed to keep the black community in political, social, and economic bondage. Furthermore, it may take two terms before a mayor can create policies or programs that generate legitimate programmatic solutions out of a de-racialized strategy. A key determinant here is to illustrate the benefit or identify a problem that has crossover appeal and that may have ameliorative or adverse effects for non-blacks as well.

The centrist Democratic Party platform can impact black candidate's seeking political office and influence some black voters to change their votes. James Jennings explicates "black activists feel that some politicians are becoming too mainstream and comfortable with the Democratic party's centrist leadership to keep calling for the need for fundamental economic and social change in America (Jennings, 1992: 179). These moderate and centrist ideals have trickled down to local level politics and some black politicians have taken advantage of the opportunity to use a race-neutral strategy by framing policy issues from the center opposed to being too far on the left or the right.

Neglected Neighborhoods

When blacks pursue policies that are overly race-specific sometimes it is difficult to create policies that produce positive results for the black community. Traditionally, white majority city councils and the business elite normally refrain from providing mass support for race specific policies that benefit non-white groups. As a result, "big-city black governments have generally pursued policies and programs of minority appointments and employment, contracts to minority business and efforts to restrain police misconduct in minority communities, but little in the way of policies that might effect the underlying problems of ghetto poverty and dispossession" (Smith, 1996: 129). Here the point made by Smith in *We Have No Leaders* is not that these issues are not important or worthy of finding solutions, but most black mayors over the years have become so heavily burdened with these same typical problems from city to city that they find it very difficult to create and implement programs and policies that would result into programmatic solutions to eradicate poverty.

Ironically, poverty remains one of the core problems confronting black mayors. Similarly, issues such as unemployment and minority contract issues and the intentional neglect of the black community produces distrust between the black community and the local government. Houston is certainly not void of these problems. *Houston Chronicle* reporter Mike Snyder provides the following explanation for some of Houston's decaying neighborhoods:

> In part, the conditions are the legacy of decades of rapid expansion in Houston with little regard to the quality of the development it brought. A local tradition of limiting services to keep taxes low, along with the inefficiencies and budgetary constraints existing in every city have helped make the problems persistent. And a recent policy shift emphasizing responses to residents' complaints has further limited the city's ability to keep up with routine maintenance. In the past 20 years, as the pace of annexations slowed, city officials turned their attention to improving conditions in long neglected neighborhoods. Through the Neighborhoods to Standard program begun by former Mayor Bob Lanier and continued under Mayor Lee Brown, for example, the city has spent almost $100 Million resurfacing nearly 2, 000 miles of streets and has replaced or Upgraded more than 31, 000 street lights at a cost of $2.5 million (Snyder: *Houston Chronicle*, 2002).

Some of Houston's poorer neighborhoods such as Acres Homes and the Fifth and Third Ward areas have suffered over the years due to neglect and annexation. For example, the end of Acres Homes country appeal came in 1971, when the city of Houston began annexing the community (Mack: *Houston Chronicle*, 2001). Although the city installed water and sewer lines for the area, some surrounding neighborhoods remain without city services, leaving the job to private companies (Ibid). Furthermore, most black mayors find it very difficult to challenge the business community to assist in eradicating inner city poverty particularly if their businesses and families are not directly impacted.

In *The Dilemmas of Black Politics*, Georgia A. Persons refers to race neutral politics as a form of "new black" politics. Persons argues that the focus on black mayoralties particularly affords illumination of the evolution of the new black politics from its early manifestation as an insurgent movement to its seeming maturation as a variant of politics as usual in which the significance of traditional racial appeals and social reform efforts apparently have been diminished (Persons, 1993: 40). Persons further articulates that

> In order to examine the collective evolution of big-city black mayoralties that they can be grouped in three specific categories. The first category is known as "a pattern of insurgency," which characterizes the challenges to the prevailing political order, embracing of a social reform agenda, and utilization of a pattern of racial appeals to mobilize a primary support group of black voters. The second group that Persons refers to is known as "a pattern of racial reconciliation." A pattern of racial reconciliation involves black candidates wooing white voters by simply diminishing, avoiding or preventing racial appeals, while in other situations black candidates exploit the images of insurgent style candidates to enhance by contrast their own appeal as racial moderates; in both instances black candidates expect to reap the benefits of racial symbolism and concomitant black voter support in a white on black

contest: the third category is called a "pattern of institutionalization," which underlies all black mayoral successes in that the number of black mayoral successes has increased over time, and their longevity and succession in office increased, reflecting their grounding, though in varied manifestations, in the systemic fabric of American politics (Persons, 1993: 40).

The second type described by Persons is applicable to the campaign that Brown conducted in Houston. An African American mayor that takes a neutral stance will often receive both praise and criticism. Sometimes this criticism comes from the very constituency that elected the candidate. It is the expectation of that constituency for black mayors to support legislation that will resolve problems that affect their community. When this is not successful then black mayors are said to be have been coopted and perceived as part of the problem rather than part of the solution. Conversely, if black mayors approach their leadership as one catering to a particular race then he or she will risk losing both economic and political support from the white power structure. As a result of these circumstances, black mayors operate in a type of dichotomous state due to this dilemma from the time they commence campaigning until their term concludes.

Enhanced Enterprise Community Program

Mayor Brown has been able to sustain the economy in Houston under some very unstable economic times due to the Enron collapse and an unpredictable national economy. One measure that the Brown Administration utilized to transform the local economy was the Enhanced Enterprise Community (EEC) program. Houston's Enhanced Enterprise Community is a twenty square mile area that is comprised of the central business district and Houston's oldest neighborhoods or wards. Some of these wards known as Third Ward and Fifth Ward, for example, maintained a heavy concentration of blacks and the neighborhoods were economically deprived. To combat these problems, Houston received a series of federal government grants. Some of this funding was used to create the Empowerment Zone/ Enterprise Community Program. This program has been key to the economic revitalization of some decaying urban communities in Houston.

Houston's EEC was designed to be culturally diverse and enhance economic opportunities. However, the EEC also has economically deprived sectors that target poverty, unemployment, lower educational levels, substance abuse problems, and crime and neighborhood stagnation. Furthermore, Houston's EEC has a population of 102,000 with 42% of the families living in poverty (E-Government Center: 1).

Mayor Brown has found other creative ways to keep the city thriving economically. Some of these initiatives include plans by the Houston Mentors and the City of Houston to construct a 7.5 million dollar rail transit line on Main

Street. The rail system was implemented in 2004. Although this rail system will more than likely be expanded at some point in the future, the critical point here is that what percentage of the African American Community will benefit from this new rail system? The layout for the initial route of this system benefited the business district, but there was no direct benefit to blacks. Second, what percentage of blacks benefited from the contracts to construct the rail system in Houston? While Blacks and other minorities received contracts, the short and long benefits of the system remained in questionable.

Brown has attempted to revitalize and empower neighborhoods through a project known as Super Neighborhoods. The Super Neighborhoods project is an initiative based on Brown's Neighborhood Oriented Government that gives communities more input into city government policy making, budgeting, planning and service delivery system (E-Government: 2). The premise here is that citizens can formulate various neighborhood councils that are supposed to be able to articulate the needs and concerns of various communities to the city council and Mayor Brown. This method provides another organized and formal means of communicating the needs of citizens to the mayor and his administration. It would be similar to interest groups articulating there needs and concerns to members of the U.S. Congress on the federal level. However, this plan can only be effective if minority communities can be encouraged to mobilize around the issues and take an active part in the process.

In most cases, the black lower class neighborhoods have the most perplexing problems along with other minority communities because they have been neglected the longest. Furthermore, if such a program only enhances the communication for white affluent or even black affluent neighborhoods then the Super Neighborhood Council should be considered non efficacious. In order for such a program to be effective, it must provide for an equal number of citizens to be represented across the board, particularly in the African American and Hispanic communities.

It is important to acknowledge that black mayors are coming into power at a time when inner cities are decaying and resources are limited. In most cases, some of these black mayors govern by employing creative visions and still try to acquire federal and state government assistance such as in Brown's EEC for the city of Houston. According to Hanes Walton, these black mayors are coming to power just as the urban crisis is peaking and they are expected to devise solutions that avert impending crises (Walton, 1997: 201). This is a critical and poignant assessment made by Walton because although some black mayors take the neutral political route into office, most inherit broken down cities from their white counterparts that are economically and socially deprived. In other words, although they may run on race neutral platforms, they inevitably end up having to put a great deal of emphasis on inner city problems that trickle down to either benefit or serve as a further detriment to blacks and other minorities. This observation makes reelection difficult for black mayors.

The key for black mayors is to be able to find creative ways to articulate the needs and concerns for the black community without over emphasizing race. In addition, not much sympathy is provided by wealthy whites or the black middle class because both groups in most cases have migrated out of areas almost literally non-impacted by incidents of high crimes, unemployment pollution, poor and inadequate educational resources and the like.

Affirmative Action and Minority Contracts

In August of 1999, Mayor Brown and the Houston City Council were facing a dead-end concerning Affirmative Action with respect to minority contracts. In fact, Brown came into office on the momentum of voter support for the city's affirmative action policy, disparaging calls by opponents to replace it with a color blind system (*Houston Chronicle* August 15, 1999). However, once in office, he was able to provide some modifications to the policy that appeared to be conservative or moderate at best. Since 1985, "the city's affirmative action contracting program has benefited only businesses owned by minorities and women. The new initiatives are based on economic status." (Ibid) The voter turnout to save affirmative action gave Brown a lead in the race for the mayor's office and in turn led to the defeat of millionaire Republican businessman Rob Mosbacher, who campaigned on the very changes to affirmative action that are now being implemented (Ibid). Thus the reality is "Brown supports affirmative action, but has supported reforms as a graduation component that would disqualify firms once they reach a certain level of success" (Ibid).

Furthermore, in 1997, during Brown's first election, the language of the Houston Civil Rights initiative (also know as Proposition A) came under extreme scrutiny. Similarly, the Houston Civil Rights Initiative collected enough signatures to place proposition A on the 1997 ballot. Under the previous law, the city of Houston set aside 20% of city contracts for women and minorities (*Houston Chronicle* August 15, 1999). Firms owned by white males are specifically excluded from 20% of Houston's city contracts, while minorities and women are allowed to bid on 100% of city contracts. Additionally, under the previous law minority and/or female owned firms are not required to be local companies, nor do they have to justify having too small or economically disadvantage businesses.

The Houston City Council subsequently altered this language. The Houston Civil Rights Initiative believed that this adjustment confused black voters in order to do away with affirmative action. However, the proposition failed at the polls. In addition, the Houston Civil Rights Initiative felt that the city had no legal right to change the language and sued the city. As a result of this activity, the city of Houston was able to keep its Affirmative Action policies in tact and at the same time Brown was able to capture the office as mayor. The mayor clearly used the momentum behind the issue of Affirmative Action to propel him into office.

Black candidates for mayor often have to take advantage of the mobilization of people around particular issues, but to be most effective the issue of race sometimes has to be de-emphasized. Nevertheless, once African American mayors are elected they are immediately expected to do more with less resources, and requested to produce more substantive policies that benefit the black community. One of the perspectives gained in the past two decades is that "mayors do not control major productive resources; they can only broker them" (Walters and Smith, 1999: 133). Thus, "they cannot intervene effectively into the cycles of despair experienced by urban blacks" (Ibid). As a result, black mayors are sometimes less effective in resolving the problems in the black community due to this lack of control. Instead, black mayors are forced to discover creative ways to negotiate and articulate their needs for grants and other sources of funding. I argue that this is a result of the cultural and historical disposition of blacks that requires a great deal of tact, diplomacy, negotiation, bargaining and management skills that are not necessarily required for white mayors. Accordingly, "this suggests a considerable distance between the institutional function of black mayors and the reward expectation of their black constituents, which are expressed more often in racial institutional rather than just institutional terms" (Walters and Smith, 1999: 133). In other words, the black masses cannot rely solely upon the institutions of the American political system to fight their battles. Rather, they have to also rely heavily upon racial institutions such as black interest groups (such as the Urban League and National Association for the Advancement of Colored People) to collaborate with black elected officials to combat their problems and articulate their issues. The black church is also a racial institution that has benefited the many causes of the black community over the years.

Racial Consciousness vs. Institutional Role

In *African American Leadership*, Walters and Smith further articulate that black mayors have to choose to put more emphasis on their institutional role as mayor. This inevitably requires them to reduce their emphasis on race specific issues as well as to de-emphasize their blackness with respect to the institutional operations of the American Political system. Herein lays the dilemma for most black elected officials. This notion is applicable to W.E.B DuBois "double consciousness theory." DuBois argued that for blacks in America, they would always have to contend with a certain two-ness: one being that of a Negro and the other that of an American. It is a peculiar sensation, this double consciousness, this sense of always looking at one's self through the eyes of others, of measuring one's soul by the tape of a world that looks on in assured contempt and pity (Gates and Oliver, 1999:11).

Walters and Smith cite contemporary examples of this institutional political dilemma. This fact was illustrated rather poignantly in the 1984 presidential campaign of Jesse Jackson. On the other hand, some mayors acted to preserve their access to the White House by supporting the candidate they perceived to be the best potential occupant, while other black mayors supported Reverend Jackson's candidacy (Walter and Smith, 1999:133). It is obvious that some black mayors both with regard to the campaign of Jackson and in other visible circumstances, operates as institutional heads rather than as race leaders. That is to say, they have weighted their roles on the side of their institutional responsibility, rationalizing this act by believing that if they are (good professionals in their institutional roles) officials, they will automatically serve their racial interests (Ibid.). This is not always the case. In fact, one may have nothing to do with the other. However, if the institutional role is pursued effectively then it can be used to facilitate and produce substantial policies that will benefit the African American community.

It is also important to acknowledge that many black mayors were able to become elected to office by using effective insurgent style campaigns. Insurgency is characterized by direct challenges to the prevailing political order, encompassing explicit criticism and attacks on elected officials, institutional processes, civic leadership structures, and the resulting mobilization of interests and bias in local political contexts (Persons 1993: 45). Persons argues that in earlier mayoral elections during the late 1960's and early 1970s, blacks were content to get a black elected to the office of mayor even if there was a void of articulation of substantial black issues or a black agenda. However, since some blacks have been very ineffective in utilizing various institutions of government to get race conscious issues at least put on the political agenda then the trend is slowly changing. This change means that black voters are now more concerned with the issues that impact their communities and it might not be enough just to elect a black in office if he or she cannot articulate and mobilize the race conscious issues pertaining to the black community.

Brown's Efforts to Reform the Police Department

The African American community and police in Houston were not unlike any other large metropolitan area. The perception of the police by the black community has historically been one of suspicion and distrust. Over the years, the legal system has been deemed as another form of white oppression against blacks particularly by lower class blacks and other minorities.

The unequal dispensation of justice is a result of the origin of legal institutions and their present operation by white citizens who do not recognize the worth of non-white cultures (Knowles and Prewitt, 1969: 58-59). Thus, the tumultuous relationship between the black community and the local police makes the job for a black mayor particularly difficult when there is a current need to ease the tensions between the two.

There are several factors that attest to this relationship. First, much of the friction between law enforcement officers and blacks stems from the overwhelming whiteness of most police departments (Ibid: 59). However, although in recent times, most local police departments have been integrated with some blacks holding high-ranking positions such as police chief or captain. Nevertheless, the organizational culture of some police departments has opposed this integration. As a result, the perception of some white police officers towards the black community is one of contempt and dismay. In the past, and at the present time, white majority police departments that patrol in black communities simply have created another form of oppressive domination over black communities that already exist under meager and inadequate conditions; posing economic and social dilemmas for blacks. In order to curtail this poor perception or augment the organizational culture of police departments; police chiefs requires the involvement of the mayor.

Second, the perception between both the local police towards the black community and vice versa has been a continuing problem. The local police have viewed the black community as one of chaos and disorder. Furthermore, inadequate resources, high incidents of crime coupled with individual and institutional racism have all contributed to the poor state of the black community. Having Brown as mayor proved advantageous; this is the case because he once held position as the chief of police in Atlanta and Houston before his quest for political office. As a result, Brown understood some of the extenuating circumstances that existed between blacks and the police.

Community Policing

Historically, the African American community and police have had a turbulent relationship. Mayor Lee Brown took the office of Mayor in Houston during a time when such distrust and ill perceived notions between the black community and law enforcement was at an all time high around the country. Police misconduct issues were on the rise in many urban areas. Police misconduct is defined as "any inappropriate behavior on the part of any law enforcement officer that is either illegal or immoral or both" (Champion, 2001: 2). Police misconduct issues like racial profiling and police brutality were prevalent issues for the black community. "Racial profiling involves law enforcement actions based on race, ethnicity, or national origin rather than on the criminal behavior of an individual" (Pampel, 2004: 3).

Most large urban cities like Houston were the center of attention for turmoil between people of color and the local police. It also made the relationship between the city mayor and its police chief more significant and at times divisive. During his tenure as the police chief of Houston, Brown was advocate of "community policing." Community policing is a strategy that includes establishing community police precincts in various neighborhoods and allows the neighborhood citizenry to become empowered by getting to know their neighborhood officers better. Community policing allows citizens to establish Neighborhood Crime Watch Programs (NCUP) that safely assist the police in curtailing some of the neighborhood crime. It calls for the police to patrol crime infested areas and riding bikes as opposed to riding in the patrol cars. In some areas the police officers patrol on horses. The idea is to allow the police to become more receptive and personable towards the citizens who live in the communities. Furthermore, it requires the citizens to be more receptive to the police presence and to take a more active role in their communities in terms of reporting suspicious and criminal activity in their neighborhoods. The premise behind neighborhood or community policing is that it serves two purposes. First, if implemented effectively the program can curtail high incidents of neighborhood crimes. Second, it may improve the poor relationship that exists between the police and the Hispanic and African American communities.

Houston has implemented Community Policing programs. However, the verdict is out on how effective these programs have been in minority communities. Community policing worked well in affluent neighborhoods and in some communities that are active and recognize involvement as apart of their civic duty. Prior to Brown's first administration, in September of 1996, there was a summit held at Rice University in Houston to discuss the creation of strategies to address the ever increasing issue of polarization between the police and the African American community (Baker Institute Study, June 1997:1). The main objective of this summit concerned developing a strategy to help close the widening gap between the police and the black community.

Brown and panel members (which consisted of scholars and urban planners) at this summit articulated several factors that could be formulated and implemented to help resolve the hostility between the black community and local police departments all over the country. First, they argued that a national commission should be appointed by President Clinton to address the issue of race in America (Ibid.). The underlying point here is that Brown and other scholars asserted that the specific problems that exist between the local police departments and the black community are an extension of a larger problem of institutional and individual racism that has existed for centuries in this country. This commission they argued should be divided into two segments: one to ensure that the issues at the local level in the communities and their police officers and police chiefs would be addressed; and second, the issue of cultural diversity in terms of training was addressed.

The premise here is that the United States has become so culturally diverse that our local law enforcement community should receive training in cultural diversity so that they can better understand the various cultural and ethnic groups with the hope of fostering more understanding and tolerance for others. In addition, the initial focus of the training should be available to anyone, but in particular, with first-line supervisors, our sergeants, which are critically important in bringing about any changes. Another recommendation deals with advancing the philosophy of community policing. This involves the community in the planning process and it means implementing creative and effective programs to involve the community, such as a citizens' academy or implementing programs to empower police officers to solve problems that have a negative impact on the people they serve (Ibid). Other recommendations include the creation of a youth citizens' academy, a youth police commission and development of a communications plan. The goal of the media led communications plan is to develop a more accurate portrayal of both the police department and the black community.

Mayor Brown was an active participant in this summit and has worked in the law enforcement industry for many years. As a result of this experience, Brown has tried to implement many of these recommendations in Houston such as the community policing strategy and opening the lines of communications between the citizens and the Houston Police Department by establishing a citizen's review board. It is also important to acknowledge that some of the problems that Houston is currently experiencing with polarization are indicative of the rise in racial profiling and the increase in incidents involving police harassment and brutality.

According to Robert Stein, Rice University Dean of Public Affairs, other metropolitan areas such as Los Angeles, Detroit or Washington D.C., for example, the issues of Houston's black communities and the local police department have been somewhat non-salient and not highly publicized which may give the impression that incidents of brutality and profiling occur at a minimum in Houston. A couple of implications can be derived from Stein's argument. One argument that can be derived from Stein's assessment is that blacks in Houston are non-assertive. Second, Stein explicates "the common perception among conservatives is that racial profiling and police brutality are considered over reactions by the black community" (Interview with Robert Stein). Conservatives usually make the argument that the police are justified in stopping black motorists because they are most likely to commit a crime. However, as a result of the lack of reporting and investigations, Stein was quick to point out that these incidents probably happen more frequently than reported in Houston.

Differential Response Team Training

Another type of policing technique that has been utilized under the auspices of the Brown administration and the Houston Police Department is known as the "Differential Response Team." The Differential Response Team Training is a new problem solving technique utilized by police storefronts. The DRT gets away from the reactionary style of policing where officers react to acts of crime and make an arrest. Instead, it focuses on problem solving and finding the causes of the crime (Vaughn: *Houston Chronicle*, 2003). A vital component of DRT involves the community policing technique. However, the DRT technique appears to take a more holistic and research oriented approach as compared to community policing. The DRT teaches the community to help itself (Ibid). In addition, the DRT model is another opportunity to build a better bridge of communication between communities and the police.

Brown's Legacy

Every mayor inevitably leaves a legacy after his or her term has expired. Brown will obviously be no exception as he approaches the end of his final term in office. One of the things that Brown should be credited with is sustaining Houston's economy. Despite the fallout from the Enron Corporation scandal, and the presence of a combative city council, Brown was able to maintain a stable economy that benefited some blacks and other communities of color. He was able to do this through the creation of jobs and the increase in some minority contracts. Employment increased as a result of the construction of athletic stadiums for Houston's professional sports teams and the revitalization of the downtown area that includes the renovation of the George R. Brown Convention Center. There are also other economic and social entities such as the three new multi-service centers. In addition, during Brown's second term, Houston appeared in *Black Enterprise Magazine* and Brown appeared on BET to highlight the city of Houston as one of the best cities for blacks to live, to conduct business and the best city to acquire jobs for young educated black professionals. These issues serve as evidence that blacks were doing relative to previous administrations.

Second, Brown was able to provide economic relief to some of the black and poor communities. As Houston's first black mayor, he can be credited with fulfilling part of his implicit promise to care for Houston's poor minority neighborhoods (Schwartz: *Houston Chronicle*, 2002). The city has spread capital funding to traditionally underserved communities with nearly $500 million slated to be spent during the next five years on capital projects in City Council districts containing some of the city's poorest neighborhoods (Ibid).

Third, Brown has exemplified his versatility by proving that he can articulate the needs of the black community, manage limited and inadequate resources, and interact effectively with both a diverse city council and business leaders. Needless to say, his extensive law enforcement background helped reconcile issues between the police department and certain communities. Certainly, Brown did not please everyone, and he received some criticism occasionally from both the black community and the white community. This reiterates the premise from my initial argument of this chapter which asserts that black mayors must be multi-dimensional in the sense that they must find creative ways to govern in order to be successful. At best, Brown has proven that he did find creative ways to govern. The downside is that they did not always favor the black community partly due to his strategy of race neutral politics and the general internal politics of any mayoral administration that includes some internal conflict with the city council. This point is exemplified in the split decision by the city council to study the issue of reparations and other issues pertinent to the African American community.

Brown was able to lead Houston through some very turbulent times with a calm and reserved demeanor. Some of these key incidents include the 2001 summer flood, the September 11th attacks and the Enron debacle. For example, although Brown was criticized on how he handled some of the incidents like the flood, observers said Brown's stolid demeanor, often seen as a drawback, was an advantage during the storm (Graves: *Houston Chronicle*, 2001). Black mayors and other black politicians have often been criticized by the black community on whether or not they create pragmatic solutions to real problems or simply represent a type of symbolic social acceptance in the American political system. The truth of the matter is that Brown and other African American mayors do represent a type of inevitable symbolic social acceptance, but some like Brown have been able to transform the symbolism into real substantive results. However, the challenge is often to determine how the social symbolism of any politician can transform the political rhetoric into practical realism that results in policies and legislation that benefits the city as a whole. Nevertheless, with black mayors, the expectation is even greater because their constituent base resides in urban areas and yet they have to focus on doing what is good for the entire governing body of a city. Brown and others have demonstrated that this can be done. Two common approaches that are being used by black mayors are deracialization and political triangulation. Deracialization allows a candidate to appeal to a broader constituency base and if it is done effectively it does not necessarily have to come at the expense of the candidate's core constituency of voters. Second, political triangulation assists in the transformation from symbolism to ameliorative practical output.

The symbolism of blacks holding political office at any level will always be apart of their legacy due to the historical and external disposition of blacks left out of the American political system. This symbolism produces good and bad consequences. On the one hand, it does the black community some good if it inspires other blacks to run for political office and represent the true consciousness of the black community. Furthermore, when black elected officials such as Mayor Brown can really make a difference then social symbolism has not failed the black community. However, social symbolism fails us if it only signals that blacks are put in positions of power simply as figure heads with no real input in the decision making process or creating change. In this instance, the symbolism of having blacks in leading political positions is non-efficacious and provides very little impact on the black community with regards to improving the economic, political and social conditions. The black community needs positive results more than they need blacks holding symbolic positions.

In closing, race neutral campaigns may be effective strategies to get more blacks elected to political office. In other words, once in office African Americans must continue to find ways to bridge together communities of color, segments of the white community and the business community to create ameliorative policies that may benefit all. Black elected officials have a duty and responsibility to give back to their communities in general because of our history of treatment as second-class citizens. Giving something back does not necessarily mean creation of all policies that are race-specific to benefit only blacks. However, it does mean that with certain issues such as Affirmative Action, education, employment, housing and minority contracts that black elected officials should find a way to give us equal percentage of access to these arenas.

References

Champion, Dean J. 2001. *Police Misconduct in America.* California: ABC-CLIO. Gates, Henry L. Jr. and Terri H. Oliver. 1999. *The Souls of Black Folk* by W.E. B. DuBois eds. New York: W.W. Norton and Company.

Graves, Rachel. June 25, 2001. "Analysis: How did Mayor's Image fare during Allison Flooding?" *Houston Chronicle.* Http://www.chron.com/cs/CDA/story.hts/storm2001/951826.Hamilton, Charles. March/April 1977 "De-Racialization: Examination of A Political Strategy." *First World.*

Houston Chronicle. August 15, 1999. "Proposition A: "Most City Leaders Back Affirmative Action Shift," Jennings, James. 1992. *The Politics of Black Empowerment: The Transformation of Black Activism in Urban America.* Michigan: Wayne State University Press.

Knowles, Louis L. and Kenneth Prewitt. 1999. *Institutional Racism in America.* New Jersey: Prentice-Hall, Inc.

Mack, Kristen. November 19, 2002. "Acres Homes As Impoverished Today as it was 10 Years Ago," *Houston. Chronicle.* http://www.chron.com/cs/CDA/story.hts/metropolitan/1665468.

Nissimov, Ron. September 19, 2002. "Some Blacks Irritated by Immigrant Influx," *Houston Chronicle.* http://www.chron.com/cs/CDA/story.hts/ec/polls/1547786.

Pampel, Fred C. 2004. *Racial Profiling.* New York: Facts On File, Inc.

Persons, Georgia A. 1993. "Towards A Reconstituted Black Politics?" In Georgia A. Persons, ed. *Dilemmas of Black Politics: Issues of Leadership and Strategy.* New York: Harper Collins.

Schwartz, Matt, November 19, 2002. "Still Waiting: Though City Touts Neighborhood Initiatives, Many Have Yet to Bring Substantial Change," *Houston Chronicle.* http://www.chron.com/cs/CD...ry.hts/special/02neighborhoods/1666396.

Smith, Robert C. 1996. *We Have No Leaders: African Americans In The Post-Civil Rights Era.* New York: State University of New York Press.

Snyder, Mike. "Neglected Neighborhoods: Hasty Annexation left a Legacy of Blighted Neighborhoods," *Houston Chronicle.* November 19, 2002. http://www.chron.com/cs.CDA/story.hts/topstory/1665530.

Starks, R. "A Commentary and Response to Exploring the Meaning and Implications of Deracialization." *Urban Affairs Quarterly,* 27: 216-22.

Vaughn, Carol E. January 29, 2003. "Holistic Approach: HPD Storefronts Focus on Solving Neighbor Disputes," *Houston Chronicle.* http://www.chron.com/cs/CDA/story.hts/thisweek/zone11/news/175605

Walters, Ronald W. and Robert C. Smith. 1999. *African American Leadership.* New York: State University of New York.

Walton, Hanes. 1997. *African American Power And Politics: The Political Context Variable*. New York: Columbia University Press.

Interview with Robert Stein, PhD, Dean of School of Public Affairs at Rice University in Houston, Texas in June 2002.

http://www.cityofhouston.gov E-Government, Houston, Texas.

Chapter 8

Political Triangulation in the Left Coast City: The Electoral and Governance Strategy of Mayor Willie Brown

Sekou Franklin

This chapter explores black politics in San Francisco, and more specifically, it investigates the electoral and governance strategy of Mayor Willie Brown (1996-2004), the city's first black mayor.[1] After a thirty-one year career (1964-1995) representing California's 18th District—located in San Francisco—Brown entered the 1995 mayoral race as one of the most influential black politicians in the country, and as one of California's most powerful democrats. The former East Texas migrant and street lawyer turned corporate lawyer, amassed a vast array of power and influence as a state legislator, and the state's longest ever Speaker of the Assembly (1981-1995).[2] As Speaker of the Assembly, Brown was a hard bargainer. His Machiavellian style and use of the bully pulpit earned him the reputation as the "Imperial Speaker" and the "Ayatollah" of the Assembly. Yet, by December 1995, Brown's decision to run for San Francisco's chief executive position and his subsequent victory, earned him a new nickname: *Da' Mayor*.

Brown's mayoral victory raised the hopes and expectations of blacks, liberals, and progressives about the possibilities of institutionalizing progressive politics in San Francisco. Yet, many liberals and progressives were cautious about Brown's candidacy because of his corporate ties and connections to pro-growth interests and commercial developers. To balance these different interests, Brown's electoral and governance style drew extensively upon, *political triangulation*, a strategy that gained wide attention during Bill Clinton's presidency, but one that has deep roots in American political history.[3] Political triangulation, as explained by social critic Christopher Hitchens, "consists of the manipulation of populism by elitism" (1999: 26). It takes place when politicians skillfully mediate competing interests within their electoral coalition. It also takes place when politicians mediate the interests of their traditional electoral coalition and those that lie outside of it.[4]

In the remainder of the chapter, I offer a historical overview of Brown's 1995 mayoral campaign and his electoral strategy during his first term. But first, I discuss San Francisco's unique political culture and how it has impacted liberal-progressive politics in the city, the status of blacks, and political triangulation.

Political Culture and Hyperpluralism in San Francisco

Political culture and subculture can impact—not determine—the types of electoral strategies utilized by mayoral candidates. Some cultural/sub-cultural variables include local and state electoral and party systems, linkage patterns between citizens and government, local political economies, and the racial/ethnic make-up or social diversity of a particular region/jurisdiction (Elazar 1966; Lieske 1993; Ferman 1985; Hero 1998).

San Francisco's political culture is best described as exceptional. Party competition is rare, elections are non-partisan (the city is overwhelmingly comprised of democrats), and the intense partisan conflicts that one finds in other cities rarely take place in San Francisco. Instead, intense political battles take place between liberals and progressives, on the one hand, and moderate/conservative democrats and republican voters, on the other hand. Bitter conflicts also take place inside of the liberal-progressive axis, often of a fractious and divisive nature.

Emblematic of the city's reform-oriented culture is the central role that citizen commissions and boards play in municipal politics. Since the city charter reforms of 1932, the citizen commission/board structure has served as an effective restraint on the power of the Mayor's office and the Board of Supervisors. When Willie Brown announced his candidacy in 1995, there were over 100 citizen commissions and boards and most of them had some autonomy over the development of their operating budgets.

Another aspect of San Francisco's political culture is the popularity of voter initiatives (also called ballot propositions). Although progressive lawmakers first implemented voter initiatives in the early twentieth century to counteract political corruption, by the 1960s, conservative interest groups began to utilize them to offset civil rights gains and liberal social welfare policies (Gibbs and Bankhead 2001). In fact Brown's exit from the Assembly occurred because of a 1990 statewide voter initiative that placed term limits on state legislators. In contrast to the statewide trend, the ballot proposition has been a friend to citizen groups and lawmakers across the ideological spectrum in San Francisco (DeLeon 1992: 184) Activists continually use voter initiatives to effect policies on land-use issues, electoral reform, and transportation.

Perhaps the most important characteristic of San Francisco's political culture is its social diversity and "hyperpluralism" (Wirt 1974; DeLeon 1992; DeLeon 1997). Across the tightly confined 49 square mile city of 750,000 people, sit 38 enclave neighborhoods and a diverse array of racial/ethnic groups, along with a relatively large and politically active gay/lesbian population (around 15-16% of the voting electorate). Although a large number of San Franciscans consider themselves liberals or progressives, the city's social diversity has made it difficult to develop long-lasting liberal-progressive governing coalition.

Richard DeLeon describes three factions that fall along the city's loose, eclectic liberal-progressive axis: liberals, environmentalists, and populists.

Liberals consist of traditional civil rights groups, blacks and other non-whites, labor, and working-class homeowners, whose policy priorities center on redistributive measures. Environmentalists, on the other hand, tend to be concerned with quality of life issues such as environmental protection, historical preservation, and ecological balance. Populists are in favor of neighborhood preservation, placing limits on commercial development, and are attracted to a grass-roots style of democracy such as citizen participation in government (DeLeon 1992: 33).

San Francisco's reform-oriented citizenry and social diversity/hyperpluralism are essential elements of the city's unique political culture. They both help to test the utility of political triangulation as office seekers/holders must balance a broad range of competing interests along the liberal-progressive axis. One consequence of this is that it has been difficult for a particular group to gain a governing coalition. At times, the city's social diversity/hyperpluralism actually serves as a restraint on the bolshevik outbursts that has earned it the reputation as the *Left Coast City*. Political battles among liberals and progressives often take place, exposing sharp cleavages along inter-racial/ethnic and inter-neighborhood lines, across sexual orientation, and between environmentalists and labor leaders. This can make it difficult to govern simply because the city's mayor has to negotiate the interests of an eclectic coalition of competing groups (Ferman 1985; DeLeon 1992: 174).

Blacks at the Dock of the Bay

In 1995 Brown returned to San Francisco to campaign for mayor after a three-decade political hiatus in the state's capitol (Sacramento). When Brown returned he found a black community whose political clout had diminished over the last twenty years as a result of the growing hyperpluralization of the electorate. As new groups moved into the city the numerical voting strength of blacks began to decline. Furthermore the loss of federal job programs after the 1970s, which had been a vehicle for black political incorporation, hurt the black community's leverage of City Hall (DeLeon 1992).

Equally devastating was the adverse impact that gentrification had on low-income blacks. Proportionately, San Francisco lost more blacks than any other large city in the country during the 1990s. In the 1970s blacks made up 15% of the city's total population. By the 1980s and 1990s their population numbers declined to 11% and 8%, respectively (Ness 2001). Black emigration also occurred as a result of rising housing costs and demolition projects of public housing. By the 1990s, San Francisco was one of the most expensive places to live in the country and commercial development in the city's downtown made it the West Coast's most attractive tourist city.

The Internet revolution further hardened conditions for blacks during the 1990s. As San Francisco became the "hub" for Silicon Valley middle-class and professional dot.com migrants the cost of housing and the land-use value of the city's downtown area increased tremendously. This set of circumstances, along with the shift from blue-collar to service industries in the city and the loss of shipping industry businesses to Oakland, created more difficulties for working-class and low-income blacks to find affordable housing in San Francisco (Ferman 1985: 17). Among those blacks that remained in the city, many of them lived in neighborhoods beset by a myriad of problems. Unemployment, poverty, environmental hazards, and rising crime throughout the 1980s and 1990s, made black neighborhoods depositories plagued by public health dilemmas and social ills typical of urban reservations.

Brown's mayoral candidacy had a symbolic appeal to many blacks who saw their political and numerical power declining. His appeal was greatest among stable working-class residents and members of moderate civil rights groups and churches, civic organizations, and labor unions. These groups received the greatest amount of benefits from political incorporation by Mayor Joseph Alioto's administration (Ferman 1985: 166-167; Browning, Marshall, and Tabb 1984: 115-116).

Brown and the Pro-Growth/Anti-Growth Tension

A source of tension inside of the liberal-progressive coalition and in urban black politics has been pro-growth/anti-growth politics and land-use issues. A major rationale for pro-growth measures has been that it will bring employment opportunities to central cities. Yet skeptics of pro-growth policies dispute this claim and argue that limits should be placed on planning and redevelopment agencies and commercial developers (Clavel 1986: 15-17; Ferman 1996; Robinson 1995; and Stone 1989). Adolph Reed, for example, argues that although commercial development has aided middle-class black business leaders and professionals it has done little to assist poor and working-class blacks: "Of the major urban constituencies of the national Democratic party, blacks had benefited least from the pro-growth framework. In fact several factors, including the racial component of real estate value, combined to make blacks the victims of pro-growth politics" (1999: 87).[5]

Over the last several decades, a formidable anti-growth/slow-growth coalition has emerged in San Francisco—perhaps the most powerful in the nation. Its most enthusiastic supporters have been environmentalists, conservationists, populists, and neighborhood preservations. In 1986, after a long, multi-year fight, growth-control advocates secured the passage of Proposition M, the nation's most liberal anti-growth/slow-growth policy for a central city (DeLeon 1992: 57-83).

Among black San Franciscans, support for growth-control measures has been mixed. Although many blacks have raised concerns about commercial development, due to fears that it will lead to gentrification, black support for growth-control initiatives has been tepid. During the height of the growth control movement, blacks voted in favor of two pro-growth measures, ballot propositions I in 1986 and H in 1990 (DeLeon 1992: 75, 146-149). Yet they voted for Proposition M (1986), which placed restrictions on the building of high-rises in the city (DeLeon 1992: 80-82).

One reason why blacks have been less enthusiastic for growth control measures is because San Francisco's mayoral leadership has been able to co-opt black leaders into planning and redevelopment agencies (DeLeon 1992: 80; Ferman 1985: 47) This has thwarted some opposition from the city's militant and progressive black leaders. Another reason is that growth-control measures in San Francisco have been largely waged in middle-class terms. Although progressives have been able to link environmental concerns and neighborhood preservation issues with the growth control movement, they have had greater difficulty in making the connection between growth control, affordable housing for low-income blacks, and redistributive policies for working-class residents in the city. This challenge points to an underlying schism within the liberal-progressive coalition, and the "neglect" by white progressives of working-class blacks (DeLeon 1992: 147).

Willie Brown's Mayoral Campaign

Willie Brown's entry into the mayoral race was a reluctant decision. He decided to enter the mayoral race only after a failed effort to overturn Proposition 140, the initiative that placed term limits on state legislators and forced him out of office.[6] Despite his corporate ties and inclination towards pro-growth policies, liberals and progressives in the city enthusiastically embraced Brown's candidacy. His record as a state legislator, in which he earned a fairly good reputation advocating for civil rights, civil liberties, and educational opportunities for marginalized residents of California (DeLeon 1997: 156; Richardson 1996; Brown 1992), provided temporary shelter from liberals and progressives who were uneasy about his pro-growth record.

Furthermore, Brown's political exploits and flamboyant personality elevated him to a celebrity status in Democratic Party circles. Traveling to San Francisco to assist Brown in the mayoral campaign were Magic Johnson and civil rights activist and former Atlanta Mayor Andrew Young, as well as members from the upper echelon of the Democratic Party (Paddock 1995: A3). Brown's campaign infrastructure consisted of his Sacramento legislative staff. He also relied on old allies in the city's working-class black neighborhoods. These included ministers, civic groups, and the local NAACP, where he was once part of a militant faction that challenged the older, entrenched leadership (Richardson 1996: 64-67). Fifty full-time volunteers carried out voter registration and mobilization activities for Brown's campaign. An additional 150 precinct captains worked the city's black communities and Brown set up campaign offices in two black neighborhoods, Bayview-Hunters Point and Ingleside (Lewis and Rogers 1995).

The mayoral contest consisted of five major candidates, yet by late summer, the race turned into a three-way contest. To the right of Brown was incumbent

Mayor Frank Jordan, the former Chief of Police, who had no prior political experience. Backed by heavy campaign contributions, Jordan fashioned himself as a conservative Democrat and a proponent of Draconian crime and anti-homeless policies. His 1991 defeat of liberal Mayor Art Agnos brought euphoria to moderate democrats and the city's diminutive republican electorate, and it was a demoralizing defeat for the city's liberals and progressives. His rise to the chief executive of the city signaled another four years of moderate and conservative policies that the city had not experienced since Dianne Feinstein governed San Francisco during the 1980s. Jordan's victory also exposed the fragility of the liberal-progressive coalition and its inability to protect Agnos from conservative mobilization efforts.

The other major candidate, to the left of Brown, was Roberta Achtenberg. In 1993, the former Board of Supervisor member was appointed to head President Clinton's fair housing division in the Department of Housing and Urban Development. Her appointment attracted national media attention, as she became the highest ranking, openly lesbian appointee in the Clinton administration. Her tough Senate confirmation hearing earned the enmity of Senator Jesse Helms of North Carolina who called her a "mean-spirited lesbian activist" (Richardson 1996: 392; DeLeon 1997: 156). What made Achtenberg impressive was her record advocating for civil rights and liberal social welfare programs. Even some members of the Nation of Islam *privately* praised Achtenberg for her congressional testimony defending the organization's security detail of inner-city public housing developments.[7]

The cast of candidates in the 1995 mayoral election attracted national attention. If Brown or Achtenberg claimed victory, the election would be considered a referendum on the conservative entrenchment that had been taking place across the nation. Both New York and Los Angeles—traditionally liberal cities—were taken over by republican administrations in 1993 (Yoachum 1995: A19). In 1994 republican victories in the mid-term elections produced the *Contract for America*, a comprehensive national conservative legislative agenda. Moreover, the ascendancy of centrists to the Democrat Party's leadership ranks in the 1980s and 1990s, as demonstrated with the Democratic Leadership Council, ushered in a wave of proposals by conservative democrats that signaled the disintegration of New Deal liberalism and liberal social welfare policies (Reed 1999).

At the start of Brown's campaign, incumbent Frank Jordan attacked him for being unethical due to his controversial business dealings. He also attacked Brown for being soft on crime. As a state legislator, Brown was a vocal opponent of harsh crime policies that disproportionately impacted poor blacks. And, earlier in his career as a street lawyer, the majority of Brown's clients were part of the city's lumpen proletariat criminal class—pimps, prostitutes, and drug dealers.

On the other hand, Jordan was a strong proponent of harsh anti-crime measures. His broad appeal in 1991 was not surprising given that the city had seen the devastation of a half a decade's worth of crack and turf wars between rival youth crews in the city's poor black communities. During his first term in office, Jordan set up a Juvenile Offender Program that targeted juveniles suspected of committing crimes. He also supported an initiative for a youth curfew that would have made it illegal for minors to be outside after 11:00 p.m. without adult supervision (Solis A16: 1995). His most controversial policy, the Matrix program, gave law enforcement officials the leeway to target the city's large homeless program. Under this program, thousands of homeless individuals found "sleeping, camping, and aggressive panhandling in public places" were arrested and detained by law enforcement officials (Millard 1995: 1).

As expected Brown's policy proposals on crime were less harsh than Jordan's. At an NAACP meeting, shortly before the election, he laid out his "comprehensive vision" for fighting crime. This included the creation of a "war cabinet" comprised of police officers, public officials, and community leaders. He opposed the Matrix program and the youth curfew ballot proposition. Furthermore, Brown said that he would shift resources to the police department's narcotics division in order to remove crack cocaine dealers off the street (*The Sun Reporter* 1995: 1). Most importantly, once elected, Brown indicated that he would fire Chief of Police Tony Ribera. This delighted blacks particularly since the city had suffered through a recent spate of police killings and shootings of unarmed black men.

Achtenberg also had a fairly progressive crime policy. Like Brown she indicated that if elected, she would fire the police chief. A major component of her crime policy entailed the implementation of beacon schools, which operate as community-centers designed to curb crime.[8]

Perhaps the most important issue in the campaign was the city's municipal transportation policy. As Mann (2001) asserts, race, class, and gender are central to municipal transportation policies. Bus/streetcar riders are disproportionately poor, people of color, and women. In San Francisco, thousands of residents used Muni (buses/streetcars) to travel to and from work. However, the Muni system was a complete failure. Buses/streetcars were crime-ridden and poorly operated. They frequently broke down on primary routes and ran notoriously late, especially in poor communities, and, morale was low among bus drivers and streetcar operators.

Hence, reforming Muni was a key issue in the mayoral campaign. None of the candidates had a convincing proposal for solving Muni's crises. Jordan endorsed handing over 20 percent of municipal transportation services to the private sector. He also planned to change the work rules of municipal bus and railway drivers, in an attempt to create a more accountable system.

Brown's transportation policy was more liberal than Jordan's but also controversial. He proposed adding more police and *surveillance* cameras to buses to curb crime. Additionally, he considered a fair work contract for bus drivers and streetcar operators. Included in his plan was a modest amount of money ($250,000) designed to "retrofit" and add cooling systems to buses. Achtenberg offered the most progressive measures for changing the transportation system. These included implementing performance and evaluation measures, creating a Muni passengers advisory board committee for oversight of the buses, and implementing a "Transit First" policy.

The Challenge of Achtenberg

Ironically, Brown's biggest challenge did not come from Jordan, but instead from an ally inside of the liberal-progressive coalition. Achtenberg's popularity, her prior record on civil rights and civil liberties, and her progressive credentials had the potential of dividing votes among liberals and progressives. Some liberals and progressives saw her as Brown's anti-thesis, given his questionable relationship with tobacco and alcohol businesses, and his unwillingness to challenge pro-growth advocates. Thus, Achtenberg and Brown's campaigns had the potential of diluting each other. This was critical since San Francisco's non-partisan elections mandated that if no candidate received over a majority (50%) of the vote in the November general election, the top two vote-getters were required to face each other in a December run-off special election.

Achtenberg's candidacy sparked an internal debate within feminist and women's activist circles, especially after she attacked Brown for retreating from liberal and gender equity issues. She criticized him for a sexual harassment case involving a long-time state assembly staffer, John Barry Wyatt during Brown's tenure as California's Speaker of the Assembly. After Wyatt was charged with sexually harassing three women, the Assembly's rules committee intervened and paid the employees a $59,000 settlement. Despite this, Brown promoted Wyatt and the three women were terminated (Paddock 1995: A3; Perry 1995: A3). Achtenberg scolded Brown for his role in the incident: "It is not enough to support legislation that addresses sexual harassment; the true test of leadership is how those policies are applied to the people you hire" (Achtenberg 1995). In defense, Brown countered by saying that he did not make the decision to fire the three women. Instead, as part of routine procedure required of the Speaker, he signed the termination papers without weighing in on the matter.

Despite the allegation, women's groups defended Brown's record on gender equity issues. He received a boost from a coalition of liberal women who paid for an advertisement in *The San Francisco Bay Times* denouncing Achtenberg's charges. They reprimanded her, stating that "We are shaken and disappointed that you have stooped to tactics we commonly associate with right wing demagogues" (Caplan, et al. 1995).

Achtenberg's candidacy was also an historic opportunity for gay/lesbian organizations to redeem the memory of gay rights activist and former Supervisor Harvey Milk, who was slain on the grounds of City Hall in 1978 by a disgruntled colleague on the Board of Supervisors. Still, it was unclear whether or not her candidacy could win support beyond the assortment of liberals and progressives willing to defect from the Brown camp and the 16% gay/lesbian electorate in the city (Bender and Ness 1995: A1). Brown's chances of temporarily uniting factions in the liberal-progressive coalition were much better than Achtenberg's, and many activists believed he represented the only legitimate chance to defeat Jordan (Ibid. A1, A21).

Furthermore, relations between the predominantly middle-class white gay/lesbian community and the working-class black community had sullied over the last two decades. As black population numbers declined and their influence in City Hall weakened, the gay/lesbian population and power rapidly grew (DeLeon 1997: 156). Despite these tensions, Brown had a reputation of being a strong advocate and defender of gay/lesbian rights dating back to his early days in the California State Assembly. His background neutralized many gay/lesbian leaders who refused to oppose him heading into the general election. In fact, in a pre-election poll given before Brown formally officially announced his intentions on running for mayor, 31.7% of gay/lesbian voters said they favored him compared to 36.5% who supported Achtenberg (King1995a: A13). Brown's campaign received an additional boost when leaders in the gay/lesbian community, such as Ann McCoy of The Alliance, attempted to convince Achtenberg not to run against him. Others such as lesbian Board of Supervisors member Carole Migden and Martha Knutzen of the Harvey Milk Lesbian Gay and Bisexual Democratic Club also expressed support for Brown (Bender and Ness 1995: A1, A21).

Jordan's Campaign Blunder and the Million Man March

Several weeks before the November election two unexpected events added fuel to Brown's campaign. First, Mayor Jordan made a tactical error when he decided to pose nude in a shower with two male Los Angeles disc jockeys. Jordan rationalized the nude photograph by stating, "As an elected official I'm squeaky clean, and have nothing to hide." The message behind this statement and the photograph was to highlight Brown's questionable financial dealings that critics charged were dirty and unethical (King and Kosova 1995: 44). The photograph was also designed to appeal to the sensibilities of the gay/lesbian constituency that showed overwhelming support for Brown and Achtenberg. However, the stunt backfired and was a public relations nightmare for Jordan campaign. It attracted national media attention and local newspapers ran the photograph for days. Most political observers viewed the picture as unprofessional, as well as a display of poor taste and opportunism on Jordan's part.

The second event that assisted Brown's campaign was the Million Man March (MMM), led by Minister Louis Farrakhan and the Nation of Islam. Leading up to the October 16th event, Brown publicly criticized Farrakhan for his previous controversial remarks about Jews and his positions on women and gays/lesbians. On the day of the event he denounced Farrakhan on the steps of Raoul Wallenberg High School, which was named after a Swedish diplomat who aided Jews in their struggle to evade Nazis in World War II (Richardson 1996: 397-398). Brown's remarks probably won him some votes, particularly among moderate and conservative San Franciscans, and re-enforced his grasp on women, gay/lesbian, and Jewish voters.

Among blacks Brown's display was not well received. The MMM had broad support among Bay Area blacks and San Francisco was a rallying point for the region's pre- and post-MMM mobilization activities. The lead organizers of the MMM and post-MMM events, Oba T'Shaka and Christopher Muhammad, brought together a number of blacks and had a base of support in the city's public housing developments. Many of these individuals were more leftward leaning than those leaders that actively campaigned for Brown.

After the MMM, Brown sensed that his earlier criticisms hurt his standing with some of the militant black leaders in the city. Realizing that this could hurt his chances in the mayor's race, Brown privately reached out to the local NAALS chapter. In meetings and conversations that went unreported in the media—due to Brown's request—he normalized relations with the March participants and solicited their support for the remainder of the campaign.[9] The group consented to Brown's request in exchange that he would hear them out on key issues that affected the black community. Based on these series of meetings and conversations, Brown was able to add another base of support to his election campaign.

It is difficult to determine how much Brown's private apologia to the local NAALS group helped his campaign. Oba T'Shaka, Co-Chair of the San Francisco NAALS chapter, believed that the organization's indigenous base in public housing developments helped to mobilize blacks that historically had not voted at high levels (Lewis and Rogers 1995). In a close three-way mayoral race that political observers predicated would be decided in a special run-off election, every vote was important in assuring that Brown would be within the top two vote getters. In a city with a dwindling black population (only 14 out of 543 predominantly black precincts), it was essential that voter turnout was higher in black neighborhoods than in previous mayoral elections. Thus, it is likely that Brown's outreach effort was a bonus to his campaign.

As predicated the general election was very close. Brown finished first with 34% of the vote to Jordan's 32%. Both Brown and Jordan outdistanced Achtenberg who finished with 27% of the vote. In heavily populated black neighborhoods, the black vote saw a significant increase from the previous election. As Table 9 indicates the vote total in the city's central black corridor—Bayview/Hunter's Point—jumped by over 10% between 1991 and 1995. Other black neighborhoods experienced similar increases.

Brown's close victory in the general election was his toughest battle in the mayoral race. Although he faced Jordan in a run-off, all signs pointed to an easy victory. Jordan's conservative ideology, Brown's colorful personality, and the closing of liberal and conservative ranks behind Brown's campaign made him the clear frontrunner in the Run-off. Brown's endorsements came from labor

Table 9 Voter Turnout in 1991 and 1995
Consolidated Municipal Elections (November)

	1991	1995
Bayview/Hunters Point	30.5	42.3
Fillmore/Western Addition	37.6	46.2
Ingleside	38.4	48.6
Visitacion Valley	31.1	36.6

Source: Office of Registrar of Voters, San Francisco, CA.

unions, environmental organizations, women's groups (National Women's Political Caucus, National Organization for Women, and the Democratic Women's Forum), the city's powerful gay/lesbian organizations, the major law enforcement organizations, education groups, civil rights groups, and black organizations. Achtenberg also endorsed his candidacy.

Black voter turnout in the special election increased in comparison to the previous run-off election in the 1991 mayoral race. As Table 10 shows, in neighborhoods with heavy black populations, voter turnout jumped between 5-10%.

Table 10
Voter Turnout in 1991 and 1995
Special Run-Off Elections (December)

	1991	1995
Bayview/Hunters Point	34.2	41.5
Fillmore/Western Addition	39.7	46.2
Ingleside	40.2	47.0
Visitacion Valley	33.2	35.4

Source: Office of Registrar of Voters, San Francisco, CA.

Although Brown ran on a liberal platform, he was also able to triangulate interests inside the liberal-progressive coalition whenever it seemed like he was in trouble. He fended off allegations of being soft on sexual harassment by reaching out to women's groups and activists who came to his defense. In terms of the Million Man March, Brown earned a double victory. His denunciations of the MMM and Farrakhan appealed to moderates in the city and demonstrated his allegiance to middle-class women's (primarily white) groups, gays/lesbians, and Jews. At the same time, Brown's private consultations with local MMM leaders after the event deterred some blacks from openly condemning his campaign. Due to his intervention, the campaigned actually gained an additional base of people who mobilized a contingent of blacks who otherwise may not have turned out for the race.

Willie Brown's First Term, 1996-1999

The real challenge that faced Brown was whether he could use his influence to implement redistributive social policies and confront the racially hierarchical elements of the city's municipal government. As political scientist William Nelson argues, black mayors have been largely unsuccessful at accomplishing these objectives: "Black mayoral leadership has not significantly challenged the institutional arrangements that produce Black subordination" (2000: 19). Despite his vast political experience, Brown's position as the Speaker of the California State Assembly made him somewhat ill-suited for San Francisco's highest office. The Speaker position provided Brown with absolute power and the bully-pulpit. He controlled the selection of committee chairs and vice chairs and used his power to allocate resources to friends and allies throughout the legislature (Clucras 1995: 21; Cohn, Schockman, and Shatie 2001: 73).

San Francisco, on the other hand, was not friendly to executive-centered mayors. The charter reforms of 1932 neutralized the power of the mayor's office and the Board of Supervisors, the city's de facto city council (Wirt 1974: 120). The revisions shifted power to a newly created Chief Administrative Officer (CAO) and an expanded body of citizen commissions and boards.

Government reformers in San Francisco considered the commission and board structure an institutionalized vehicle for deliberative and participatory democracy. However, the influence of the commissions/boards and the CAO, did not sit well with Brown. Therefore, he was pleased that political reformers placed a ballot initiative—Proposition E—before the voters in the November 1995 election that called for a new city charter. The passage of this initiative led to the largest reforms in city government since 1932.

The new city charter eliminated the CAO position and replaced it with a City Administrator that was more accountable to the mayor's office. The new charter also shifted power back to the mayor's office. It gave the mayor's office jurisdiction over the city's budget and control over the city's departments. In addition, the new charter increased the political stature of the Board of Supervisors. It gave the Board the authority to increase spending on budget items, and with two-thirds of the vote, the power to reject mayoral appointments to the city's commissions (Ballot Simplification Committee 1995: 58; King 1995b).

Many black leaders endorsed the new charter, yet some in the liberal-progressive coalition opposed it. They feared that it gave the mayor too much authority over the citizen commissions. Business leaders applauded the initiative because the old charter guaranteed "specific work rules, pay levels, overtime rewards and pension provisions for which public-employee unions have, over the years, won the citizens' approval" (*Economist* 1995). They believed that an executive-centered government would allow them to leverage the mayor to create a more business friendly atmosphere in the city.

Brown's most important political coup was his defeat of a proposed referendum to replace the procedure for electing the Board of Supervisors from an at-large to a single-member district system. For years liberals and progressives in the city expressed their opposition to at-large elections, especially since single-member districts had the potential of diversifying the Board of Supervisors and increasing the representation of non-whites and less affluent candidates.

Shortly before the mayoral campaign, momentum began to build for supplanting the at-large system. In 1994 voters approved an initiative that created a committee to develop proposals for implementing a single-member district (Levy 1995: A1). Within a year the city's Elections Task Force of San Francisco issued a report recommending that the Board of Supervisors place a two-part referendum before the city's voters that would eliminate the at-large system.

Notwithstanding the strong sentiments among many progressives for a single-member district plan, one of its toughest opponents was Brown. He believed a new electoral system would prevent him from appointing allies on the Board of Supervisors. Under the at-large system, the mayor had the authority to appoint interim supervisors when seats were prematurely vacated. With the expected departure of two supervisors in 1995, two in 1996, and a potential seat vacated if Terence Hallinan was elected the city's District Attorney, the new mayor would be given the opportunity to appoint their own allies on the Board (Ibid.).

Sensing a mayoral victory, especially with pre-election polls indicating that he would easily defeat Jordan in the run-off election, Brown set out to scuttle the single-member district plan even before he was elected. To replace the at-large system, the Board of Supervisors had to agree through a majority vote, to put the proposed plan before the voters in the form of a ballot proposition. Despite the earlier support for single member district elections among most of the liberal Board members and leaders in communities of color, the Board split its vote (5-5). As a result, the district plan failed to reach the voters in the form of a ballot proposition.

Interestingly, the Board members who opposed the initiative were two representatives from communities of color, two lesbians, and a neighborhood advocate, all of whom had expressed prior support for district elections (Ibid.). Supervisor Tom Hsieh, a supporter of district elections, stated that Brown "was the reason" why the Supervisors changed their votes (Ibid.). Ruth Holton, executive director of California Common Cause, stated that Brown's influence on the final vote could best be explained as "speakerized." This meant that he "directed something behind the scenes to get things done" (Ibid.). In one instance Brown convinced Supervisor Mabel Teng, a member of the Rainbow Coalition, to change her vote. In another instance he leveraged Supervisor

Carole Migden to vote against the plan. Migden planned to resign and run for Brown's old Assembly seat and needed his endorsement.

The defeat of the district elections was a major blow to the liberal-progressive coalition and to election reformers. In the plethora of voting rights studies that emerged since the passage of the Voting Rights Act of 1965, it has been well documented that at-large elections often dilute the black vote and other underrepresented groups (Davidson 1984; Grofman and Davidson 1992). The fact that the majority of supervisors who voted against the opportunity for San Franciscans to accept or reject a single-member district plan was a sad commentary on their unwillingness to challenge Brown's attempts to consolidate power and control.

The collapse of the electoral reform campaign underscores the downside of political triangulation. First, as stated earlier, the anti-democratic nature of this strategy points to the manipulation of populist initiatives by elites. Second, and perhaps more troubling is that this approach depends upon the capitulation by some political activists who are supposed to protect liberal and progressive interests. In this case, liberal members of the Board of Supervisors changed their votes when pressured by Brown.

Brown's Governance Strategy

During Brown's first two years in office his energies were directed toward accomplishing his campaign goals and accommodating the diverse interests of his electoral coalition. Shortly after his run-off victory, the police chief resigned due to Brown's pressure. He replaced him with Fred Lau, one of the highest ranking Chinese Americans ever to be hired to lead a big city police department. Brown also hired Robert Demmons to lead the fire department. This was an important victory for Blacks, since Demmons led a decade long civil rights battle to combat the racist hiring practices of the San Francisco fire department. In addition, Brown resided over a mass marriage ceremony of gays/lesbians in the city.

One of Brown's most significant policy proposals was his health care plan: one of the most progressive by a big city mayor. In his first nine months in office he convened a city health summit. At the summit he introduced a "cradle-to-grave" government run health care system that consisted of universal access, comprehensive health coverage, and choice of doctors and hospitals (Hospitals & Health Networks 1996: 76-81). Although Brown's vision for health care was never implemented, he later joined forces with the Health Consumer Alliance to educate consumers about how they might receive affordable health coverage.

Notwithstanding Brown's early activism, and despite the new city charter and his defeat of the single-member district plan, he expressed frustration with the constraints placed on the mayor's position. In contrast to the free-lancing that he was afforded as the Speaker, Brown believed that the rigidity of municipal politics handicapped him from enacting far-reaching reforms. As Brown stated in an interview to his political biographer, "You have a lot less flexibility budget-wise. You cannot pay people what they're worth, and you cannot reduce people who are not worth it if they are already at a certain level" (Richardson 1998: 32). Brown's frustrations increased in August 1996 after he failed to push through an amendment to the new city charter that would have given him greater power and the unions more leverage over contract talks (Stein 1996: 11).

In some respects, Brown's complaints were invalid. Most of San Francisco's previous mayors had to navigate the stubbornness and incrementalism of city government. On the other hand, Brown had more flexibility to carry out his agenda than previous mayors, as a result of the new city charter and his command over the selection of supervisors. Furthermore, Brown received an unexpected gift in his first two years in office. The growth of the national economy and the Internet revolution gave the city an unexpected $100 million budget surplus, which allowed him to hire 1,000 new government employees.

One explanation for Brown's disillusionment with the machinations of municipal politics is that he wanted to deflect attention away from the difficulties he faced in implementing his policies. On the front burner were concerns among San Franciscans about the broken down municipal transportation system. To his credit, Brown ordered more police patrols of Muni to curtail crime on buses and streetcars. He increased Muni's budget by 5.7% in 1997 and 7.7. % in 1998 and started a capital program designed to replace broken door Muni streetcars. Yet, Brown was playing catch-up. His budget increases were nullified by earlier reductions. In the previous decade leading up to Brown's first term, Muni's budget had been reduced by $30 million dollars (Rescue Muni 1999).

By his sophomore year in office Muni was an albatross for Brown's administration. In 1997 federal officials scolded Muni's safety record despite Brown's early attempts to combat crime. Bus riders also continued to express disillusionment with the Muni system. In two surveys (conducted in 1997 and 1998) administered by the San Francisco Planning and Urban Research Association and Rescue Muni, a transportation reform group, bus and streetcar riders said that services did not improve under Brown's tenure as mayor. Buses and streetcars still ran notoriously late, particularly in poor communities of color, and bus schedules were unreliable. In August 1998 disaster hit the transit system when Muni experienced a complete meltdown and grinded to a halt. Brown received much of the blame for these problems, especially since a year earlier he urged riders to soften their criticisms of Muni (Lewis and Gordon 1999).

The continuing failures of Muni clearly hurt him among voters. In several polls conducted by local newspapers, Brown's popularity sharply declined in his last two years in office, much of which was due to their dissatisfaction over Muni.

Willie Brown and the Liberal-Progressive Coalition

Brown's electoral strategy had mixed results during his first term in office. In addition to his health care policy proposal and budget increases for Muni, he appointed blacks and other non-whites to key positions in city government. He also mobilized support for $100 million dollar affordable housing bond. On the issue of homelessness, Brown was somewhat insensitive. After claiming that homeless residents did not live in the renowned Golden Gate Park, he was forced to issue a public apology after local media proved that his statement was false. Moreover, despite Brown's promise to eliminate the harassment of the homeless population that occurred under the Matrix program, they continued to be targeted and detained by law enforcement officials.

Brown's economic proposals were unimpressive. During his mayoral campaign, he spoke sporadically about his economic program for the city. Although he occasionally talked about his economic agenda, Brown really did not broadly articulate his economic program until the run-off election, after it was apparent that he would defeat Frank Jordan. His first economic initiative entailed a regional economic summit comprised of business leaders, labor, and non-profit groups (Brown 1995: A19). The summit was designed to re-enforce the confidence of business leaders in Brown's leadership.

As many predicated Brown's commitment to the pro-growth interests brought forth new development projects in the city. In 1997, he mobilized voters to back a stadium bond issue for the San Francisco 49ers, and in 1998, Brown pushed through an initiative to redevelop the Mission Bay area. Indicative of Brown's triangulation strategy was his enlistment of labor leaders to campaign for his redevelopment and pro-growth initiatives. In exchange, union contracts almost doubled during Brown's first term in office.

Brown's Re-Election Campaign

Heading into his re-election campaign, Brown's support among voters fell to an all-time low. Six months before the election a *San Francisco Examiner/KTVU Channel 2* poll showed that almost 70% of the respondents did not approve of his performance. The low approval rating was attributed to the continuing problems with Muni. Because Brown faced no serious challengers to his seat, his confidence was unshaken (Gordon 1999: A1). Yet, several weeks before the general election, Brown faced an unsuspected challenge from Supervisor Tom Ammiano who entered the race as a write-in candidate.

As an openly gay supervisor and former teacher, Ammiano had far reaching influence among gays/lesbians and educators. He had strong ties to tenants' rights activists and leftists in the city, which urged him to challenge Brown in the 1999 mayoral race. Ammiano was also more progressive to Brown. As a supervisor he drafted legislation for an $11.00/hr living wage for San Francisco workers. He advanced progressive taxation initiatives that included small taxes on stock transfers to help overcome the city's budget crises (Gallagher 2000). He also proposed taxes on downtown businesses to fund the city's transit authority.

Despite being a write-in candidate Ammiano amassed 25% of the vote in the general election, finished second in the race, and forced a special election run-off with Brown. His showing in the mayoral contest attracted wide attention and revealed cracks in Brown's armor. In order to counteract Ammiano's campaign leading up to the December run-off election, Brown accepted assistance from the conservative, pro-business San Franciscans for Sensible Government (SFSG), which joined forces with labor leaders and attacked Ammiano's political record. Interestingly, Brown's long-time rivals and political enemies also closed ranks behind his campaign. Following the November general election, the San Francisco County Republican Central Committee (RCC) voted to endorse Brown's run-off against Ammiano. In commenting on the decision, RCC Chairperson Don Casper said, "You deal with the world as you find it, not as you wish it to be....There are now two poles: Willie Brown and Tom Ammiano. Thus, it would be irresponsible for Republicans not to vote for Willie Brown" (Epstein 1999:A1). The decision won approval from top state republican leaders, Insurance Commissioner Chuck Quackenbush and Senate Minority Leader Jim Brulte. Other endorsements came from former republican Governor George Deukmejian and George Schultz, former Secretary of State under Ronald Reagan, whose wife was a San Francisco socialite and director of protocol under Brown (Gallagher 2000).

Brown's reelection campaign was another example of his use of political triangulation. In order to maintain political power, he was more than willing to receive help from old political enemies, many of whom opposed ameliorative and redistributive social policies. This group filled the vacuum left by liberals and progressives who defected to Ammiano's campaign. Brown could afford taking this risk because he had allies within moderate black and labor leaders who campaigned heavily for him in their respective communities. This strategy proved to be successful as he defeated Ammiano by a 60-40% vote.

Conclusion

A major objective of this chapter was to provide a brief historical sketch of Willie Brown's mayoral campaign and first term in office. The second objective was to demonstrate how Brown used political triangulation as an electoral and governance strategy. Triangulation occurs when a candidate is able to skillfully balance competing interests inside of her or his electoral coalition(s). Another form of political triangulation is when a candidate is able to mediate the interests of her or his electoral coalition and those interests that lie outside of it. In short, Brown performed both tasks in his mayoral campaign and first term in office.

To a large extent, most politicians triangulate competing interests against each other. Overall, despite the use of various electoral strategies (e.g., triangulation, deracialization), black mayors are likely to increase social spending for redistributive policies (Brown 1999). Yet, when political triangulation is central to one's campaign and takes precedence over a framework designed to expand the opportunity structure and challenge racially hierarchical regimes, then it creates many problems.

This strategy reveals larger ideological tensions in electoral coalitions, even those comprised of liberals and progressives. To maintain power, politicians may triangulate by recruiting a moderate and conservative collective of black leaders and civic activists to represent the interests of black and working-class communities. Simultaneously, triangulation tends to offset more militant and progressive activists who are likely to raise issues that could upset the balance of the electoral coalition. Triangulation also assumes that the broader electorate is docile and subject to the maneuverings of political elites and skillful politicians.

Alternatives to political triangulation include those efforts that seek to carry out meaningful black political power. By this I mean the development and rigorous implementation of an agenda that attempts to ameliorate poverty and challenge racially hierarchical and exclusive municipal governments. This occurs not simply when mayors appoint blacks to positions in city government or when they make symbolic appeals to the black rank and file, but more importantly, whey they advocate for the implementation of redistributive policies, such as employment opportunities to low-income blacks, living wages, affordable housing, adequate health care service, and other similar social policies (Jennings 1992; Reed 1999; Orr 1992; and Nelson 2000).

Willie Brown's electoral strategy is instructive for assessing the types of electoral strategies utilized by black leaders in the thirty-five years since black mayors were first elected to major urban cities. His tenure as mayor points to the difficulties that black mayors may face governing cities beset by hyperpluralism, social diversity, and a political culture that requires, to some extent, skillful politicians, who have to balance different competing interests.

Brown's triangulation strategy attempted to accommodate three major interests: the material-based policy concerns of blacks (and other non-whites and labor); the pro-growth regime's pressures for assuming control over the city's commercial development projects; and the progressive reform measures offered by the eclectic, assortment of citizen-based groups, gays/lesbians, environmentalists, and neighborhood preservations.

By the end of his first administration the major dilemma that Brown faced was the defection of a faction of white liberals and progressives (i.e., environmentalists, citizen groups, gays/lesbians, neighborhood preservationists, etc.) to Tom Ammiano's camp in the 1999 mayoral election. In addition to Brown's close ties to commercial developers, his support for a new city charter that reduced the influence of citizen's groups and his opposition to a single-member district election plan for the Board of Supervisors, angered many liberals and progressives. Although Brown was damaged by this defection, he was able to stave off the attacks by these voters by mobilizing support from moderate democrats and republicans.

Perhaps Brown's greatest challenge was balancing his pro-growth agenda with the material-based policy concerns of blacks (other non-whites and labor). Although Brown was hardly the champion of black power radicalism, many blacks and others along the liberal-progressive axis, supported him because of his ties to the old, liberal Burton machine, and because he served as an alternative to the likes of incumbent Mayor Frank Jordan. Brown's connection to the NAACP and other black civic groups, his accommodation of moderate black leaders, flamboyant style, support for liberal social welfare policies as a state legislator, and prior history as a street lawyer, also earned him the backing of black voters. Furthermore, Brown was very good at articulating the importance of redistributive and social welfare measures, even if he was less successful and far less committed to implementing them.

Despite the support that Brown had among blacks and other non-whites, he also worked hard to earn the trust of commercial developers who saw him as uniquely positioned to implement pro-growth policies. The irony is that Brown saw no contradiction with these two frameworks (material-based/redistributive and pro-growth) operating or coexisting under the same umbrella. This was problematic since many activists believed that the pro-growth regime had little regard for improving the material conditions of poor and working-class blacks, who were among the hardest hit by commercial development projects.

The pro-growth regime's policies contributed to the exorbitantly high housing prices, to the gentrification of black neighborhoods, and the subsequent emigration of blacks out of the city. Certainly, this was not entirely Brown's fault. The pro-growth regime's steam roll began before Brown announced his candidacy for mayor. Yet some activists who reluctantly endorsed Brown's candidacy hoped that he might put up some resistance to the pro-growth regime. Unfortunately, he failed to do this. Hence, Brown's legacy as San Francisco mayor—at least in regards to low-income residents and blacks—he may have less to do with what he accomplished, than what he didn't accomplish. In fact, he may be remembered most for residing as mayor during a period that saw one of the largest exoduses of poor and working-class blacks out of the city.

Endnotes

1. Sam Jordan ran for mayor in 1963. He was the first major black mayoral candidate.
2.Brown was recruited to run for political office by Phillip Burton, a former state legislature and congressman, and perhaps San Francisco's most influential politician from the 1960s-1980s. Along with his brother John, Phillip Burton organized one of the most powerful political machines in San Francisco during the twentieth century. The Burton machine as it was called, and is still called today, developed a cadre of liberal politicians in the city that continuously challenged conservative policies. Sam Jordan ran for mayor in 1963. He was the first major black mayoral candidate. Brown was one of the

Burton machine's first recruits and some argue that today he is the de facto leader of the loose organization. For a detailed assessment of the Burton machine, see Jacobs (1995).
3. See Forsmisano's (2001) discussion of the Jefferson presidency.
4. In the three decades since black power ushered in the first wave of black mayors to the top offices in central cities, black politics has seen a diversification of electoral strategies. Over the last decade, many black mayors and mayoral candidates have rejected policy agendas tied to race-specific demands or redistributive justice, and instead engage in electoral and governance strategies designed to accommodate white and black middle class voters (Persons 1992; McCormick and Jones 1992, Smith 1990, Reed 1999; Perry 1996).
5. Political scientist Adolph Reed (1999) is one of the most vocal critics of the "neoliberal" agenda now advanced by the Democratic Party and many black democrats.
6. Many political observers believed that Proposition 140 was specifically designed to remove Willie Brown from office.
7. In a Nation of Islam meeting that I attended in the summer of 1995, Nation of Islam Minister Christopher Muhammad praised Achtenberg for defending the organization's security force. He contrasted this with Brown's capitulation to alcohol corporations
8. Beacon schools are school-based community centers. Although beacon schools operate across the nation, they gained wide popularity in New York City. They generally operate 12-13 hours out of the day and many beacon schools/centers are open seven days a week. The beacon schools were implemented specifically to steer adolescents away from crime in neighborhoods that had high rates of drug and criminal activities.
9. In Richardson's (1996) acclaimed political biography of Brown, he mentions Brown's exploits at Wallenberg High School, but fails to mention his meetings and conversations with black leaders from the NAALS organization. This is not surprising. Based on informal conversations with participants in the initial NAALS meeting, there was a concerted effort on the part of the organization's leaders to make sure that the local media and Brown's political enemies were not informed about his meeting and conversations with the group.

References

Ballot Simplification Committee. 1995. *New City Charter*. San Francisco, CA.

Bender, Kandace and Carol Ness. 1995. "Mayoral Race a Dilemma for S.F. Gays." San Francisco Examiner (April 14): A1, A21.

Brown, Robert E. September 1999. "Race and Politics Matter: African American Urban Representation and Cities' Social Spending During the 1970s and 1980s." Paper Prepared for the Annual Meeting of the American Political Science Association. Atlanta, Georgia, September.

Brown, Willie L. 1992. Interview. Regional Oral History Office, Bancroft Library, University of California. Berkeley, CA.

Brown, Willie L. (Editorial). 1995. "Economic Growth Is Key to Budget." *The San Francisco Chronicle* (November 27): A19.

Browning, Rufus E., Dale Rogers Marshall, and David H. Tabb. 1984. *Protest Is Not Enough: The Struggle of Blacks and Hispanics for Equality in Urban Politics*. Berkeley, CA: University of California Press.

Caplan, D. et al. 1995. "Open Letter to Roberta Achtenberg. Reprinted from *The San Francisco Bay Times*. (November 2).

Clavel, Pierre. 1986. *The Progressive City: Planning and Participation, 1969-1984*. New Brunswick, New Jersey: Rutgers University Press.

Clucas, Richard A. 1995. *The Speaker's Electoral Connection: Willie Brown and the California Assembly*. Berkeley, CA: IGS Press.

Cohn, Matthew Alan, H. Eric Schockman, and David M. Shatie. 2001. *Rethinking California: Politics and Policy in the Golden State*. Upper Saddle, NJ: Prentice Hall.

Davidson, Chandler (ed.). 1992. *Minority Vote Dilution*. Washington, D.C.: Howard University Press.

DeLeon, Richard E. 1991. "The Progressive Urban Regime: Ethnic Coalitions in San Francisco." In Byran O. Jackson and Michael B. Preston (eds.) *Racial and Ethnic Politics in California*. Berkeley, CA: IGS Press.

_____. 1992. Left *Coast City: Progressive Politics in San Francisco, 1975-1991*. Lawrence, KS: University Press of Kansas.

_____. 1997. "Progressive Politics in the Left Coast City: San Francisco." In Rufus P. Browning, Dale Rogers Marshall, and David H. Tabb (eds.) *Racial Politics in American Cities*, Second Edition. White Plains, NY: Longman Publishers, 137-159.

Economist. "Willie's New Stage." *Economist* vol. 335, no. 7918 (June 10): 2.

Elazar, Daniel. 1966. *American Federalism: A View From the States*. New York: Thomas Y. Crowell.

Epstein, Edward. 1999. "Republicans Grit Teeth, Back Brown." *The San Francisco Chronicle* (November 9): A1.

Ferman, Barbara. 1985. *Governing the Ungovernable City: Political Skill, Leadership, and the Modern Mayor*. Temple, PA: Temple University Press.

_____. 1996. *Challenging the Growth Machine: Neighborhood Politics in Chicago and Pittsburgh*. Lawrence, KS: University Press of Kansas.

Franklin, Sekou M. 1997. "The Federal Government's Demolition and Revitalization of Public Housing." Unpublished Paper.

Forsimano, Ronald P. 2001. "State Development in the Early Republic: Substance and Structure, 1780-1840." In Byron E. Shafter and Anthony J. Badger (eds.) *Contesting Democracy: Substance and Structure in American Political History, 1775-2000*, 7-35.

Gallagher, Tom. "The San Francisco Voter Revolt of 1999." *Social Policy* vol. 31, no. 2 (Winter 2000): 24-34.

Gibbs, Jewelle Taylor and Teiahsha Bankhead. 2001. *Preserving Privilege: California Politics, Propositions, and People of Color*. Westport, CT: Praeger.

Gordon, Rachel. 1999. "Mayors Grip Slips." *San Francisco Examiner* (May 16): A1.

Grofman, Bernard and Chandler Davidson (eds.). 1992. *Controversies in Minority Voting: The Voting Rights Act in Twenty-Five Year Perspective*. Washington, D.C.: Brookings Institution.

Hero, Rodney E. 1998. *Faces of Inequality: Social Diversity in American Politics*. Oxford: Oxford University Press.

Hitchens, Christopher. 1999. *No One Left To Lie To: The Triangulations of William Jefferson Clinton*. London: Verso.

Jacobs, John. 1995. *A Rage for Justice: The Passion and Politics of Phillip Burton*. Berkeley, CA: University of California Press.

Jennings, James. 1992. The Politics of Black Empowerment: The Transformation of Black Activism in Urban America. Detroit: Wayne State University

King, John. 1995a. "S.F. Mayor Poll Puts Achtenberg in Third Place." *The San Francisco Chronicle* (April 24): A1, A13.

_____. 1995b. "New S. F. Charter Gives Brown a Stronger Hand." *The San Francisco Chronicle* (December 27): A1.

King, John and Susan Yoachum. 1995. "Candidates Pledge No New Taxes: Jordan's, Brown's Plans for Balancing the Budget." *The San Francisco Chronicle* (November 29): A1.

King, Patricia and Weston Kosova. 1995. "The Real Slick Willie. *Newsweek* (December 1): 11.

Levy, Dan. 1995. "Brown Already Calling Shots." *The San Francisco Chronicle* (December 19): A1.

Lewis, Gregory and Dick Rogers. 1995. "The Black Vote." *San Francisco Examiner* (November 15): A1.

Lewis, Gregory and Rachel Gordon. 1999. "Mayor Gets Mixed Reviews." *San Francisco Examiner* (June 13): A1.

Lieske, Joel. 1993. "Regional Subcultures of the United States." *The Journal of Politics* vol. 55, no. 4 (November): 888-913.

Mann, Eric. "Building the Anti-Racist, Anti-Imperialist United Front: Theory and Practice from the L.A. Strategy Center and the Bus Riders Union." *Souls* (Summer 2001): 87-102.

Nelson, William Jr. 2000. *Black Atlantic Politics: Dilemmas of Political Empowerment in Boston and Liverpool.* Albany, NY: State University of New York Press.

Ness, Carol. 2001. "Blacks Fear Losing Their Political Clout in State." *The San Francisco Chronicle* (June 17): A1.

Orr, Marion. 1992. "Urban Regimes and Human Capital Policies: A Study of Baltimore." *Journal of Urban Affairs* vol. 14, no. 2, 173-187.

McCormick, Joseph and Charles E. Jones. 1993. "The Conceptualization of Deracialization: Thinking Through the Dilemma." In Georgia Persons (ed.) *Black Politics: Issues of Leadership and Strategy.* New York: Harper Collins College Publishers, 66-84.

Millard, Max. 1995. "Mayor Jordan, Willie Brown: Two Views of Homelessness." *The Sun Reporter* (August 17): A1.

Paddock, Richard C. 1995. "A Watershed Event in S.F." *Los Angeles Times* (November 5): A3.

Perry, Huey L. (ed.). 1996. *Race, Politics, and Governance in the United States.* Gainesville, FL: University Press of Florida.

Perry, Tony. 1995. "State Settles Aides' Harassment Suit." *Los Angeles Times* (December 31): A3.

Persons, Georgia A. 1993. "Black Mayoralties and the New Black Politics: From Insurgency to Racial Reconciliation." In Georgia Persons (ed.) *Black Politics: Issues of Leadership and Strategy.* New York: Harper Collins College Publishers, 38-65.

Reed, Adolph. 1999. "Introduction: The New Liberal Orthodoxy on Race and Inequality." In Adolph Reed (eds.) *Without Justice for All: The New Liberalism and Our Retreat from Racial Equality.* Boulder, CO: Westview Press.

Rescue Muni. February 1999. *The Muni Reform Initiative.* San Francisco, CA.

_____. 1998. *Muni Riders' Survey Results.* San Francisco, CA.

_____. 1997. *Muni Riders' Survey Results.* San Francisco, CA. Richardson, James. 1996. *Willie Brown: A Biography.* Berkeley, CA.

_____. 1998. "San Francisco's Mayor Has Been on the Job Now for Two Years. How Does He Size Up His Performance?" *California Journal* (August): 31-33.

Robinson, Tony. 1995. "Gentrification and Grassroots Resistance in San Francisco's Tenderloin." *Urban Affairs Review* vol. 30, no. 4 (March): 483-513.

Smith, Robert C. 1990. "Recent Elections and Black Politics: The Maturation or Death of Black Politics." *PS: Political Science and Politics* vol. 23, no. 2 (June 1990): 160-162.

Solis, Suzanne Espinosa. 1995. "Teens Rally Against S.F. Curfew Measure in Mock Election, High School Kids Vote for Brown." *The San Francisco Chronicle* (November 4): A16.

Stein, M.L. 1996. "*Brown* Sees Red." *Editor & Publisher* vol. 129, no. 33 (August 17): 11-12.

Stone, Clarence. 1989. *Regime Politics: Governing Atlanta, 1946-1988.* Lawrence, KS: University Press of Kansas.

Wirt, Frederick W. 1974. *Power in the City: Decision Making in San Francisco.* Berkeley, CA: University of California Press.

Yoachum, Susan. 1995. "As U.S. Tilts Right, S.F. Tilts Left: Brown, Hallinan Wins Buck Conservative Trend." *The San Francisco Chronicle* (December 14): A19.

PART IV

THE CONGRESSIONAL

BLACK CAUCUS:

THE DISAPPEARING VOICE?

Chapter 9

Symbolic Linkages and the Congressional Black Caucus

Richard Seltzer, Sekou Franklin, and John Davis

Introduction:

In his seminal work *Public Opinion and* Democracy, V.O. Key viewed political linkage as a dyadic relationship involving authoritative decision making elites in government who "must seek willing acceptance and conformity from most of their citizens" (1964: 412). Key speculated that the political organizations responsible for mediating the relationship between government and the masses could provide some restraint on political elites who may otherwise make decisions without considering the interests of their constituents. Similarly, Eulau and Prewitt believed that strong political institutions and electoral competition could help to close "the distance between the average citizen from the political leadership" (1973: 22).

Linkage theorists generally identify political parties as the primary instigative units" that link the concerns of an active citizenry with the policy formulation and outputs of the state (Lawson, 1980: 13; Martin and Hopkins, 1988: 184). Notwithstanding the responsibility that parties have as instigative units, they often fail to meet the concerns of their key supporters and the broader electorate. Although they provide what Lawson calls an "interactive communication," between elite decision makers and a politically attentive mass, party functionaries may also oppose certain types of political activities (i.e. protest), as well as moderate the public policy preferences of an active citizenry. When this happens, alternative linkage mechanisms emerge to replace or compliment the activities of parties (Walton, 1994; Eulau and Prewitt, 1973: 20; Lawson, 1988: 3-13; Baer and Bositis, 1993). Even when parties succeed in integrating the policy preferences of an active citizenry into government, alternative organizations, leaders, or linkages are needed to guarantee democratic governance or political participation.

This is often left to citizens, vis-à-vis minor political parties, grassroots organizations, lobby/pressure groups, and civic groups. As Lawson writes, "In the final analysis, only an informed and assertive citizenry can compel parties— or any other organization—to adopt the structures and practices necessary to aggregate their interests; to recruit responsible, electable, and effective leadership; and to transform reasoned wishes into public policy" (1980: 24).

In the case of blacks, party failure is not the only reason why alternative organizations and leaders have been important in linking their concerns with authoritative political institutions. Historically, institutional racism, electoral arrangements, voter dilution mechanisms, and segregation patterns have prevented blacks from fully participating in the political process. Thus, as Walton states, alternative organizations emerge "first to expose and propagandize the weaknesses of the major parties, second to attempt to place their own representatives in power" (1988: 377).

In this chapter we revisit Walton's (1994) concerns regarding the need to understand linkage patterns that connect citizens to "the overall thrust of black politics." We are interested in assessing what we call *symbolic* linkage patterns between the black electorate and national level political figures, particularly the Congressional Black Caucus (CBC).[1] Formed in 1971 the CBC's formation was the logical outgrowth of the Civil Rights and Black Power movements. Often called the "Conscious of Congress" the CBC's initial objective was to advance a legislative agenda for African-Americans, and in many cases, an agenda that was equally beneficial to other non-whites, progressives and liberals, and poor people (Barnette, 1982; Miller, 1979). The linkage patterns assessed in this chapter are largely *symbolic* because they measure the popularity and approval ratings of the black electorate towards the Black Caucus, as well as their closeness to and knowledge of the lobby organization.[2]

A major argument of this chapter is that black congressional representatives serve as important instigative units for linking blacks to the national political process. However, this linkage pattern is somewhat limited; it has not fully extended to the black subpopulations that experience the most alienation (low income blacks, those who have very little trust in the economy, non-voters, etc.). Therefore, while a cohort in the black community feels close to the CBC and view it as useful for articulating policy preferences, especially when compared to white congressional leaders, some blacks feel detached from the Black Caucus.

The first part of this chapter looks at the challenges and dilemmas that face the CBC. Second, we discuss our data and methodological approach. This is followed by a discussion of the findings. We conclude this chapter with a discussion of important concerns facing the Black Caucus and national level black political leadership.

Context and the Congressional Conscious

In his edited volume *Linkage Politics* (1969), J.N. Rosenau argued that "linkage phenomena" must look at how contextual factors strengthen or weaken the connections between authoritative decision makers and citizens of a particular community or sub-community. Although Rosenau's study focused primarily on world politics and "the interdependence of national and international systems," it is difficult to ignore the author's warnings when analyzing Black Politics. Contextual factors and events that are external to the black community can have a dramatic impact on the ability of black leaders and organizations to instigate effective linkages for their constituents (Walton, 1997). Finally, we discuss several contextual factors that have shaped and limited the CBC's effectiveness in articulating public policy preferences beneficial to blacks and poor people.

Whither the Mass Movement

The formation of the Black Caucus in the early 1970s signaled the institutionalization of Black Politics and the increasing desires by black legislators to influence national politics (Smith, 1981a). Yet, without a mass movement and outside pressures to help the CBC maximize its influence, it has been difficult for the Caucus to influence the passage of major substantive legislation that is beneficial to poor African-Americans. Davis hints at this problem:

> .....it may have been noted, if not explained, that the presence of 40 black legislators (all but one members of the Democratic party, which then controlled both the House and the executive branch of the government), could not sway enough votes to pass a measure critical to black interests. Conversely, the 1964 Civil Rights Act and the 1965 Voting Rights Act were passed with only five or six black members present respectively, *and* with 3 million fewer black voters (Davis, 2000: 582).

Ideally, black legislators who substantively represent the interests of their constituents would be able to influence the passage of legislation that concentrate on redistributive social welfare policies, civil rights, employment, affordable housing, and a health care system that provides a safety net for the poor (Swain, 1994; Whitby, 1996; Walton and Smith, 2003: 168). However, attempts by the CBC to advance legislative packages such as these have often failed or been ignored. For example, the CBC could not convince its Democratic Party allies to support meaningful full employment legislation and to endorse the CBC's alternative budgets, which focused on social and economic reforms (Smith, 1996; Smith, 1992: 113-118). One would hope that these failures would be minimized, to some extent, if there were massive grassroots pressures designed to hold the Black Caucus and its Democratic Party colleagues accountable to a progressive legislative agenda. These pressures might increase the Caucus's own leverage vis-à-vis its own political party.

Dilemmas of Pluralist Democracy

The concerns that Davis alludes to underscores an additional difficulty that the CBC faces, which is the failings of the American pluralist design to accommodate a substantive legislative agenda that benefits poor African Americans (Berg, 1994). This design is based on the assumption that certain ethnic groups that have been historically or systemically oppressed undergo politically and economically assimilation, once they undertake periods of conflict and competition with other groups, who are in power and in charge of economic resources.

Once assimilation has been achieved, pluralist theory contends that ethnic identity or race-based formation would no longer be needed as an organizing principle for that particular group (McClain and Garcia, 1993: 251). It assumes that once assimilation (or political incorporation) occurs, black legislators can and will exercise their political influence in a fashion similar to older immigrant groups (ethnic whites) despite the fact that these groups have different histories and structural locations in American society than blacks (Berg, 1994). Pluralism contends that black legislators will experience as much success or failure as their white counterparts at turning their legislative agenda into policy outputs. This success would be dependent on how well CBC members learn the "rules of the game" that are essential to the workings of Congress (i.e. compromise, bargaining, coalition-building, obtaining seniority on committees, parliamentary procedures, crafting legislation, etc.).

As pointed out by many students of Black Politics, the major defect of pluralist theory is that it fails to account for the limited opportunity structure that blacks face as a result of institutional racism (Pinderhughes, 1987; Jones, 1972). Furthermore, comparisons between black and white legislators based upon the assumptions of pluralist theory does not account for the "historical and extant constraints imposed on blacks, serving as a standard against which the political progress of blacks was measured" (McClain and Garcia, 1993: 251).

For example, in contrast to white legislators, CBC members typically represent urban districts, many of which were economically devastated by de-industrialization and suburbanization during the 1970s. They also come from districts with constituencies that are largely working-class, and in some cases, very poor (Levy and Stoudinger, 1976: 31; Smith, 1981b: 204; Johnson and Secret, 1996). CBC members represent what Singh (1998:11) calls an "exceptional constituency"—one in which the policy preferences and priorities of African-Americans are distant from those of the average American voter and his or her representative. As a result, most CBC members tend to support liberal social welfare policies that attempt to address the needs of their constituencies.

Rising Tide of Conservatism

A major challenge to the CBC's effectiveness is that its maturation took place amidst fading support among the American electorate for liberal social agendas. Many voters, beginning in the 1960s and culminating with the election of President Ronald Reagan, shifted to the right and became antagonistic to liberal programs (Edsall and Edsall 1991). The conservative shift in the nation, along with the reorganization of the right wing in the 1960s and continuing into the present, fundamentally reshaped the trajectory of the Democratic Party (Lowi, 1995; Edsall and Edsall, 1991). It weakened the New Deal coalition and pushed the Democratic Party away from its traditional support of liberal policies. By the late 1980s, the Democratic Leadership Council, a coalition of centrist and conservative leaders, began to dominate the Democratic Party's agenda, despite the protests of many black and progressive party activists.

The conservative shift in the nation had a dramatic impact on the CBC's attempt to mobilize support for progressive public policies that the electorate was reluctant to support. As a result, students of Black Politics face a different set of realities when measuring the effectiveness of Black Caucus members, even the most conservative among them (moderate/conservative Democrats), along the same lines as white representatives.

The conservative shift in the American body politic also uncovered ideological fissures within the CBC, which previously, had a strong history of racial solidarity and voting cohesion (Gile and Jones, 1995; Bonitos, 1993: 31-35; Canon, 1999; Whitby, 1997; Singh, 1998). By the mid-1990s, some Black Caucus members were unwilling to oppose legislative packages that were adverse to the interests of many African-Americans, such as the 1994 Crime Bill (Violent Crime Control and Law Enforcement Act, P.L. 103-122) and the 1996 Welfare Bill (Personal Responsibility and Reconciliation Act P.L. 104-93) (Singh 1998). In addition, black legislators made overtures to and in some cases joined moderate and conservative political groups that were antagonistic to liberal policies and civil rights. By the mid-late 1990s, some Black Caucus members began to work closely with organizations such as the Democratic Leadership Council, the Blue Dogs, the Fair Rules and Openness Group, the Mainstream Forum, and a southern bloc of legislators closely aligned with the tobacco and defense industries (Bositis, 1994: 38-39; Derfner, 2000). In addition to the CBC's ideological diversity, its member's policy preferences have been influenced by their own unique regional (North, South, West, Midwest) and jurisdictional (large urban, small urban, and rural) concerns, as well as by the racial/ethnic composition of their districts (Whitby, 1997: 139-141).

Despite the divisions inside of the CBC that have blossomed in recent years, it would be premature to conclude that they have totally disrupted the group's cohesiveness, and ability to link the black electorate with state-sponsored support of traditional civil rights and social welfare policies (Whitby,1997). As Bositis states, a "broad gulf continues to separate the Caucus—including its more conservative wing—from white southern Democratic legislators on several important issues" (1993: 40).

Data and Methods

Data for this study were obtained from the Inter-University Consortium for Political and Social Research (ICPSR) Roster of United States Congressional Officeholder (1997) and the Americans for Democratic Action's (ADA) 1995 and 1996 congressional scorecards, which measured the liberal ideology of the congress members. In addition, we used data from the 1996 National Black Election Study (NBES) (Principal Investigator, Katherine Tate). The data consists of 1,216 respondents who were interviewed prior to the 1996 presidential election. We matched the respondents with 252 house districts and 34 of the 39 congressional districts that had black representatives.[3] Data from the ICPSR Congressional Officeholder and the NBES were merged into a single SPSS file.[4]

To assess linkage patterns between the black electorate and black members of Congress we conducted four separate measurements that assess the CBC's popularity and approval (according to mean thermometer scores) among the surveyed respondents. First, we examined the relative popularity ratings of black congressional representatives, in comparison with the popularity scores of prominent leaders and events that were widely known in black America during the 1990s.

Our second measurement evaluates the approval scores that the respondents gave to their congressional representatives. The independent variable controls for race of the congressional representatives, their party affiliations (white republican, white democrat, black democrat), and their tenure in Congress (0-4 years v. 5+ years).

Third, we conducted a series of cross-tabular analyses that measured the approval of, closeness of, and knowledge that the respondents have of their congressional representatives. Our independent variable combines race and political party of the representative. The three dependent variables for these cross-tabular analyses are:

(1) A question that measures whether the respondents approve of the way their Representative is handling his/her job. (The question asks: Do you approve or disapprove of the way Representative [Name] has been handling his/her job?); (2) A question which assesses the relationship between the representative and his or her constituents. (This question asks: How good a job would you say U.S. Representative [Name] does of keeping in touch with the people in your district?); and (3) A question that measures the respondents' knowledge of their congressional representatives.

Our fourth measurement uses a regression analysis to measure the popularity of the CBC (dependent variable).[5] Our independent variables for the regression analysis falls under three different categories: socio-demographic characteristics, party allegiance and political ideology, and political participation and alienation.

Socio-Demographic Characteristics

First, we control for a number of socio-demographic characteristics, including age, gender, region (where the respondent lives), and socioeconomic status. We use four measures of socioeconomic status as our independent variables: education, income, occupation, and a variable that measures whether the respondent has been on public assistance. We expect some differences to exist primarily across age and socioeconomic lines. Earlier studies indicated that younger and low-income blacks tend to be more disillusioned with electoral politics (Cohen and Dawson, 1993; Dawson, 1994; Tate, 1994). Thus we expect younger and low-income respondents to express the greatest amounts of disillusionment with the Black Caucus.

Party Allegiance and Political Ideology

The regression analysis includes several independent variables that offer some insight into party allegiance and political ideology. We look at attitudes toward President Bill Clinton and Reverend Jesse Jackson as proxies for measuring different dimensions of liberalism and party allegiance. Furthermore, we account for whether or not the respondents reside in districts governed by liberal congressional representatives, according to the ADA's liberal-conservative congressional scorecards. Nationalist sentiments are measured by the attitudes of the respondents toward Minister Louis Farrakhan of the Nation of Islam and whether or they support the formation of a black political party. We use an additional variable that looks at the respondents' attitudes toward the Million Man March (MMM), the protest rally called for by Farrakhan on October 16, 1995. Instead of using the March as a proxy for assessing nationalist sentiments, we use it to assess a different dimension of liberal attitudes among the respondents. As we discuss later on in this chapter, many mainstream black leaders endorsed the March. Also, many of the March participants were not nationalistic, but liberal in their political outlooks (McCormick, 1997; Morris, 1997: 13; McCormick and Franklin, 2000: 323).

Political Participation and Alienation

We look at a number of measures that assess political participation and alienation. These include whether the respondents attended church on a regular basis; their beliefs about racial equality; and whether they voted in the 1996 election. We conducted additional factor analyses on ten questions that measured political alienation and one's interest in politics. From this list two factors emerged: (a) one's trust in Congress and government; and (b) one's trust in people. Two additive indices were created from these factors. We expect the respondents who have high levels of trust in Congress, the government, and in people to also have favorable outlooks of black congressional representatives.

Findings

Our first task is to look at how the respondents view the Black Caucus and other prominent national political figures. As Table 11 indicates the

Congressional Black Caucus (73.7) received higher favorable ratings than the entire Congress (59.9). It also received higher scores than civil rights leader Jesse Jackson (69.8), General Colin Powell (most recently the Secretary of State in the administration of President George W. Bush) (66.7), NAACP President Kweisi Mfume (69.0), and the Minister Louis Farrakhan (31.0). Only Bill Clinton, the Democratic Party, and the NAACP received higher scores than the Black Caucus.

Table 11

Rating Scales of Prominent National Leaders (Scale 0-100)

	Average
NAACP	78.6
Bill Clinton	76.2
Democrats	75.7
Million Man March	75.6
Congressional Black Caucus	73.7
Average Black Democrats	72.3
Jesse Jackson	69.8
Kweisi Mfume	69.0
Colin Powell	66.7
Average all Representatives	59.9
Clarence Thomas	41.6
Republicans	38.9
Bob Dole	35.7
Louis Farrakhan	31.1

Clinton's high rating among blacks is not that surprising. Clinton was successful at mobilizing black voter support, despite his promotion of policies that have had an adverse impact upon low-income blacks and poor people (i.e. the 1994 Crime Bill and the 1996 Welfare Reform Bill). Clinton has also used a coterie of prominent, moderate black churches and religious leaders to mobilize black voters (Lusane, 1994).

The NAACP's highest ranking is somewhat surprising. This probably reflects the respondents' familiarity with the NAACP as a well known lobby group and as the nation's most influential civil rights organization. Furthermore, the NAACP is one of the few national black organizations with both a national and a local presence throughout the country.

The data further suggests that the Million Man March turned out to be more accommodating to mainstream black politics than was reported in the media. In fact the event had higher approval ratings in the NBES ratings scale than the CBC, despite the very poor rating that the event's organizer, the Minister Louis Farrakhan, had among the respondents (more on this later in the chapter).

As Table 12 shows the respondents view black congressional representatives in a much more favorable light than white democrats and republicans. Whether this was a function of race by itself or by party and ideology is difficult to assess. It may very well be a function of race since white republicans (58.9) with over five years of experience received stronger approval ratings from blacks than did those living in congressional districts governed by white democrats and white republican leaders with fewer than five years of experience.

Table 12
Approval Rating by Race, Party of Representative, and Tenure

Mean Thermometer Rating	
White Republican (0-4 Years)	43.4
White Republican (5+ Years)	58.9
White Democrat (0-4 Years)	42.9
White Democrat (5+ Years)	48.7
Black Democrat (0-4 Years)	78.4
Black Democrat (5+ Years)	69.6

In addition to the high favorable ratings for black congressional representatives, short term black congressional representatives seem to resonate more positively than long term incumbents. Those living in congressional districts governed by black democrats with no more than five years of experience had the strongest approval ratings (78.4). Black incumbents with over two-terms of experience received a lower approval rating of 69.6 (0-100 thermometer scale).

One reason that helps to explain this pattern is that in order to win election new members of Congress are forced to campaign harder and pay careful attention to the concerns of their constituents. On the other hand, incumbents who rarely face serious challenges to their seats generally do not to spend a lot of time and energy on campaigning, and thus, respond to their constituents in different ways than newer members of Congress. Some scholars argue that in comparison to white incumbents, black incumbents tend to assume the role of trustees of their electoral districts, rather than as representatives who routinely consult with and mobilize their constituents (Swain, 1994; Fenno, 1978). However, this is debatable. The incumbency advantage benefits both blacks and whites. Absent of political battles that may result from redistricting, competitive campaigns, and controversial or divisive pieces of legislation, both black and white incumbents are probably less proactive in mobilizing their constituents than new congress members.[6]

A closer look at the approval ratings among the black electorate offers additional insight into how the respondents view their congressional representatives. Table 13 looks at three questions that assess the respondents' approval of, closeness to, and knowledge of their congressional representatives.

Black congressional representatives received higher approval ratings (60%) than white democrats (36.9%) and white republicans (24.7%). Moreover, the respondents in the NBES generally believe that black democrat congressional representatives did a better job of keeping in touch with their constituents than white congressional representatives. They also had greater knowledge of black democrat congressional representatives than they had of white congressional members. For example, almost 22% of the respondents living in districts governed by black congressional leaders were able to name their representatives. This is in comparison with slightly under 10% of those living in districts governed by white democrats and slightly over 6% of those living in districts governed by white republicans.

Table 13
Approval Ratings by Race and Party of Representative

Do you approve or disapprove of the way Representative [Name] has been handling his/her job?

Type of Congressional District	Strong Approve	Not Strong Approve	Not Strong Disapprove	Strongly Disapprove
White Republican	24.7%	30.8%	17.6%	26.9%
White Democrat	36.9	35.8	15.1	12.3
Black Democrat	60.4	3.9	8.3	7.4

How good a job would you say U.S. Representative [Name] does of keeping in touch with the people in your district?

Type of Congressional District	Very Good	Fairly Good	Fairly Poor	Poor
White Republican	13.8%	38.5%	21.3%	26.4%
White Democrat	20.9	43.9	15.8	19.4
Black Democrat	41.7	42.5	7.7	8.1

Knowledge of Congressional Representative by Race and Party of Representative

Type of Congressional District	Correctly Name Rep.	Know Rep.'s Party	Know Rep.'s Race
White Republican	6.3%	29.1%	54.8%
White Democrat	9.3	35.8	63.3
Black Democrat	21.9	56.6	78.5

Note: Data comes from the National Black Election Studies (1996). The results point to the type of congressional districts measured in this study.

These findings suggest that the black electorate continues to look to black congressional representatives to articulate their concerns at the national level. This linkage pattern is not merely a function of party loyalty, but also one influenced by racial identification.

Finally, we conducted regression analysis to further assess the CBC's role as an instigative unit. Although the popularity ratings displayed in Table 13 do not measure the effectiveness of the CBC, or even its utility in articulating progressive policies, they nonetheless help us understand how connected the black electorate feels to the lobby organization.[7]

Earlier in this chapter we suggested that the most alienated cohorts would express more disillusionment with the CBC because of their antipathies toward the political process and the perception that the group is ineffective in advocating for ameliorative social policies. Our findings suggest otherwise. When measuring popularity ratings of the CBC, there were no differences between the most marginalized respondents (low-income and politically alienated blacks) and middle-class blacks, and those who have positive political and economic outlooks. As Table 14 indicates, there was no relationship between attitudes toward the CBC and age, education, gender, region, voter participation, church attendance, political ideology, one's attitudes toward Congress, and one's support for a black political party.[8]

Table 14
Popularity of the Congressional Black Caucus

	B	Beta	p-value
QM2C-attitudes toward Million Man March	.28	.34	.0000
QM1D-attitudes toward Jackson	.22	.25	.0000
QM1A-attitudes toward Clinton	.45	.18	.0000

R Square = 0.40

Note: Results are from data that merged the ICPSR Congressional Officeholder and the National Black Election Study into a single SPSS file. See Footnote No. 8 for a listing of non-significant variables.

Where differences do emerge is when one looks at the role that leadership plays as a proxy for measuring different dimensions of liberalism. The findings point out that civil rights leader Jesse Jackson and former President Bill Clinton helped to re-enforce one's support (or popularity) for the CBC. Furthermore, the respondents who had the highest amounts of support for the Million Man March (both men and women respondents) were more inclined to look favorably upon the CBC.

The strong showing for the CBC among Clinton supporters was expected, in part, due to the strong Democratic Party identification among blacks. Another reason why Clinton supporters were closely allied with the CBC is because the former president has been afforded a high status among blacks. This is due to a variety of reasons, all of which are widely known: Clinton's ability to triangulate the interests of the left and the right; his outreach to black churches and radios; his appointment of blacks in his cabinet; his visit to Africa; and the good state of the economy during the Clinton years (Wickham, 2002; Bositis, 2000; Staples, 1998). Furthermore, Clinton's much dramatized childhood and his ability to *exploit* his marginal working-class upbringing has garnered him broad sympathy among blacks who contrast him with the largely elite, wealthy origins of many prominent politicians.[9] Consequently, blacks were (and still are) Clinton's most loyal constituency. And notwithstanding the criticisms that the CBC levied towards Clinton and his centrist policies, the lobby group was one of his staunchest supporters in Congress. Whether Clinton has mere symbolic or substantive value as an instigative unit is a question that goes beyond the scope of this research. However, symbolic representation or reassurances—though often skewed—can go a long way in influencing political attitudes and behavior (See Pitken, 1967: 96-102; Dye and Ziegler, 1996: 194-213).

Jackson supporters were also more likely to give the CBC a high popularity rating. Since the early 1970s Jackson has fashioned himself as a broker of sorts of black interests inside of the elite ranks of the Democratic Party. His two presidential campaigns registered a number of new black voters in the 1980s (Tate 1994), as well as helped to usher in a number of blacks into local and statewide political offices. Furthermore, Jackson and the CBC have worked together over the last two decades on a number of issues. Thus Jackson supporters do not necessarily view him as someone who operates outside of the Democratic Party framework, but instead as an influential political figure who is able to link their concerns with the Democratic Party and the CBC.

Finally, Million Man March supporters were just as likely to support the Congressional Black Caucus as were Jackson and Clinton supporters. This may come as a surprise to some, given that the Million Man March was organized by Minister Louis Farrakhan, and considering his low ratings in comparison to other leaders and organizations (See Table 11). Yet those who attended the MMM were drawn to the event not necessarily because of Farrakhan, but were propelled by the social and political climate of the time–heightened conservatism as seen with the 1994 Republican Party takeover of Congress, as well as rollbacks in affirmative action and social welfare programs (McCormick, 1997; McCormick and Franklin, 2000: 319-320). The high level of support for the event was probably attributed to its ability to capture the concerns of many liberal blacks that were attempting to offer a response to the conservative legislative agenda that shaped the country during this period.

Furthermore, the March attendees and many supporters of the event were not economically marginalized or politically alienated—those who one might suspect to be the least likely to look to mainstream black political groups for linkages. The average median income of the March attendees was about $43,000 and about 60% had some experience in college or technical school (22.7% completed four years of college) (McCormick, 1997: 146). In fact there were strong similarities between the Million Man March attendees and the regular black Democratic Party activists. In his intriguing comparative study of Million Man March participants and black delegates at the 1992 Democratic National Convention, Morris (1998) found almost identical socioeconomic backgrounds and policy preferences between these two groups.

Leading up to the October 1995 event, a few CBC members expressed dissatisfaction with the Million Man March because Farrakhan was its chief organizer. The most outspoken critic was former civil rights activist and Georgia congressman John Lewis. Yet, some Black Caucus members supported the event. Two of the Caucus's most visible leaders spoke at the March, including Charles Rangel (D-New York) and John Conyers (D-Michigan). In some respects, the Million Man March was not an independent black political movement or larger social change initiative designed to create a *permanent linkage* that articulated black interests outside of the two-party system or as an organized response to it. Instead it attracted CBC members, moderate church leaders, and members of the civil rights community who helped to mobilize black voters during the presidential elections.

Linkage and Alienation

At the outset of this study we suggested that levels of support for the CBC would differ across socioeconomic groups. Our findings suggest otherwise. We found very little heterogeneity in respondents' views toward their individual congressional representatives and the CBC when controlling for socioeconomic status. This was unexpected. We initially would have concluded that low-income and less educated blacks would show significantly more disillusionment toward Black Caucus members than middle-income, affluent, and well-educated blacks. We expected this because low-income/less educated members of the electorate tend to be less enthusiastic about elections and often pessimistic about the ability or willingness of politicians to articulate policy concerns that are beneficial to poor people.

There are two explanations why socioeconomic differences were not as transparent as we had originally predicted. First, party identification and loyalty seem to influence the respondents' attachment to Black Caucus members more than their socioeconomic backgrounds. Despite the Democratic Leadership Council's dominance of the Democratic Party's national agenda, blacks continue to believe that the Democratic Party is a better advocate for liberal social welfare issues than the Republican Party. They believe that *black* democrats situated in high-level positions are in the best position to advance their interests, at least in the national political arena. Hence party identification, along with racial identity and the ability of both the CBC and the Democratic Party to use surrogates (Jesse Jackson, Bill Clinton, and the Million Man March) to mobilize blacks, are all instrumental to understanding linkage patterns between blacks and the national political arena.

Another reason why there were no discernable differences across socioeconomic lines was because most black members of Congress benefit from an incumbency advantage (Gerber, 1996). Incumbency often masks underlying class differences that may exist when trying to understand outlooks toward congressional representatives and politicians. When incumbents face few serious challenges to their electorate districts it can create the perception that homogenous linkage patterns, excluding party identification, exist between the black electorate and black congressional representatives. Several scholars argue that discernable differences or linkage patterns between lower class and middle-class voters generally emerge in ideologically, competitive races, in which one candidate campaigns on a class-based, liberal social welfare agenda (Hill, Leighley, and Hinton-Anderson, 1995; Hill and Leighley, 1996). Absent of this type of competition, linkages with black congressional representatives will most likely appear to be stable and homogenous.

Conclusion

This chapter looked at symbolic linkage patterns between the Black Caucus and the black electorate. Despite the ideological diversity that has grown inside of the CBC it is still largely viewed as a cohesive unit that articulates the interests of blacks inside of Congress. The respondents in the survey ranked the CBC high on their list of national political leaders and organizations. The respondents were also more likely to approve of black congressional leaders, as well as have knowledge of and feel close to them, when compared to white congressional representatives. The congressional representatives tenure in office seemed to have some affect on the respondents' attitudes toward them. Recently elected black congressional representatives received higher scores from the respondents than senior black democrats.

Initially we expected that distinct differences would emerge between middle-class and low-income/less-educated in terms of their viewpoints toward the CBC. We also expected those who were the most politically alienated to look less favorably upon the CBC. Surprisingly, we found very little differences across socioeconomic lines and among those involved in and alienated from the political process. The most significant variables that were able to connect the black electorate to the CBC were political ideology and party allegiance. We used several proxies for measuring liberalism, including the respondents' attitudes toward Jesse Jackson and Bill Clinton supporters, along with those who supported the Million Man March. All of the respondents who looked favorably towards these variables were more inclined to rank the CBC high on the popularity rating scale.

Despite these results, political scientists should be cautious about making broad generalizations about linkage patterns between black legislators and the black electorate. Our study measures *symbolic* rather than substantive linkage patterns. Nonetheless, symbolic linkage patterns can help to reassure blacks that their congressional representatives are and will be responsive to their policy preferences.

Endnotes

1. On this point there has been very little research conducted measuring black attitudes toward groups like the National Black Caucus of State Legislators, the National Black Caucus of Local Elected Officials, the U.S. Conference of Black Mayors, and the National Association of Black County Commissioners.

2. *Substantive* or *concrete* linkage patterns look more closely at how Black Caucus members sponsor specific policy preferences of the black electorate. As Walton and Smith state: "*Symbolic representation* concerns the extent to which people have confidence or trust in the legislature, and *substantive representation* asks whether the laws passed by the legislature correspond to the policy preferences of the people" (2003: 168).

3. All of the black members of Congress in this study are democrats.

4. The NBES is useful for measuring attitudes toward the Black Caucus, as well as other organizations, leaders, and highly publicized national events (i.e., elections, Million Man March, etc.) that are widely known in the black community. However, using this data raises serious concerns. National surveys measuring political opinion toward black leaders rarely include black organizations and leaders that lie outside of the political mainstream (excluding the Nation of Islam). These surveys tend to exclude organizations or leaders that operate at the sub-national and local levels and organize the black rank and file on the street corner, at the factory, in the fields, and on college campuses. Because of these shortcomings, specific data on black or multiracial groups, grassroots organizations, environmental organizations, women and feminist associations, gay/lesbian, and youth groups have been virtually overlooked in national surveys measuring mass black political behavior. Consequently, black respondents are given very little information and data on how these groups might feel about policy issues that shape the life circumstances of low-income blacks (See Walton 1988; 1994; Reed 1999).

5. The thermometer scale for the congressional representative's popularity was the only dependent variable that was interval level.

6. When controlling for their numbers in Congress, there are proportionately more senior black democrats, than there are white ones (blacks comprise about 20% of the most senior democrats in Congress) (Gerber 1996). Furthermore, the black congressional delegation tends to be dominated by incumbents rather than new members of Congress. These factors may bring additional scrutiny to black incumbents than to white incumbents. Furthermore, they may create the perception that distinct differences exist between black and white incumbents, when patterns of mobilization by both groups may actually be quite similar.

7. It is important to mention that popularity and approval ratings do not necessarily measure the effectiveness of the congressional representatives. High popularity and approval ratings can be achieved through symbolic appeals, media attention, and the introduction of key legislation. Effectiveness can be determined by looking at congressional behavior (e.g., the ability to pressure other congressional representatives and the president, the ability to mobilize one's constituents, etc.).

8. The independent variables that were not statistically significant were region (South or North), education, age, gender (male), church attendance, whether blacks will ever

achieve full equality, trust people index, pro congress index, attitudes toward Farrakhan, whether blacks care who wins the next election, support formation black party, vote in last elections, on public assistance, and conservative-liberalism scale.

9. Nobel Laureate and novelist Toni Morrison referred to President Clinton as "our first black president" (Jackson 1998: A25). Writer/poet Ishmael Reed stated that Clinton is a "white soul brother" (Connolly and Pierre 1998: A1). These references are used to describe Clinton because of his marginal, working-class origins and the attacks that he received from his political enemies, which were likened to the attacks that blacks suffer due to institutional racism.

References

Baer, Denise L. and David Bositis. 1993. *Politics and Linkage in a Democratic Society.* Englewood Cliffs, NJ: Prentice Hall.

Barnett, Marguerite Ross. 1982. "The Congressional Black Caucus: Illusions and Realities of Power." In Michael Preston, Lenneal Henderson, and Paul Puryear (eds.) *The New Black Politics.* New York: Longman, 29-52.

Berg, John C. 1994. *Unequal Struggle: Class, Gender, Race, and Power in the U.S. Congress.* Boulder, CO: Westview Press.

Bositis, David A. 1994. *The Congressional Black Caucus and the 104th Congress.* Washington, DC: Joint Center for Political and Economic Studies.

_____. 2000. "Gore's Problem With Black Voters." *The Plain Dealer* (August 18): 11B.

Canon, David T. 1999. *Race, Redistricting, and Representation: The Unintended on Sequences of Black Majority Districts.* Chicago: University of Chicago Press.

Cohen, Cathy J. and Michael Dawson. 1993. "Neighborhood Poverty and African American Politics." *American Political Science Review* vol. 87, no. 2 (June).

Connolly, Ceci and Robert E. Pierre. 1998. "Clinton's Strongest Constituency; To African Americans, President's Record Outweighs Personal Problems." *The Washington Post* (September 17): A1.

Davis, Donn. 2000. Book Review, *The Journal of Politics* vol 62, no. 2 (May): 580-582.

Dawson, Michael C. 1994. *Behind the Mule: Race and Class in African American Politics.* Princeton, NJ: Princeton University Press.

Derfner, Jeremy. 2000. "The New Black Caucus." *The American Prospect* (March 27-April 11) vol. 11, no. 10.

Dye, Thomas and Harmon Ziegler. 1996. *The Irony of Democracy: An Uncommon Introduction to American Politics.* Belmont: Wadsworth Publishing.

Edsall, Thomas Byrne with Mary D. Edsall. 1991. *Chain Reaction: The Impact of Race, Rights, and Taxes on American Politics.* New York, New York: W.W. Norton & Company.

Eulau, Heinz and Kenneth Prewitt. 1973. *Labryrinths of Democracy: Adaptations, Linkages, Representation, and Policies in Urban Politics.* Indianapolis, Indiana: The Bobbs-Merrill Company, Inc.

Fenno, Richard E. 1978. *Home Style: House Members in Their Districts.* Boston: Little, Brown and Company.

Gerber, Alan. 1996. "African Americans' Congressional Careers and the Democratic House Delegation." *The Journal of Politics* vol. 58, no. 3 (August): 831-845.

Gile, Roxanne L. and Charles E. Jones. 1995. "Congressional Racial Solidarity: Exploring Congressional Black Caucus Voting Cohesion, 1971-1990." *Journal of Black Studies* vol. 25, no. 5, 622-641.

Hill, Kim Quaile, Jan E. Leighley, and Angela Hinton-Anderson. 1995. "Lower-Class Mobilization and Policy Linkage in the U.S. States." *American Journal of Political Science* vol. 39 no. 1 (February): 75-86.

Hill, Kim Quaile and Jan E. Leighley. 1996. "Political Parties and Class Mobilization in Contemporary U.S. Elections." *American Journal of Political Science* vol. 40, no. 3 (August): 787-804.

Jackson, Derrick Z. 1998. "Clinton's Unpaid Debt to His Black Defenders." *Boston Globe* (October 7): A25.

Johnson, James B. and Philip E. Secret. 1996. "Focus and Style of Representational Roles of Congressional Black Caucus and Hispanic Caucus Members." *Journal of Black Studies* vol. 26, no. 3 (January): 245-273.

Jones, Mack H. 1972. "What is Black Politics? A Frame of Reference for Black Politics." In Lenneal J. Henderson (ed.) *Black Political Life in the United States; A Fist as the Pendulum.* San Francisco: Chandler Publishing Company, 7-20.

Key, V.O. 1964. *Public Opinion and American Democracy.* New York: Alfred A. Knopf, Inc. Lawson, Kay (ed.). 1980. *Political Parties and Linkage Politics: A Comparative Perspective.* New Haven: Yale University Press.

_____. 1988. "When Linkage Fails." In Kay Lawson and Peter H. Merkl (eds.) *When Parties Fail: Emerging Alternative Organizations.* Princeton, New Jersey: Princeton University Press, 13-38.

Levy, Arthur B. and Susan Stoudinger. 1976. "Sources of Voting Cues for the Congressional Black Caucus." *Journal of Black Studies* vol. 7, no. 1 (September): 29-46.

Lowi, Theodore J. 1995. *The End of the Republican Era.* Norman, Oklahoma: University of Oklahoma Press.

Lusane, Clarence. 1994. *African Americans at the Crossroads: The Restructuring of Black Leadership and the 1992 Elections.* Boston: South End Press.

Martin, William C. and Karen Hopkins. 1980. "Cleavage Crystallization and Party Linkages in Finland, 1900-1918." In Kay Lawson (ed.) *Political Parties and Linkage: A Comparative Perspective.* New Haven, CT: Yale University Press, 183-203.

McCormick, Joseph P. 1997. "The Messages and the Messengers: Opinions from the Million Men Who Marched." *National Political Science Review* vol. 6, 142-164.

McCormick, Joseph P. and Sekou Franklin. 2000. "Expressions of Racial Consciousness in the African American Community: Data from the Million Man March." In Yvette M. Alex-Assenoh and Lawrence J. Hanks (eds.) *Black and Multiracial Politics in America.* New York: New York University Press, 315-336.

McClain, Paula D. and John Garcia. 1993. "Expanding Disciplinary Boundaries: Black, Latino, and Racial Minority Group Politics in Political Science." In Ada W. Finfter (ed.) *Political Science: The State of the Discipline II.* Washington, DC: American Political Science Association, 247-279.

Miller, Jake C. 1979. "Black Legislators and African-American Relations, 1970-1975." *Journal of Black Studies* vol. 10, no. 2 (December): 245-261.

Morris, Lorenzo. 1998. "The Million Man March Participants and National Politics: Similarities Among 1995 Demonstration Participants in Electoral and National

Politics." Center for Urban Progress, Howard University, Working Paper Series, Working Paper 98-03.

Pinderhughes, Dianne. 1987. *Race and Ethnicity in Chicago Politics: A Reexamination of Pluralist Theory*. Urbana: University of Illinois Press.

Pitkin, Hannah. 1967. *The Concept of Representation*. Berkeley: University of California Press.

Reed, Adolph. 1999. *Stirrings in the Jug: Black Politics in the Post-Segregation Era*. Minneapolis: University of Minnesota Press.

Rosenau, J.N. 1969. *Linkage Politics: Essays on the Convergence of National and International Systems*. New York: Free Press.

Singh, Robert. 1998. *The Congressional Black Caucus*. Thousand Oaks: Sage Publications.

Smith, Robert C. 1981a. "Black Power and the Transformation from Protest to Politics." *Political Science Quarterly* vol. 96, no. 3 (Autumn): 431-444.

_____. 1981b. "The Black Congressional Delegation." *Western Political Quarterly* 34: 203-221.

_____. 1992. "Politics" Is Not Enough: The Institutionalization of the African American Freedom Movement. In Ralph C. Gomes and Linda Faye Williams (eds.) *From Exclusion to Inclusion: The Long Struggle for African American Political Power*. Westport, CT: Greenwood Press.

_____. 1996. *We Have No Leaders*. Albany, New York: State University of New York Press.

Swain, Carol. 1993. *Black Faces, Black Interests: The Representation of African-Americans in Congress*. Cambridge, MA: Cambridge University Press.

Walton, Hanes. 1988. "The National Democratic Party of Alabama and Party Failure." In Kay Lawson and Peter H. Merkl (eds.) *When Parties Fail: Emerging Alternative Organizations*. Princeton, New Jersey: Princeton University Press, 365-388.

_____. 1994. "The Nature of Black Politics and Black Political Behavior." In Hanes Walton (ed.) *Black Politics and Black Political Behavior: A Linkage Analysis*. Westport, CT: Praeger, 3-10.

_____. 1997. *African American Power and Politics: The Political Context Variable*. New York: Columbia University Press.

Walton, Hanes, Jr. and Robert C. Smith. 2003. *American Politics and the African American Quest for Universal Freedom*.

New York: Addison Wesley Longman, Inc. Wickham, Dewayne. 2002. *Bill Clinton and Black America*. New York: The Ballantine Publishing Group.

Whitby, Kenneth J. 1997. *The Color of Representation: Congressional Behavior and Black Interests*. Ann Arbor: University of Michigan Press.

Chapter 10

The CBC and Foreign Policy:
Strategy and Politics in a
Conservative Political Culture

John Davis

Introduction

This chapter explores the strategy and politics utilized by the Congressional Black Caucus in their efforts to influence U.S. foreign policy during an era of a conservative political culture that spanned the years 1992-1999.[1] This period consisted of the following characteristics: (1) dominated by Republican Presidents and their legacies (Reagan and Bush), (2) "republican control of congress" during periods when democratic President Bill Clinton occupied the White House, and (3) during a new era in international relations described as the post-Cold War, post-Apartheid, and post-Haiti periods whereby realism occupied the central axis of American foreign policy.[2] The central concern of this chapter is to access whether the CBCs "coalition-cooperative strategy"—utilized during this period—was successful and at what cost to the interests of the Caucus and whether this strategy will prove productive during the twenty-first century.[3]

The Caucus and Foreign Policy: History and Objectives

The interests of the Congressional Black Caucus in foreign policy consists of four components: (1) the singular interests of its senior leadership, (2) the correlation of the interests of African Americans with that of the African Diaspora, (3) increasing American economic assistance to Africa, and (4) an intense struggle by black politicians designed to confront institutional racism in American foreign policy (Miller, 1979).

Initially, during its infancy CBC interest in U.S. foreign relations were directly linked to its senior leadership. Two examples are instructive. CBC co-founder Representative Charles Diggs became the first African American to serve on the House Foreign Affairs Committee (he later became chairman in 1969). Diggs maintained a strong concentration in African affairs, in particular, U.S. economic assistance to the region. Throughout his tenure, Diggs remained an outspoken detractor of U.S. policy towards Africa. On this point, the representative offered the following statement:

We are particularly well aware of the imperfections regarding American foreign policy in Africa. We have stood out among its most severe critics. We have offered constructive alternatives. We have counseled our government and the American people about the significance of Americas economic and security interests (Ibid).

Another senior leader involved in U.S. foreign relations was the venerable Mervyn Dymally (CBC Chairman 1987-1988). Dymally was born in Trinidad and his natural interest concerned American foreign policy in the Caribbean (Copson, 1996). Dymally was concerned about the increasing Cold War rhetoric that had the potential to turn the region into another superpower playground. According to the representative, the way to ease the tensions and simultaneously preclude Soviet advancement required greater American attention and focus to the seeds that produced anti-Americanism in the hemisphere.

The interests of these and other representatives produced a backlash from critics who charged the CBC with "Balkanizing" U.S. foreign policy. This criticism occurred on two fronts. First, it arose from critics who disagreed with the over-emphasis of race as an instrument of caucus objections to U.S. policy and strategies towards Africa and the Caribbean and its ill-advised disparagement of the American invasion of Grenada. Observers argued that the incessant employment of race has only clouded the focus of black politicians and delayed constructive criticism with the end-result of producing a change of U.S. policy, particularly in Africa. On this point, Donald McHenry, a former black official at the Department of State, offered the following opinion:

Why build a policy toward Africa on so fragile a base as race when there are already sufficient grounds for a thorough reevaluation and change in policy on the basis of broader American interests, if only American policy makers would free themselves of outmoded concepts about defense, communism, and economic, political and social systems which differ from our own (McHenry, 1974).

This argument proved significant because it surfaced during caucus defeats but not during its triumphs. From the perspective of several CBC members, they thought it odd since the interests of the caucus were best served when it spoke out against injustices, particularly those in foreign countries where race was a salient variable in American policy. Many relied upon the words of Civil Rights leaders, particularly Martin Luther King, Jr., who remarked without "our input" into the decision making process, "I don't believe we can have world peace until America has an "integrated" foreign policy" (Henry, 2000).

Additional clamor arose over caucus opposition to the American-led invasion of Grenada. After the successful American military intervention, detractors within the executive branch and blacks in academia charged senior members of the CBC with excessive and unjustifiable support for the communist regime (Editor, 1984). Two examples are instructive: Rep. John Conyers was critical of the invasion on the grounds that it violated international law and Rep.

Julian Dixon declared that U.S. troops "weren't defending anyone. They were the aggressors" (Editor, 1984). In lieu of the tepid international support for the invasion in the region (there was opposition among American allies and elsewhere around the world), among Granadian's, and with Americans, there were those who thought caucus criticism suspect and without justification (Copson, 1996).

The correlation of the interests of African Americans with that of the African Diaspora continues to be a significant component of caucus strategy. On this supposition, 1982 Caucus Chair Rep. Walter Fauntroy, offered this conclusion:

> Black Americans and people from the island nations of the Caribbean are brothers and sisters caught in an involuntary African Diaspora. We are cousins in the African family [and] here in North America are a valuable constituency for Black people whatever they may be (Copson, 1996).

The CBC posited its vigilance in both areas was consistent with the interests of its constituency. Similarly, the actions on the part of the caucus in these two regions of the world represented a new reality: the maturation of the black politicians. Martin Weil addressed this issue in his seminal article, "Can the Blacks Do For Africa What Jews Did for Israel?" His thesis was rudimentary: someday the United States would have to accept the reality of the emergence of a "black challenge" towards its policy in Africa and elsewhere. Success, he argued, depended upon the following:

> A movement for reform of American policy toward Africa must be perceived as a vehicle for exporting American ideals. It must be an affirmation of black faith in the United States and a demonstration of black ability to manipulate the fine structure of American politics with the astuteness and finesse of previous practitioners. Blacks may identify with Africa, but it is only as Americans that they can change United States policy in Africa. If Afro-Americans ever gain leverage in foreign policy, it will be those black politicians who are most successful within the system who will do so—those who can command the respect of their black constituents and reassure white America at the same time (Shain, 1995).

It is ironic that after living up to this prediction black politicians continue to confront a dual dilemma: criticism from within the black community and from the establishment uncomfortable with its burgeoning influence and the presence of another lobby that endeavors to challenge American policy.

The third corollary interest was brilliantly articulated by Representative William Gray: "As blacks, we share many common heritages, struggles, and concerns" that require the United States to devote considerable resources to economic development and curbing burgeoning human rights violations within Africa (Copson, 1996). As such, he believed it was the obligation of the CBC to lend its voices and presence in lobbying for a dramatic increase in U.S. economic assistance to the region.

The fourth component involved an intense struggle by black politicians determined to end institutional racism in American foreign policy. This particular grievance unified the interests of the Congressional Black Caucus, and other black organizations, namely TransAfrica and Africare, to alter U.S. policy during the late seventies in Angola and Rhodesia. Their efforts encouraged greater executive awareness in both countries. The CBC had an ally in President Jimmy Carter who worked assiduously for a solution to the internal unrest involving a minority white government in Rhodesia that oppressed its black majority population. In spite of these triumphs, the CBCs most significant accomplishment followed its indifference to the Reagan administration's policy of "constructive engagement" in South Africa. Following the battle over US policy, critics of the caucus missed the aftermath of this struggle: the CBC, along with the efforts of a host of organizations from the free South Africa movement, not only won a dramatic victory but equally important concerned the fact that its most influential effort (during the 80s) to influence American foreign policy came at the expense of a republican administration—Ronald Reagan—during the height of the Cold War.

In order to implement its objectives, in its relatively short history the CBC employed a number of instruments to affect U.S. foreign policy.[4] Those instruments include: coalition building with members of both political parties, cooperation with the executive branch, and when these two measures failed, black politicians utilized a number of confrontational measures that brought attention to its causes (Copson, 1996).

The avenues open to CBC are far ranging. They include the following: Private letter's designed to lobby the president, sponsoring legislation on matters of critical importance to the caucus, black politicians have been arrested for protesting in front of the White House, caucus members have utilized the Supreme Court on occasions where the CBC viewed actions of administrations (usually republican) as unconstitutional, and finally, whenever appropriate, the CBC offered its own alternative policy.

In the case studies that follow, the author illustrates these and other strategies that the Caucus employed in their efforts to influence and eventually alter American foreign policy in a way consistent with the interests of the Black Diaspora.

Somalia

In late 1992, the last year of the administration George H.W. Bush, the CBC made overtures to enlist American involvement to end the humanitarian crisis in Somalia. In a letter sent to Secretary of State James Baker, the caucus argued that the United States should "take the initiative in the United Nations in forcefully advocating a high-level U.N. presence in Somalia" (Johnston and Dagne, 1993). In spite of caucus efforts to influence administration policy, the republican administration remained hostile to direct U.S. participation, contending the increasing chaos in the African failed state was not within the "fringes" of American national interests.

Although elements within the CBC continued to press the administration, the caucus was by no means unified on the issue. Indeed, the ongoing ethno-political conflict in the East-African country remained a divisive question: there were those within the caucus that favored intervention, beyond that displayed by the U.N., and another faction who thought any support for American intervention on the continent violated long-standing CBC opposition towards U.S. military adventurism. As the crisis worsened, the CBC adjusted its policy. While a number of its members remained opposed to intervention, those on the House Foreign Policy Committee took the initiative. Two individuals—Representative Donald Payne and Representative John Lewis—were pivotal in CBC attempts to influence American policy towards Somalia.

To comprehend the genesis of CBC policy, we must consider the efforts of Senator Nancy Kassebaum. Senator Kassebaum was the first to propose the introduction of U.S. troops into war torn Somalia, an idea bitterly opposed by the Bush administration, and, at that time, a majority of the CBC. After the Kassebaum initiative floundered, Payne admitted that he had been a long time proponent of humanitarian intervention. Events in Somalia forced a dramatic modification of his political philosophy. As the violence escalated and the death toll continued to climb, Payne decided to take decisive action. His first achievement concerned the passage of S. Con. Res. 132, the result of which required the use of force permitted under Chapter VII of the UN Charter:

> In August I brought to the floor of the House the resolution on Somalia calling for the expansion of aid and deployment of United Nations security guards to assure the delivery of relief. Then, in September 6, when the Subcommittee on Africa held a hearing on Ethiopia, I questioned the distinguished Assistant Secretary for Africa concerning the possible use of Marines that were then reported off the shore of Somalia. Following my return from Baidoa, Somalia, in late November, I was one of the first members of Congress to publicly request the U.S. Armed Services for the humanitarian intervention in Somalia.[5]

Payne's legislative success notwithstanding, the following statement demonstrated his commitment to the issue: "We cannot sit by and actually allow a country to commit suicide before the world."[6] Two months later, Rep. John Lewis began a separate initiative. In order to bring further attention to the issue, Lewis led a large congressional delegation to Somalia. Soon after his return, the representative introduced H. Con. Res. 370, which called for the following actions from the President of the United States:

> Express to the United Nations Security Council the desire and willingness of the United States to participate, consistent with applicable United States legal requirements, in the deployment of armed United Nations guards, as authorized

by the Security Council, in order to secure emergency relief activities and enable greater numbers of international and Somali organizations and people to provide relief and rehabilitation assistance.[7]

The non-binding resolution successfully passed the Senate and House chambers. Following several congressionally sponsored "high-level consultations with executive branch officials," the CBC, with Payne and Lewis performing essential roles, successfully participated in the transformation of administration policy. These meetings formed the basis of the "meeting of the minds" between the executive and legislative branches. On December 4, 1992, President Bush announced—one day after the U.N. Security Council passed resolution 794 authorizing "all necessary means to secure the environment"— Operation Restore Hope, the humanitarian intervention of the United States to feed the famine-stricken people of Somalia.[8]

Following the direct action of two of its members, the CBC—introduction of legislation, letter-writing campaign to senior executive officials, along with meetings with top administration foreign policy advisors, and cooperation with members of congress (on both sides of the isle)—proved beneficial in the eventual deployment of American troops into the region.

If the caucus actions proved significant on the front end of the intervention, its actions were less visible during the withdrawal of U.S. forces. To put this statement into perspective, consider republicans expressed lukewarm support for the last-minute Bush administration "changed-policy" directive to intervene Republican support dissipated when the Clinton administration assumed control of the White House. The new administration quickly altered U.S. policy. At the close of the Bush administration, the United Nations implemented a Security Council resolution that called for disarming of all clan-factions in Somalia. The Bush administration dismissed this portion of the U.N. initiative, warning the factions instead that American troops were given strict rules of engagement— short of disarmament—to "do what it takes" to deliver humanitarian assistance to starving Somali's.

With its policy of "multi-nationalism," the Clinton administration was determined to carryout nation building in Somalia. In order to ensure the success of this objective, the administration understood the necessity of disarming the various factions. Significantly, while discussing its new policy, the administration ordered a dramatic reduction in U.S. military forces, leaving many to question how the administration intended to carry out this initiative in a considerably altered environment.[9]

On this subject, the CBC was largely silent noting any American involvement to assist the oppressed people of Somalia would prove eventful in the final analysis. However, in time, there were signs of open hostility towards the policies of the Clinton administration.

The caucus at this time was not speaking with one voice. Indeed there was considerable evidence of fragmentation. In collaboration with other members of Congress—many of which were republicans—several members of the caucus expressed "misgivings" towards the administration's decision to pursue Mohammed Farah Aideed the renegade warlord responsible for the deaths of twenty-three Pakistani peacekeepers. Under the leadership of Payne, this faction within the CBC wanted the administration to adhere to the policy guidelines proscribed during the Bush administration, which was to provide security that allowed for the delivery of humanitarian relief.

Another faction led by Ronald Dellums within the CBC articulated its desire for the administration to support a long-term political settlement in Somalia. This same group remained concerned about the possibility of American military casualties. This fear symbolized "casualty phobia": the notion that U.S. military deaths could end an American foreign policy initiative. On September 29, 1993, the majority of caucus members supported an amendment to the Defense Department Authorization, requiring the Clinton administration "to report to congress" on administration objectives in Somalia and required the executive branch to seek congressional approval for deployment of U.S. forces beyond November 15 (Merida and Cooper, 1993).

In a letter sent to the president in October, Ronald Dellums, the Chairman of the House Armed Services Committee, warned Clinton of the dangers of American military activities in Somalia. According to Dellums, "the Army Rangers had been more apart of the problem than the solution" (Copson, 1996). On October 9, 1993, following a firefight (on October 3-4) between U.S. Army Rangers (along with a contingent of Delta's) and forces loyal to warlord General Mohammed Aideed, the CBC began to shift its support for Clinton's policy following the death of 18 American soldiers.[10] This event occurred a few days after Dellums' letter to the president. Once again fragmentation was visible. Queried on the subject of whether U.S. forces should withdraw or remain in Somalia, Rep. Kweisi Mfume, the caucus chair, stated: "The days of unanimity are over for the Congressional Black Caucus because of our diversity." (Devar, 1993)

The death of American military personnel was more than enough to alter public opinion. Case in point, the dragging of a U.S. serviceman—an event pictured on CNN—shocked the public and congress. In a relatively short period both sides of the political spectrum called for the rapid withdrawal of American troops. In spite of the growing domestic pressure, several caucus members retained their support for a U.S. military presence in Somalia. As he did in the beginning, Payne remained a vocal proponent of American involvement. In an extraordinary statement to the House Foreign Affairs Committee, Payne endeavored to send a message: American forces must remain engaged in Somalia and complete their task:

> Everyone regrets the loss of human lives, regardless of how many, but we do want to let the warlord Aideed return the country to death and destruction, malnutrition and sorrow? I say no. I witnessed this tactic on a recent trip to Mogadishu during the Fourth of July recess. Six United Nations civilian

workers and four members of the international press had just been killed by Aideed's hidden gunmen, like those who killed the 23 Pakistani troops. And bless their courageous hearts, yesterday Pakistan announced that they were sending 200 more troops to Somalia. They are not withdrawing, and I think that this shows real commitment on their side, and the United States and some of our lawmakers ought to look at what is happening when a small country like Pakistan is being shown, and hope that we do not weaken in our courage. Finally, the world is looking to our continued leadership in the support of the United Nations' effort.[11]

In spite of the efforts of Payne and other members of the caucus, the United States withdrew its forces in March of 1994. The CBC strategy ultimately failed. There were attempts to build coalitions and pass supportive legislation, but in the end, the inability of the caucus to sustain its multiple partnerships—due in part to a number of factors: the lack of unanimity within the CBC, a strong anti-humanitarian/nation building faction among conservative republicans and democrats, and ineffectual leadership from the White House—precluded assertive, if promising action on the part of members of the Caucus. In the final analysis, the CBC never employed, nor did the opportunity arise to utilize its time-honored "protest tactic"—a hallmark of its approach to end South African Apartheid—as a means to secure a definitive U.S. commitment in Somalia.

Rwanda

Months after the withdrawal of U.S. forces from East Africa, a crisis in Central Africa embroiled the CBC in another major foreign policy event. The situation in Rwanda tested caucus strategy like no other event in post-Cold War world. This position is taken for a number of reasons: (1) With events in Rwanda moving rapidly, the CBC had little time to devise a credible strategy, (2) the absence of time preclude the CBC from sponsoring legislation to guide overall U.S. foreign policy, and (3) the Clinton administration's memory of the events in Somalia induced a reluctance to support another large scale international peacekeeping operation. Collectively, lacking coalition partners (from the left or right), White House inertia, and republican warnings against U.S. involvement in another African ethnic conflict, the CBC employed a direct and confrontational strategy aimed at forcing the Clinton administration into some form of assertive policy with the desire to prevent further bloodshed between the Hutu and Tutsi ethnic factions.

The civil unrest in Rwanda accelerated on April 6, 1994 following the plane crash that killed President Juvenal Habyarimana (a member of Hutu majority) in the Kigali Airport. Violence erupted throughout the country with Hutus taking out their revenge on the Tutsi minority and those suspected of supporting them. The United Nations reported that nearly 800, 000 to one million Rwandan's, primarily Tutsi, were slaughtered. In late July of 1994, in response to the escalating hostility, the Rwandan Patriotic Front (RPF), a predominantly Tutsi militia, and assumed control of the government. Concerned with retribution, over 700, 000 Hutu refugees fled to neighboring Zaire. In the State Department and the United Nations, there was increasing fear of duplication of genocide in Burundi, a country that had an identical ethnic make up as Rwanda. Besides this activity, the U.S. government maintained a "hands off" approach to the situation in Kigali, ignoring the pressure of the CBC.

Recent evidence indicates that the United States had an opportunity to prevent the genocide in its early phases. However, bureaucratic inertia, the misperception that this was a peacekeeping and not a humanitarian situation, along with republican opposition prevented decisive American participation. It appears that the genocide orders were issued via radio broadcasts in early April and June by the military high command and party leaders to extremist Hutu elements that were responsible for carrying out the killings. Holly Bukhalter offered the following disturbing information:

> Pentagon experts have informed me that the Department Defense possesses the capacity to jam such broadcasts and could have done so at any point during the genocide. Yet, even as messages were aired urging Rwandan Hutus to kill all Tutsi—to ethnically cleanse and recleanse areas to be sure that all children had been killed—the Clinton administration took no action. According to Pentagon sources, the decision of whether or not to jam the radio broadcasts was not theirs to make: as a political matter, it was properly the decision of the State Department or the NSC. Yet it appears that neither the State Department nor the NSC pursued the idea seriously, and that the Pentagon discouraged serious inquiry into it by making it sound as if it were a technical impossibility. In any event, the Clinton administration, through its inaction on the radio broadcasts, failed to take the one action that, in retrospect, might have done the most to save Rwandan lives (Bukhalter, 1994).

Unaware of this information, one could only imagine the reaction of the CBC had it known of the existence of this evidence. This evidence exposed the dilemma that confronted the caucus in their attempt to influence administration policy: they made the same mistake as the president. Both the CBC and the administration misjudged the crisis from the beginning. Nonetheless, the response of the CBC, in terms of its criticism of administration policy (and the U.N. effort), concerned the failure of President Clinton to take the lead on the introduction of American peacekeeping forces in Rwanda.

In a letter dated May 4, 1994, caucus Chairman Mfume and Rep. Payne issued a statement acknowledging the CBC met and voiced its "urgent concern about the terrible situation in Rwanda," and observed the president's personal attention was required to bring the crisis to an end. Having received no response to its original letter, the caucus issued a subsequent communiqué. The second communication contained the following language:

> The caucus had not received a reply by June 16, when Mfume and Payne wrote the President again to criticize what they regarded as "mixed signals" from

administration officials and the alleged slowness of the Department of Defense in deploying armored personnel carriers that had been promised to peacekeepers. This letter was particularly critical of the U.S. Ambassador to the United Nations, Madeline Albright. Anger over the pace of administrations' response to the Rwanda crisis was a key factor in the caucus threat to boycott the June 1994 White House conference on Africa.... At his June 30 press conference on Rwanda, Payne accused Albright of "participating in one stalling maneuver after another" to delay a U.N. response to the Rwanda crisis (Copson, 26).

Payne's criticism was unceasing. In his August 4 White House meeting (attended by Secretary of State Warren Christopher, National Security Advisor Tony Lake, UN Ambassador Albright, and Brian Atwood, Administrator of the Agency for International Development) with Clinton, the administration exhibited no credible leadership throughout the crisis and the representative dismissed the president's statement: "We've been working since May and I have done all I knew to do [sic]," as window dressing. The United Nations commenced its peacekeeping mission in Rwanda (UNIMIR) without major American support. As the crisis unfolded, the Clinton administration limited its involvement to the support of UN Security Council Resolutions, but refused direct American participation in their implementation. The absence of administration leadership minimized Western contribution in the peacekeeping operation. However, on July 22 the administration ordered U.S. troops to the region in what it called an "immediate and massive increase" of American humanitarian assistance. Dubbed Operation Support Hope, U.S. participation was limited to 2,600 troops, with the vast majority remaining off shore aboard American naval vessels. Even worse, from the perspective of the CBC and the people of Rwanda, President Clinton issued orders that U.S. forces were to withdraw on September 30, 1994.

The confrontational lobbying strategy of the CBC failed to alter American policy. The caucus attempt to influence U.S. policy was predestined from the start. In their search for democratic allies, the caucus found few converts. Efforts to reach across the isle to republicans proved equally ineffectual. In the final analysis, the Congressional Black Caucus was isolated—accept for their relationships with relief organizations, such as Africa Care—and were therefore unable to change the attitudes of an administration obsessed with casualty phobia and republican disparagement of their amorphous multilateralism.

Haiti

The crisis in Haiti symbolized caucus strategy and politics. As the crisis widened, the CBC's—more so than its strategy during the Reagan years that secured the end of constructive engagement and apartheid—activity was visible from the start and produced the most significant change of American foreign policy to date, one that forced the Clinton administration to accept the caucus alternative. If one were to explore the genesis of U.S. policy toward the

Caribbean country, one would assume that the aforementioned hypothesis was overstated. During the Bush administration, the caucus exhibited open hostility towards a U.S. refugee policy that some argued precluded a clearly defined approach to deal with the unfolding events in Port Au Prince.

The CBC considered the Bush administration's policy of refugee interdiction and return to the island nation, a "cruel policy." Representative Alcee Hastings was particularly critical of the administration's "dual treatment," whereby Cuban's were permitted entry and Haitians were returned. According to the representative, he and other members of the caucus interpreted administration policy as clearly one of blatant racial discrimination (James, 1994).

The Clinton administration policy was in response to the ouster of elected President Jean Bertrand Aristide. Elected in December of 1990, Aristide held power for nine months before the military, which had support from the business elite (both were concerned that Aristide's policies threatened their power base), ended his reign. Days after the military came to power, Secretary of State James Baker observed the junta would "be treated as a pariah, without friends, without support, without a future" (Morley and McGillion, 1997). At this point, administration policy was consistent with other countries of the region whose polices had a singular purpose: the restoration of the Aristide government. However, according to two observers, the administration shifted its policy in response to concern over Aristide's populist orientation:

> The White House was ambivalent about supporting an elected leader who was committed to empowering the poor through changes in the economy, the regime and the state. And as the policy unfolded, it soon became clear that support for Aristide's return was predicated on the latter's willingness to accept specific limitations on his presidential powers, not least because his efforts to democratize the Haitian state were perceived as a potential threat to long-term U.S. objectives: the restoration of political stability; the survival of an, albeit reformed, military institution with its external linkages to the Pentagon intact; and the promotion of an open economy and a development strategy that accorded foreign investors a central role (Morely and McGillion, 1997).

Inside the caucus, there was no visible indifference to the policy shift. This new policy remained in effect until well after the conclusion of the Bush administration. However, during the 1992 Presidential Campaign the caucus did react positively to then candidate Governor Bill Clinton's campaign pledge to assist Haitian's requesting asylum in the United States. Indeed, many had hoped when the Clinton administration commenced, the president-elect would hold to his pledge. The CBC was nonetheless disappointed to learn the democratic president continued the Bush administration's policy of forcible repatriation, thereby contravening his campaign promise. The shift followed an internal administration review that warned the president if he went forward with his refugee plan, the United States would be confronted with up to 200, 000

Haitians seeking political asylum. In the days following the review, Clinton privately acceded to the continuation of the Bush strategy.

In its attempt to limit the political fallout, and certain CBC criticism, the Clinton administration announced a series of steps designed to return Aristide power: (1) the administration selected Ambassador Lawrence Pezzullo as the Special Envoy to Haiti, (2) they wanted an internal political solution that culminated in the return of Aristide, and (3) the administration offered a carrot and stick strategy to end the crisis. In the form of the carrot, the administration offered the troika—Army Chief of Staff Lt. Gen. Raoul Cedras, deputy chief of staff Gen. Philippe Biamby, and the Port Au Prince Police Chief Michel Francios—a seat at the negotiating table. The stick took the form of a threat to tighten bilateral, regional, and global sanctions (Ibid). On July 3, 1993, this strategy culminated in the Governors Island agreement. The goal of the agreement called for re-democratization: the return of Aristide, a reconstituted parliament, reforms for the military, police and the judiciary, political amnesty for those responsible for the coup, and finally, the end of economic sanctions.

In spite of the plaudits and the momentum that surrounded the agreement, Clinton's Haitian policy fell into disfavor with Aristide, republicans, democrats (particularly the CBC), and elements within the administration. On the internal dissension within the administration, consider the following *Newsweek* excerpt:

> Aristide wasn't even talking to Pezzullo; Christopher, Lake and other senior foreign policy advisers began to have meetings without him. The strategy "just collapsed," says a senior White House official who was clearly exasperated by Pezzullo. "Larry wanted to continue along that line. There was always another initiative, the second cousin of the head of the Parliament who believed he could get Cedras. It became clear we were just chasing butterflies." Led by Lake and Berger, National Security Council officials pushed for aggressive action against the military regime. They wanted to crank up the sanctions and lay the groundwork for possible invasion. They were joined by senior adviser George Stephanopoulos and Strobe Talbott, the new deputy secretary of state, who had been handed the Haiti brief and soon decided that sanctions alone were unlikely to drive Cedras from power. On the other side were Pentagon officials who thought it foolhardy to threaten invasion—and who took cover behind the argument that planning an invasion was unnecessary because Pezzullo was making progress with his diplomatic strategy (Barry and Breslau, 1994).

In recognition of administration confusion, the CBC was ready, as one insider claimed, to "hijack American Haitian policy."[12] The CBC had its own dilemma: polarization over the course and direction of U.S. policy towards Haiti left the caucus in disarray. The Congressional Black Caucus remained unified in their efforts to confront Bush and Clinton on American refugee policy (Gomis, 1999). On the question of sanctions and U.S. military intervention, the caucus symbolized a house divided. Those in favor of intervention confronted several dilemmas. First, the American people were opposed to the use of force and the

CBC was unable to stir public interest. Second, in direct criticism of Clinton, Representative Charles Rangel warned, "we don't have the will because we don't have the leadership" (James, 1994). Third, the caucus was isolated, with democrats and republicans opposed to Clinton's approach to the situation in Haiti, and a preponderance of members from both sides of the isle were equally opposed to intervention. Finally, the CBC had another hurdle to clear: President Clinton resisted the idea of invasion.

On the other end of the political spectrum, republicans were bitterly opposed to administration policy, owing to the fear of another Somali style fiasco. In addition, conservative elements complained the administration failed to make its case that Haiti was in the vital national interests of the United States. Without meeting this basic foreign policy procedure, they argued the administration had no justification to consider the option of invasion. Finally, the individual the administration and the CBC wanted to liberate—Aristide— was vehemently opposed to intervention. The deposed president made the following instructive comment on *National Public Radio*: "I am against intervention. Never, never, never would I agree to be restored to power by an invasion" (Ibid).

These issues notwithstanding, as was the case in their approach to Somalia, the inability of the forty member caucus to speak with one voice created fragmentation, with some opposing invasion and another faction indifferent to the continuation of ineffectual sanctions. Representative Watt lamented, "Some of us have real misgivings about an invasion. Representative Mfume posited, "We hope that [the invasion] would not be a necessity. We would hope any police action in Haiti would be brief" and Rep. Maxine Waters called for invasion to topple General Cedras.

Inside the caucus, the voice that carried considerable weight on foreign policy matters belonged to the venerable Payne. Payne thought it appropriate to offer a deadline: "We've got to come back to the drawing board by the end of June to see if there's any bending on the part of the [Haitian] military. If there's "no bending, our only option is to go in" (Ibid). In taking this position, according to Payne, the proponents of invasion were breaking new ground:

> We have not been, generally speaking, a group that supported gun barrel diplomacy, but we are seeing a changing a world. I don't think any of the members of the caucus initially supported military intervention and there are still some who oppose it. But I do think the majority of the members are slowly moving toward the point where it might be the only solution at the present time (Holmes, 1994).

There was little doubt about the infighting, prompting Representative Rangel to acknowledge, "We don't speak with one voice in the Black Caucus. We haven't had any policy that relates to Haiti" (Cohn, 1994). It remains unclear how the differences of opinion were resolved, but at some point a consensus emerged and thereafter the CBC presented what can best be described as its "alternative policy."[13] The CBC strategy consisted of multiple components: (1) Thirty nine members introduced a bill to "impose swift and severe" economic sanctions on the military regime; (2) called upon the United States to sever its commercial air links with the island nation; (3) "halt the interdiction and summary repatriation" of refugees; (4) freeze all financial assets, and (5) when all else failed, the caucus expressed its support for invasion. Following a cold administration reception to their proposal, on March 18, 1994, the CBC sent a private letter to President Clinton. The letter was explicit:

> We believe that the combination of these measures will demonstrate the profound resolution of the United States against [the junta]. We are convinced that you share our determination: it is high time to modify our Haitian policy drastically. We remain unfailingly committed to the propositions delineated above. We are prepared to work with you in order to bring about the application of this social challenge (Adopted unanimously by the Black Caucus).[14]

Having made its position known, the caucus expressed concerned about the republican response to its initiative. On this point, Representative Watt stated: "The conservatives would like to be able hang this on us, especially if it goes wrong" (Taylor, 1994). Democratic members of the CBC did not issue a response; they remained focused on their goal: pressuring the administration to change their approach to the situation in the Caribbean.

In spite of the CBC's efforts, the president did not alter US-policy toward Haiti. It would take additional prodding by the CBC, with assistance from TransAfrica, before President Clinton changed his approach. Having received no word on their letter, the caucus "made Aristide's return a litmus test for its relations with an administration desperate for votes on the crime bill and health-care reform." (Barry and Breslau) With the administration in desire straits on two critical pieces of legislation, the Congressional Black Caucus was willing to push the envelope (Cohn, 1994). The caucus focused attention on the crime legislation. In the view of most caucus members, the health-care reform initiative faced certain defeat. However, the $30 billion crime bill seemed headed for certain passage with republicans and democrats prepared to offer their support. One obstacle remained: the caucus. The CBC recognized the president would do everything to appease them. To test Clinton's sensitivity to their growing concerning over administration policy, the caucus attempted to attach a controversial amendment to the crime bill: the Racial Justice Act. The act required "death row inmates argue that they were being unfairly subjected to the death penalty if statistics showed that capital punishment fell disproportionately on minorities" (Cohn, 1994). The bill and the caucus amendment sailed through the House but faced certain defeat in the republican-controlled Senate. Republicans complained they saw through the hidden caucus agenda, which called for support on the crime bill if the administration altered its policy in Haiti. The administration considered the idea but refused to change its policy. Thereafter, the caucus strategy became more confrontational and unyielding.

Several weeks later, a number of caucus members, along with Spike Lee, Robert De Niro, and Julia Roberts, were arrested while protesting administration policy in front of the gates of the White House. In a separate strategy, Randall Robinson, head of Trans-Africa went on a hunger strike that began in April of the same year. His strike marked the second phase of an intensified and coordinated response to administration intransigence. This phase called for the caucus and TransAfrica to expose "the humiliating character" of administration policy with the intension of cutting the president off from his democratic allies in congress. The strategy worked. Following the hospitalization of Robinson, the embattled administration commenced a series of unprecedented meetings with the CBC that were designed to end the "siege" surrounding Clinton's Haitian policy.

On May 8, after considerable concessions, the White House announced major changes to their policy. In a salient concession to the CBC, William Gray, a former member of the caucus, assumed the position as Presidential Envoy to Haiti, replacing Lawrence Pezzullo (Jones and Lowery, 1994 and Corn, 1994). After further deliberation within the administration, the president adopted all of the strategy options contained in the CBC House bill.

By the end of the day, the transformation of U.S. policy identified the obvious: President Clinton capitulated, caving into relentless pressure from the CBC (Holmes, 1994). In the final analysis, senior members of the administration argued that the CBC strategy became "the unwelcome blueprint" for Clinton's policy, ultimately resulting in invasion.

This statement represented the first of a series of complaints that accompanied the caucus victory. Critics inside and outside the beltway intimated that "the White House became captive to liberal groups":

> We are talking disproportionately with members of the Black Caucus, and not enough to the relevant congressional committees who have the expertise," says one source. Berger and Lake spent hours with members of the caucus. Key players with defense and foreign policy knowledge were marginalized, according to Clinton insiders unhappy with the way the Haiti policy developed. "The administration was responding to a very narrow constituency," says Rep. Robert Toricelli, chairman of the House Subcommittee on the Western Hemisphere Affairs. He said his advice was "rarely sought and almost never accepted" (Barry and Breslau).

To be sure, caucus influence over administration Haitian policy was highly visible. However, in the aftermath of their triumph the caucus faced considerable condemnation. The internal dispute produced the first public debate within the CBC over its strategy, forcing the caucus to admit—even though some of the same fragmentation existed over the CBC approach to Somalia—it does not speak with one voice. Second, members of the Clinton administration, and others from the Democratic Party openly criticized the CBC for their unceasing pressure on the president in the pursuit of its objectives. Finally, considerable infighting among caucus and non-caucus democrats resulted in a triumphant lobbying effort for the Congressional Black Caucus. However, during a period where democratic control of the House was on its last leg, the caucus was about to confront their most daunting test.

The African Growth and Opportunity Act

The republican sweep of the 1994 Congressional Election ended democratic control of the congress and ushered in the era of Contract with America. For the caucus, the transformation within congress occurred at an inopportune time. During the period 1992-1994, the CBC was at the zenith of its power. Its membership was at an all-time of high 40 members (39 representatives and 1 senator), many caucus members chaired influential committees, and the CBC was coming off its most successful venture (Haiti) in international affairs, a direct challenge which forced the president into accepting their alternative foreign policy strategy. The republican victory altered the political landscape, forcing the caucus "to shift from the being a political player on major legislation" to reverting to its original role: "the conscience of the Congress" (Cooper, 1994). According to some political observers, the decreasing role of the CBC placed the body on unfamiliar territory, threatening to further dismantle its already tempestuous cohesion:

> House members in the overwhelmingly Democratic caucus have lost Chairmanships of three committees and about 20 subcommittees, as well as four coveted seats on the Ways and Means, Appropriations and Rules Committees. A plan that the new Republican majority appears determined to implement is likely to cost the caucus, one of the oldest in Congress, its office, staff and budget (Cooper, 1994).

David Bositis, a senior researcher at the Joint Center for Political and Economic Studies, observed, "They're going from their peak. The 103rd Congress was their most influential time ever. The 104th is really going to represent a wholesale shift in the way things are done" (Ibid).

The changing political winds in Washington coincided with an issue that represented a critical segment of the caucus constituency: public sector financial assistance to Africa. With a republican controlled congress, the CBC had three problems to confront: the republicans wanted to restrict and decrease direct American foreign aid to Africa, and second, the new leadership in Congress wanted to follow the Reagan approach, which called for a shift in U.S. policy from public to private sector sponsored development. Third, the caucus had to devise a strategy to protect its African constituency. In the end, political convergence allowed the caucus to retain some of its waning clout. Ronald Walters viewed the issue this way:

> One of the more interesting aspects of this shift is that it represents an example of "political convergence" between Republicans and a sector of the Democratic Party, but also involving many Black Democrats as well. Nevertheless, the shift prompted a political conflict initiated by the difference of opinion between those who favored it, for whatever reasons, and many Africa-oriented groups and politicians who favored the maintenance of economic development strategies (Walters, 2001).

In this environment, the CBC had few options, cooperation or confrontation with the republicans. According to Bositis the choice was an easy one: "In a confrontation between the Congressional Black Caucus and the Republican's, I don't see what the Black Caucus had to gain" (Cooper, 1994).

The debate had the usual suspects: coalitional building by the CBC and internal dissension within its ranks. However, in contrast to previous struggles the caucus had the opportunity to shape the outcome of the legislative battle from the beginning. In June of 1996, Democratic Rep. Jim McDermont "noted that American policy toward Eastern Europe in the post-Soviet era was shaped by fundamental economic directions" and questioned why a similar proposal was not made available to the countries of Africa" (Walters, 2001). CBC Rep. Rangel and Republican Rep. Phillip Crane introduced the African Growth and Opportunity Act (AGOA) on April 24, 1997. The bill contained the following particulars: (1) $150 million equity fund and another $500 million infrastructure fund, (2) An Export-Import Bank initiative for the expansion of loans for the development of private sector businesses, and (3) elimination of trade quotas on African textiles (Dagne and Sek). On May 21, 1997, continuing the bipartisan spirit, Republican Senator Richard Lugar introduced a similar piece of legislation (S. 778).

The legislation had the support of the White House from the beginning. The administration acknowledged that AGOA could do for Africa what the Asian Pacific Economic Cooperation (APEC) accomplished for Asia, namely free trade and bustling independent economies. According to Susan Rice, Assistant Secretary of State for Africa, "Africans need this bill. They don't want a handout. They want the hand of a partner.... The African Ambassadors in Washington have repeatedly urged Congress and the President to enact this legislation." After issuing these talking points, the administration pressed Congress to enact AGOA.

A promising development soon turned ugly. Once again, a divisive caucus became the center of gravity. The caucus members, along with several special interest groups (the most significant being Trans-Africa), opposed to the legislation were concerned about several issues including the emphasis on "conditionalities." Second, the bill did not possess any measures to preclude labor and human rights abuses, and third, caucus opponents emphasized the legislation offered no measures to assure the poorest of households in Africa benefited from the initiative.

On the matter of conditionalities, several caucus members opposed the legislation on the grounds it violated the political sovereignty of African countries. In order to receive the assistance African states had to meet four eligibility requirements: (1) African states were not permitted to trade with Libya, Cuba, and Iraq; (2) states had to eliminate barriers to trade (government protection for national industries); (3) they had to demonstrate movement towards democratic institutions; and (4) illustrate a clear indication of liberalization of trade and definitive movement towards the World Trade Organization (WTO).

The leading opponent of AGOA was none other than Jessie Jackson, Jr. This in and of itself proved interesting, especially since Jesse Jackson, Sr., held the portfolio as President Clinton's Special Envoy to Africa. Rep. Jackson sent a letter to Rep. Rangel (the chief CBC advocate of the bill) and a separate correspondence to President Clinton, expressing his opposition to the legislation. In his letter to the president, Jackson argued "the bill will force 48 sub-Saharan African nations into a straightjacket of economic austerity and deepening poverty in order to benefit transnational financial institutions, wealthy investors and large corporations" (Malveaux, 1998). After his letters failed to persuade the proponents of the bill, Rep. Jackson offered up his own bill and this dissenting opinion:

> This is not the first trade policy with Africa. The first Africa trade policy was initiated in 1619 and involved African Kings and potentates selling other Africans to white-owned shipping companies.... We do not need a deal between undemocratic and permanently entrenched Kings and Presidents-for-life in Africa and multinational businesses in the United States and elsewhere that do not hire, promote or value African American employees at home.... Why should we trust the people who discriminate against us and disparage affirmative action at home to be respectful of African workers (1998)?

In another attempt to dissuade proponents of AGOA, on February 23, 1999, Jackson introduced H.R. 772, better known as the Human Rights, Opportunity, Partnership, and Empowerment for Africa Act (HOPE). HOPE was distinguished from AGOA in three respects: (1) it "included extensive debt relief," (2) set a minimum level of "appropriations for U.S. development assistance" in sub-Saharan Africa and (3) it removed any conditionalities for the receipt of aid (Dagne and Sek, 2000).

Jackson's attack represented an attempt to split the so-called unholy alliance between conservative republicans and members of the CBC. His other supporters, each taking a less confrontational stance, were Rep. John Conyers, Rep. Maxine Waters, and Rep. Sanford Bishop (and others) criticized the legislation because it threatened American jobs; this appeal represented an effort to position organized labors' opposition to AGOA (Woellert, 1998).

The Jackson-led caucus opposition to AGOA did not succeed. CBC advocates of the legislation constructed a solid coalition. The coalition included unyielding support from House Speaker Newt Gingrich, Senator Richard Lugar, Jack Kemp and other republicans. On the democratic side, former Mayor of New York, David Dinkins, non-caucus democrats, and a majority of the caucus, led by Rep. Rangel, backed the legislation. To offer additional support, the coalition depended upon the leadership of President Clinton, and when necessary, waiting in the wings, this group could count on the African countries themselves. AGOA passed on a voice vote in the House and later approved in the Senate with little opposition.

The success of the caucus in this venue requires further qualification. Initially, the lobbying efforts ought to be applauded owing to the fact this legislation passed during a period of declining American foreign assistance and burgeoning deficits. Second, in era of complete republican control of congress, the CBC was nonetheless successful in their efforts to reach across the isle to the opposing party and build a strong coalition to defeat opponents of the measure. Lastly, one should be mindful that AGOA passed both houses of congress during a period when the caucus was split on the matter and where its influence decreased as a result of the republican gains in congress.

Conclusion

This study indicates that CBC efforts to influence American foreign policy during the post-Cold War period were mixed. Similarly, the evidence for this study indicated that caucus strategy and politics during an era of conservative political culture attempted to force the executive branch to reconsider intervention in Somalia and Rwanda. In spite of their lobbying and legislative efforts in these two countries, the CBC was unable, in the final analysis to affect U.S. policy. This breakdown was due to burgeoning fragmentation within the CBC; the fact that the caucus could no longer act with one voice, including timidity and the altered policy approach by the Clinton administration and the unforeseen deaths of American military personnel in Somalia.

On the matter of Haiti and AGOA, the CBC—despite the presence of fragmentation—was able to have its way. In the case of Haiti, its most confrontational postwar endeavor, the caucus was able to force the Clinton administration into accepting its alternative policy, while simultaneously pressuring the administration to permit one of its former members (William Gray) to lead the diplomatic initiative to force out the ruling junta in Port au Prince. Collectively, these concessions represented an unprecedented victory for the CBC and will serve as a model for future engagements with the executive branch. With respect to AGOA, despite the presence of republican control over congress and divisions within its ranks, the caucus assembled coalitions inside congress and throughout the NGO community, which permitted the successful passage of legislation vital to one its constituencies. In the final analysis, the foreign policy events involving the caucus yielded a startling conclusion. Known as the conscience of congress, with the advent of continued fragmentation and the inability of the CBC to speak with one voice on major issues of the day as events in the international arena continue to unfold the caucus will likely have a far-more difficult task in confronting the executive branch on issues relevant to the Black constituency.

The dilemmas confronting the caucus do not end here. In a period of burgeoning ethnic and tribal conflict (particularly in Africa and most certainly in Darfur, Sudan) the CBC has yet to put forward its own strategy on the issue. This failure makes it highly unlikely that the caucus will be in a position to force the executive branch into supporting greater cooperation on matters that affect the CBC's constituency. Similarly, in the ever-changing post-Cold War world the CBC has criticized the Clinton administration and butted heads with conservatives over narco-terrorism and other transnational issues that affect the Black Diaspora. Once again, with no strategy and no alternative policy to speak of, along with conservative claims that the CBC has improperly injected race as a substitute for national security interests, black politicians are unlikely to mount a major challenge in this area.

Finally, on matters of defense spending fragmentation and a new mood among the new generation of caucus members, where jobs play an important role to their constituency, these new dynamics threatens the CBC efforts to curb defense spending, and as a by-product, reduce caucus efforts to channel money to areas that benefit its constituency (health care, education, job training, etc.). As the conservative political culture continues well into a new millennium, CBC strategy and politics envisages new and unforgiving challenges.

Endnotes

1. There is currently a host of new incidents or crises in Haiti, Liberia, Sierra Leon, and Darfur, Sudan. Each of these issues has unfolded in a new conservative political culture. That is, the period of focus for this study—1992-1999—represents more traditional conservatism. The current administration is dominated by the so-called neo-conservatives, whereby the Pentagon, and not the State Department, is the vicar of US foreign policy. This is indeed significant. With two African American's—Colin Powell at State and Condeleeza Rice within the White House as the National Security Advisor—one would have thought that the Caucus would have had greater access and influence on US foreign policy. In fact the opposite is true. With the polemical 2000 presidential election as a catalyst, President George W. Bush has not had a "formal meeting" with the CBC and as a result this lack of access to the president, the CBC is unable to exert any influence on issue in foreign relations that may impact countries in Africa, the Caribbean or other aspects of the Diaspora. Nonetheless, the CBC has been vocal on such issues as Liberia, the Patriotic Act and the attendant profiling of minorities, HIV/AIDS, and at the time of this writing, Darfur, Sudan. It remains unclear, at the moment, to discern the impact the caucus may have in the aforementioned areas.

2. This requires some qualification. In actuality, institutionally speaking, complete republican control of both houses of congress did not occur until the1994 congressional elections. Nonetheless, while the democrats controlled Congress from 1992-1994 (covering the Bush and Clinton years), on issues concerning foreign policy at every turn republicans criticized Clinton administration policy and argued that the administration, on what were considered marginal issues (i.e., Somalia, Haiti, and Bosnia), repeatedly damaged American credibility. Second, it should be noted that the republicans chided Clinton for undermining the legacies of Reagan and Bush. Third, even in a period of democratic control of congress, the democrats were the "party in exile," out of power for twelve years and desperately trying to formulate and implement foreign policy strategies to overturn or replace the remnants of policy initiatives begun by Reagan-Bush. Finally, during this conservative culture, the congressional black caucus endeavored to challenge this political culture, and whenever appropriate, confront the policies of the Clinton administration if and when they impacted their constituency. It is for the aforementioned reasons that the author employs the word "control" in this context.

3. By "costs" the author is making reference to the following: (1) To what extent has the division within the CBC on an assortment of foreign events impacted its overall objective to influence U.S. foreign policy; (2) does the fragmentation indicate maturation and an unexpected event: the CBC is now operating like the democratic, women's, and even the Hispanic caucus where division is common and representative of politics in an era of partisanship; (3) as an indicator of a generational dispute within the caucus whereby a new generation of CBC members are less likely to follow the directions and leadership of its proven cadre; and (4) Or in the final analysis, it may be argued that in spite of fragmentation, the CBC maintains the ability to frustrate, defeat, and where appropriate, offer an alternative policy initiative of its own as a means to demonstrate their ability to affect policy in the international arena.

4. It should be noted that from the outset, the caucus does not involve itself in every foreign policy issue. It is for this reason that the author has been selective in choosing case studies that match the description of issues relevant to the interests that meet CBC objectives, interests of African Americans, and where on occasion they overlap with American national interests.

5. Statement taken from, The Crisis in Somalia. Hearing before the Committee on Foreign Affairs, House of Representatives, One Hundred Second Congress, Second Session, December 17, 1992. Markup on S.J. Res. 45 Authorizing the Use of U.S. Armed Forces in Somalia, One Hundred Third Congress First Session, May 5, 1993. Washington, DC 1993.

6. Ibid.

7. Ibid, 194.

8. It should be noted that Congress as a whole was not supportive of Bush's decision to intervene. Indeed, the intervention was well timed, coming at the point when Congress was adjourned.

9 During the Bush administration, Operation Restore Hope, or United Nations Task Forces (UNITAF) operated with 28, 000 U.S. troops (and another 10, 000 foreign forces) deployed to Somalia with a rudimentary purpose: provide humanitarian relief to the Somali people and restore order in southern Somalia. This phase began December 9 and lasted until May of 1993. During the next phase, United Nations Operations in Somalia

(UNOSOM), what was described as the handoff phase from U.S. control of operations to United Nations leadership; during this phase, American forces were reduced to 4,500. Yet in a new environment whereby American forces were asked to disarm the warring factions, hunt down Aideed, many questioned the wisdom of Clinton's policy. Moreover, Bush maintained a close watch of the situation in Somalia. By contrast, the Clinton administration reduced American supervision of events at U.N. headquarters in New York, eliminated the State Department Task Force that oversaw events, and Clinton was said to be not in the loop on majors decisions, particularly during the firefight in Mogadishu on October 9, 1993. For more on this point, see the following, Kenneth Allard. 1995. *Somalia Operations: Lessons Learned.* Washington, DC: National Defense University Press; Lester Brune. 1998. *The United States and Post-Cold War Interventions: Bush and Clinton in Somalia, Haiti, and Bosnia, 1992-1998.* Claremont, CA: Regina Books, and *The United Nations and Somalia,1992-1996.* 1996. New York: United Nations Department of Public Information.

10. Helen Devar describes the situation this way: The Congressional Black Caucus, which is divided over Somalia, has requested a meeting with Clinton and Les Aspin, Secretary of Defense, "to get a clarification of U.S. policy. The caucus discussed the situation in Somalia at its weekly luncheon yesterday but did not emerge with a consensus. Caucus Chairman Kweisi Mfume said there were eight or nine recommendations, ranging from pulling out U.S. troops to staying and finding a political solution. A task force was appointed to sift through the recommendations." For more on this point, see her article, "Senate Vote Pullout Delayed: Opponents of Immediate Withdrawal Warn Against Precipitous Action." 1993. W*ashington Post*, October 7.

11. Recent Developments in Somalia, Hearing before the Subcommittee on Africa of the Committee on Foreign Affairs, House of Representatives, One Hundred Third Congress, first session, July 29, 1993.

12. Interview with former State Department official, November 2001.

13. The CBC is well known for its alternative domestic budgets, but rarely is there ever any mention of an alternative external policy.

14. In an unusual move, the CBC enlisted several actors to its cause. They had their own statement attached to the CBC letter. "We, the undersigned, entreat you to put our Haitian policy into action as last by adopting the directions specified by the members of the Black Caucus in the clear and remarkable letter [above] and addressed to you on March 18, 1994. We implore you to respect your promise to restore democracy and to send to the rest of the world a message recalling our commitment to respect for human rights and to the democratically elected government in Haiti." Some of those who signed the letter were: Robert Altman, Harry Belafonte, Francis Ford Coppola, Robert De Niro, Richard Gere Steven Spielberg, and Spike Lee, to name a few. The letter may be found in Carrol F. Coates. 1996. *Dignity: Jean-Bertrand Aristide, President of the Republic of Haiti.* Virginia: University Press of Virginia, Appendix 6-Letter from the Black Caucus to the President William J. Clinton, 18 March 1994, 183.

References

Allard, Kenneth. 1995. *Somalia Operations: Lessons Learned.* Washington, DC: National Defense University Press.

Barry, John and Karen Breslau. 1994. "How Did We Get Here?" *Newsweek*, September 26.

Brune, Lester. 1998. *The United States and Post-Cold War Interventions: Bush and Clinton in Somalia, Haiti, and Bosnia, 1992-1998*. Claremont, CA: Regina Books.

Bukhalter, Holly. 1994. "The Question of Genocide: The Clinton Administration and Rwanda." *World Policy Journal*. Fall.

Coates, Carrol F. 1996. *Dignity: Jean-Bertrand Aristide, President of the Republic of Haiti*. Virginia: University Press of Virginia.

Cohen, Richard. 1993. "Blacks Look Abroad," *Washington Post*. November 2: A19.

Cohn, Bob. 1994. "Buying Off the Black Caucus," *Newsweek*. August 1.

Cooper, Kenneth J. 1994. "Black Caucus Tries to Cushion the Fall From its Height of Influence," *Washington Post*, December 16: A21.

Copson, Raymond W. 1996. "The Congressional Black Congress and Foreign Policy: 1971-1995," *CRS Report for Congress*, July 18.

Corn, David.1994. "Pressure Drop." *Nation*. May 30: 737-35.

Dagne, Ted and Lenore Sek. 2000. *African Trade and Investment: Proposals in the 106th Congress*, CRS Issue Brief for Congress, August.

Devar, Helen. 1993. "Senate Vote Pullout Delayed: Opponents of Immediate Withdrawal Warn Against Precipitous Action," *Washington Post*, October 7.

Editorial. 1998. "African Trade-Offs," *Nation*, April 6. Editors Comments. 1984. "The Black Caucus and the Danger of Balkanizing U.S. Foreign Policy," *Lincoln Review*, Winter: 4-11.

Gomis, Henriette. 1999. "The Impact of the Congressional Black Caucus on U.S. Foreign Policy: Haiti and the Haitian Refugees, 1991-1994, Unpublished Dissertation.

James, Daniel. 1994. "The Divided but Revealing Views of the Congressional Black Caucus." *The Washington Times*. June 30.

Jones, Joyce and Mark R. Lowery. 1994. "Bill Gray's Haitian Mission," *Black Enterprise*, August.

Johnston, Harry and Ted Dagne, 1993."Congress and the Somalia Crisis." In *Learning from Somalia: The Lessons of Armed Humanitarian Intervention*. Edited by Walter Clarken and Jeffrey Herbst. New York: Westview Press.

Malveaux, Julianne. 1998. "What Price Will Africa Pay For Growth And Trade?" *Crisis*. July: 31-33.

Marable, Ronald, Colonel USA, Ret. 1994. "Congressional Black Caucus and American Foreign Policy." Industrial College of the Armed Forces.

McHenry, Donald. 1974. "Captive of No Group," *Foreign Policy*, Summer 15.

Merida, Kevin and Kenneth J. Cooper. 1993. "As the Crisis Grows, the Support of Black Politicians Fragments." *Washington Post*, October 9, A15.

Miller, Jake C. 1979. "Black Legislators and African-American Relations, 1970-1975," *Journal of Black Studies*. Vol. 10 no. 2, December: 249-261.

Morley, Morris and Chris McGillion. 1997. "Disobedient Generals and the Politics of Redemocratization: The Clinton Administration and Haiti." *Political Science Quarterly*, Fall: 4.

Remarks at a Congressional Black Caucus Luncheon for President Mandela, October 5, *Weekly Compilation of Presidential Documents*, Washington. 1992. October 10.

Shain, Yossi, 1995. "Multicultural Foreign Policy." *Foreign Policy*. Fall: 69-88.

Statement Taken From, The Crisis in Somalia. Hearing before the Committee on Foreign Affairs, House of Representatives, One Hundred Second Congress, Second Session, December 17, 1992. Markup on S.J. Res. 45 Authorizing the Use of U.S. Armed Forces in Somalia, One Hundred Third Congress First Session, May 5, 1993. Washington, DC 1993.

Taylor, Ronald A. 1994. "Black Caucus Split on Haiti," *The Washington Times*, September 16: A12.

The United Nations and Somalia,1992-1996. 1996. New York: United Nations Department of Public Information.

Walters, Ronald. 2001. "The African Growth and Opportunity Act: Changing Foreign Policy Priorities Toward Africa in a Conservative Political Culture." In *Foreign Policy and the Black (Inter) National Interest.* 2001. New York: State University of New York Press. Edited by Charles E. Payne.

Woellert, Lorraine. 1998. "Black Caucus Divided On African Trade." *The Washington Times.* February 26: A4.

List of Contributors

Donn G. Davis, Ph.D. is an associate professor of political science at Howard University. His research and teaching are in the areas of Constitutional Law, Black Politics, and American Judicial and Legislative process. He has written monographs, book chapters and journal articles in these areas. In addition to the legal area, much of his work has centered on leadership and ideology, and his present research is on a comparative analysis of affirmative action in the US, Brazil and other societies with historically evolved racial and class distinctions.

John Davis, Ph. D., Howard University. His interests include US Foreign Policy, National Security, International Terrorism, International Law, American Government and Black Politics. He has authored several articles, chapters in books, and has edited several books to include: *The Global War On Terrorism: Assessing the American Response, Presidential Policies and the Road to Second Iraq War*, and *Africa and the War on Terrorism.*

Sekou Franklin, Ph.D., Middle Tennessee State University. He has authored numerous articles on Black Politics that include among others: "Conflicts in the Coalition: Challenges to Black and Latino Political Alliances" (co-authored), "Social and Political Attitudes on the Black Predicament: Data from the Million Man March," (co-authored).

Kevin L. Glasper, Ph.D. Glasper recently completed his doctorate at Howard University. His dissertation was titled "Black Interest Groups' Responses to Police Brutality and Racial Profiling: An Analysis of Organizational Behavior, Constraints, Resources, and Policy Influence, 1995-2005." His research interests include Black Politics and the American Government.

Mack Jones, Ph.D., Clark Atlanta University, Retired. Jones (a major contributor to Black Politics) is the author of several major works that include *A Frame of Reference for Black Politics, African Americans and the American Political System* (co-authored), and *Political Science and the Black Political Experience.*

Georgia Persons, Ph.D., Georgia Institute of Technology. With much of her research focused on Black concerns she is the editor of *The National Political Science Review;* she is the author of numerous articles and several important books to include, *Contemporary Patterns of Politics, Praxis, and Culture,* and *Dilemmas of Black Politics: Issues of Leadership and Strategy.*

Frank Pryor, Ph.D. Student Howard University. His research interests include Black Politics and the American Government and Politics; he is currently employed with the Center for Peace and Justice Education at the University of Villanova.

Richard Seltzer, Ph.D., Howard University. An author of numerous books to include *Contemporary Controversies and the American Racial Divide* (co-authored) and *Sex as Political Variable* (coauthored); additionally, he has authored or co-authored numerous articles.

Robert C. Smith, Ph.D., San Francisco State University. He is the author of several major books, including *Racism in the Post-Civil Rights Era: Now You See It Now You Don't, We Have No Leaders: African Americans in the Post-Civil Rights Era.*, and has most he has recently written an encyclopedia of African American Politics; additionally Smith has numerous articles to his credit on the subject of Black Politics.

Ronald Walters, Ph.D., University of Maryland., College Park. Another major contributor to Black Politics, Walters has authored a number of important studies to consist of *Black Presidential Politics In America: A Strategic Approach, African American Leadership* (co-authored), *Jesse Jackson's 1984 Presidential Campaign: Challenge and Change in American Politics* (co-authored).

Hanes Walton, Ph.D., University of Michigan. One of the most respected scholars in the field, he is the author of numerous books on elections, race, and African-American politics, to include *African-American Power and Politics, American Politics and The African American Quest For Universal Freedom, The Political Philosophy of Martin Luther King, Jr, Black Political Parties; An Historical and Political Analysis, The Native-Son Presidential Candidate: The Carter Vote in Georgia,* to name a few.